Revised Edition

HAUNTED WISCONSIN

MICHAEL NORMAN AND BETH SCOTT

Trails Books
Black Earth, Wisconsin

Library of Congress Catalog Card Number: 2001093465
ISBN: 1-931599-04-1

Editor: Anne T. McKenna
Copy Editor: Jerry Minnich
Design: Colin Harrington
Cover Design: Kathie Campbell
Cover Photograph: R.J. & Linda Miller
Back Cover Photograph: Al Denninger

Printed in the United States by McNaughton & Gunn
07 06 05 04   6 5 4

Trails Books, a division of Trails Media Group, Inc.
P.O. Box 317 • Black Earth, WI 53515
(800) 236-8088 • email: books@wistrails.com
www.trailsbooks.com

TABLE OF CONTENTS

PART II. Southern Specters

PREFACE TO THE 1980 EDITION

Nobody knows when, where, or why the first ghost walked this earth. But from the time that earliest man gathered around a circle of fire, words were whispered about unreal presences in the night ... shadows of the dead which refused to die. The stories were passed down through the ages, from culture to culture, and eventually adapted and elaborated upon until mankind grew increasingly fearful of "seeing a ghost." We remain fascinated by the possibility of encountering these things that defy scientific explanation.

Are there really such things as ghosts? Our rational minds tell us that "ghost stories" are just that—fiction created to scare little boys and girls and the faint-hearted. We can accept computers, space travel, holography, and molecular photographs much more readily than "things that go bump in the night." Cynics place ghost stories into the category of UFOs, Big Foot, and the Loch Ness Monster and scorn anyone reporting an encounter with any of them. How then can we explain studies that indicate that over one half of the people surveyed believe in ghosts?

Literally thousands of people in every nation of the world have reported encounters with ghosts. What is it they have seen?

The most accepted definition of a ghost is that it is a disembodied spirit, usually of a dead person, which haunts a person or former habitat. All ghosts are not the same. G.N.M. Tyrrell, in his classic British study, *Apparitions*, says ghosts are of four distinct types:

(1) a "crisis apparition" that occurs when a living person sees, hears, or feels the presence of another person who is experiencing a serious difficulty; (2) an apparition that occurs when a living person has tried deliberately to place his image before another person in a distant place; (3) one that appears long after the person represented by the vision has died; and (4) one that appears in a certain house, or other locale, often giving it the reputation of being "haunted."

If we are to accept the possibility of ghosts, how can they be explained? Parapsychologists attribute this psychic phenomenon to one of two explanations:

(1) the ghost is the actual spirit of a dead person, and the person experiencing the haunting has no role in creating the vision; (2) the ghost is produced primarily by the human being experiencing the apparition. The latter view is much more widely held by scientists investigating psychic happenings. Just as television pictures are transmitted through radio waves, so a person may be able to transmit a telepathic image through space to a receiver. The picture is then reconstructed by the human being receiving the mental image. Tyrrell's crisis apparition ghost would fit this explanation, as would cases of telepathic transmittal of images between individuals.

But what of ghosts that appear long after death? The psyche (or spirit or mind) of a person may be able to survive physical death, researchers say. The body and psyche separate after death. The spirit may then survive in a different dimension with the capability of manifesting itself in a pseudo-physical form. This would partially explain why ghosts are often transparent, leave no footprints, and are unencumbered by the laws of nature, e.g., being able to move through solid objects.

No one has been able to "prove" beyond doubt that ghosts exist, just as it has been impossible to verify the existence of UFOs, the Abominable Snowman, or the Loch Ness Monster. Those who deride the notion of ghosts echo the words of Ebenezer Scrooge when he said Marley's ghost was only "a slight disorder of the stomach ... an undigested bit of beef, a blot of mustard, a crumb of cheese, a fragment of an underdone potato."

Are the stories on the following pages true? We can't "prove" their accuracy. However, we believe that the participants in the stories believe sincerely in what happened to them. The people you will read about, and the writers of this book, cannot explain the events. Nor have we tried. We are reporting what happened. We have tried to present the stories in a nonjudgmental way, leaving it up to you, the reader, to draw your own conclusions.

Alas, there are no truly famous or prominent ghosts among the five dozen stories we've collected. As far as we know, there is no ghost permanently ensconced in the governor's mansion, no ephemeral actresses still trodding the boards of abandoned theaters long after death, and no phantom cavalry troop still parading at Fort McCoy. But, many of the ghosts that follow are (or have been) very much in evidence. Some historical ghosts attracted the attention of newspapers in their day, and their shenanigans were widely reported.

Preface to the 1980 Edition

Professor Robert Gard, the noted Wisconsin folklorist, has said that Wisconsin may have more ghosts per square mile than any other state. We emphatically agree!

There is an amazing collection of haunted houses, poltergeists, apparitions, and other unexplainable phenomena in a state known more for its cheese and vacation resorts.

The specters and stories you'll encounter include:

- the Ridgeway Ghost, which has mystified residents of the windchoked valleys of southwestern Wisconsin for 150 years.
- a possessed servant girl in early Milwaukee.
- the lingering specter of a long-dead woman in a house her husband built.
- a flamboyant grandmother who came back as a ghost to check up on the relatives.
- a poltergeist in St. Croix County that attracted a crowd of over three hundred spectators.
- two sisters who share a strange ability to attract representatives of the spirit world.
- two Ojibway ghosts that visited an Indian family one winter day and stayed for months.
- a gentle southern lady who came back to help her descendant find missing branches of the family.
- several spirits that refused to leave some early Wisconsin hostelries even after the inns were shuttered.
- a phantom horse that signaled death during the pioneer days of the Wisconsin Dells region.
- a ghost that takes its modus operandi from the fertile imagination of Washington Irving.
- a German-born farmer who returns to his tragedy-plagued farm near Waukesha even today.
- the strange events in a Cedarburg house that drove a young family to the brink of hysteria.
- the ghost of a devoted wife who returned nineteen years after her death on the very night her husband died.

You will read about not only ghosts and apparitions, but mysterious footsteps in the night, swinging railroad lanterns held by unseen hands, sounds that defy explanation, and a house that would burst into flame for no earthly reason. There is even a case of demonic possession, which ended only after the ancient rite of exorcism was performed in a Watertown church.

We have often been asked what prompted our interest in the ghosts of Wisconsin. Our objectives in writing the book are threefold. First, we wanted to entertain, to offer compelling stories that would engage the imagination. Second, we sought to fill a niche in the state's folklore/historical legacy by writing on a subject that had never before been covered in detail. Perhaps this skein of tales, woven into the fabric of Wisconsin's history, will give us a firmer appreciation of our regional character. And, last, we wanted to contribute to the vast body of ghost lore extant, with the hope that some of our stories might be significant.

Because no body of research existed for us to draw upon, we created our own. We wrote to nearly every newspaper in the state, inviting readers with information on ghost lore to tell us their stories. We also contacted selected county historical societies and every student newspaper in the University of Wisconsin system. The responses were encouraging, both in quantity and quality. Where possible we interviewed respondents in order to tape-record their stories. We were impressed by the sincerity of the people we interviewed, by their willingness to share with us their experiences. On numerous occasions we were told that we were the first persons, outside the immediate family, to hear the story. The fear of ridicule and derision prevented the telling to others. We vividly remember one young woman who was so traumatized by the recounting of the unexplainable events that her hands trembled as she served us coffee. And this was four years after the haunting!

Where time or distance made personal interviews difficult, we mailed detailed questionnaires to the subjects to evaluate their material.

Other contemporary and historical tales included in this book were gleaned from many sources. We consulted the Manuscript Collection at the State Historical Society of Wisconsin; city, county, and state histories; copies of nineteenth- and early twentieth-century newspapers; books and magazines of folklore and parapsychology. We excluded from consideration most material centering upon the famous Spiritualist Movement in Wisconsin, feeling that it was beyond the scope of this book.

Any book is the result of numerous contributions. We received assis-

Preface to the 1980 Edition

tance from many sources, some of whom prefer to remain anonymous. We wish to acknowledge the help that the following people provided:

Tim Ericson, assistant director of the Golda Meir Library, UW-Milwaukee, for his invaluable bibliographic insights and encouragement; Paul Woehrmann, Milwaukee Public Library; Willis Miller, former editor, *Hudson Star-Observer*; Jim Bednarek, writer-photographer, *Germantown Press*; Betsy Doehlert, freelance writer, Madison; Tom Heinen, reporter, *Milwaukee Journal*; Jeanie Lewis, author of *Ridgeway Host to the Ghost*, and C. W. Orton, two indefatigable pursuers of the Ridgeway ghost; Marjorie M. Davies, librarian, Kilbourn Public Library, Wisconsin Dells; Mrs. Verne Worthing, Evansville; Richard Heiden, Milwaukee; Ervin Kontowicz, Milwaukee; and the dozens of people who told us their ghost stories and without whom this book would have been impossible. Most of all we would like to thank our editor, Mark E. Lefebvre, for his wise guidance and unfailing enthusiasm.

We hope that you have as much fun reading about haunted Wisconsin as we have had chasing the ghosts from the coulees to the farms, from the wooded northland to the city streets. Elusive creatures they are — we never met a single one! At least, we don't think so.

Beth Scott
Michael Norman
September 1980

The letter arrived at Post Office Box 352, River Falls, Wisconsin, and was dated August 22, 1977. At the bottom was the signature of someone named Mark E. Lefebvre, editor-in-chief, of what the letterhead identified as Wisconsin House, Ltd., Book Publishers, of Madison.

"Dear J. M. Norman," the missive began, "I read with considerable interest your letter in a recent issue of *The Capital Times* requesting information of hauntings which originate in Wisconsin ... "

Lefebvre's six-paragraph letter went on to state that although he had no personal experiences to share, his company would be very interested in reading any manuscript that might result from "your research." A follow-up paragraph included words any writer longs to hear: "I would very much like to read it for possible publication."

He then noted that Wisconsin House was merging with Stanton & Lee and that "if you wish to contact me in the future, share progress reports, whatever, you can contact me at ... " and here he listed the mailing address. His final words were: "If you go elsewhere, best of luck. I hope your research is rewarding and the project is fulfilled."

Well, to say that my coauthor, Beth Scott, and I were pleased to receive this unanticipated letter is to severely understate our reaction. I was in London when the letter came, so Beth called my wife, who then relayed the information to me. I don't remember if the phone dropped from my hand, but I do know it shook so that it kept a rhythmic beat against my ear and I spoke in a tone of voice much louder than staid Englishmen are used to hearing. (It was also while I was in London that my wife telegraphed the news—yes, in those days one could still send a Western Union—that she was pregnant. I thought that if these are the kinds of things that happen when one travels, I should leave the country more often!)

Some background is necessary.

Earlier in 1977—and it's so hard to think that it's been nearly a quarter of a century ago—Beth and I had resolved to write a book together. She was a friend, a neighbor, and a successful professional writer for

Introduction to the 2001 Edition

nearly three decades. It seemed such a simple decision, one that I am sure is made daily by thousands of would-be authors. But looking back now, I see how naïve we were, how little we understood that here had occurred a life-altering moment that would shadow us until our collaboration ended with Beth's untimely death some seventeen years later.

The first problem to solve was this: About what subject should we write?

We had narrowed down the process to something nonfiction and something about Wisconsin. Both of us had "adopted" the state, neither of us a native, and we had grown quite fond of this chunk of earth.

As we wrote in the introduction to the original 1980 edition, eminent Wisconsin authors Robert Gard and L. G. Sorden eventually sent us on the trail of the supernatural when we saw in their *Wisconsin Lore* their claim that the state " ... contains, if the yarns are an indication, more ghosts per square mile than any state in the nation."

Hmmm, we thought. How can that be? To think of Wisconsin was to think of bratwurst and beer, Colby cheese and dairy cows, vacation resorts with world-class fishing lakes, Badger football, and Titletown U.S.A. Where in this world or any other could tales of ghouls, ghosts, and haunted houses possibly fit in? Sure, international news coverage of Plainfield's unlikely handyman/cannibal Ed Gein, or the best-selling *Wisconsin Death Trip*, had given Wisconsin a certain macabre reputation, but old Ed was a real human monster, and stark photographs of corpses dressed in their Sunday best or small-town news stories of particularly grisly demises were light-years from traditional American ghost lore.

But the more we thought about it, the more we kept coming back to this question: Why not a collection of ghost stories? They're always popular. It hadn't been done before. And if enough scout troops and schools bought such a book, we might even sell a few hundred copies. There's nothing like the sound of ringing cash registers to focus working writers' minds on what needs to be done.

We then decided to write letters to newspapers around the state, asking readers to send us their favorite local ghost stories, or to tell us about their own personal experiences. One such letter appeared in the *Capital Times*, and thus that encouraging letter from the man named Lefebvre.

And so I wrote to him at Wisconsin House on September 6, 1977, saying, in as cool and professional a tone as I could muster, that, well, yes we would be pleased to send him some sample chapters and an outline. What

Haunted Wisconsin

I wanted to shout was: Are you mad? Are you toying with our fragile writers' egos? Do we wish to contact you in the future? Of course we wish to contact you in the future! And, if necessary, we will hire Brinks to safely deliver the manuscript the 240 miles between our homes and Madison.

Nearly twenty-four years have passed from that time to the appearance of this, the first revised edition of the book which came to be *Haunted Wisconsin*. Through six publishing houses, umpteen printings, and twenty-plus years in print, *Haunted Wisconsin* had a good deal of life in it, so to speak. What Beth and I had considered possibly a "one-hit wonder" turned into a small cottage industry of ghost story collections published over the following fifteen years: *Haunted Heartland* was published by Stanton & Lee in hardcover in 1985 and is now a Warner Books paperback. *Haunted America* (1994) and *Historic Haunted America* (1995) were published in hardcover and paperback by TOR, a division of St. Martin's Press.

Furthermore, that letter from a man I did not know turned out to be "the beginning of a beautiful friendship."

Mark Lefebvre began as our publisher and then, after leaving the book business for a more profitable and stable career elsewhere, he became our agent. But much more than that, he became our treasured friend, indispensable ally, and loyal confidant. Following Beth's untimely death in 1994, Mark helped me navigate the deep waters of New York publishing as I completed writing and editing those final two books on which Beth and I would collaborate.

I think the hardest part of moving on to new projects without Beth Scott as my writing partner, colleague, editor, and gentle friend, is learning to speak not as a "we" but as an "I." Our writing styles were so analogous, our goals so similar, our temperaments so perfectly suited for the sometimes-disastrous process of collaboration, that it almost seemed we often thought as one. We were a plural but we wrote as a singular.

There are new stories in this edition, and revisions to some of our original tales. A few stories were dropped for various reasons. I tried in the new stories to bring more contemporary material into this edition, and thus I would like to thank the following individuals who gave of their time to sit down for interviews with me or for giving me permission to write about them: Dennis Boyer, Dodgeville; Al Denninger, Milwaukee; John Dettloff, Indian Trail Resort, Couderay; Stacy Kopchinski,

Introduction to the 2001 Edition

Chances Restaurant, Rochester; Barb McMahon, Golden Fawn Lodge, Hayward; Kathy Olson, journalist and photographer, Stone Lake; Mr. and Mrs. Dick Owens, Renton, Washington; Dr. Don Petzold, professor of geography, UW–River Falls; Gerald Schneider, Milwaukee; Debbie Schuerman, Chances Restaurant, Rochester; and Ezra Zeitler and Micah Zeitler, geography students, UW–River Falls.

I also wish to thank those several individuals who told me their most amazing ghost stories but who wish to remain anonymous.

My deepest thanks and appreciation also go to Jerry Minnich and Prairie Oak Press for initially believing that *Haunted Wisconsin* still had plenty of life; to Anne McKenna and Trails Books for seeing this volume through to completion; to the University of Wisconsin–River Falls journalism department and administration for agreeing to provide me with the leave of absence necessary to work on this project; and to my friend and agent Mark Lefebvre for his unwavering support.

And finally to Beth Scott. Without her, none of these books would have been possible. I trust that she continues to watch over me, and all that I write.

However, this revised edition passed through my hands alone, so any errors of commission or omission are my singular responsibility.

Michael Norman
River Falls, Wisconsin
August 2001

Grateful acknowledgement is made to Brandon Press, Boston, for permission to adapt material from Tomorrows Unlimited, *by Marion Stresau, Copyright 1973, by Brandon Press, Inc.*

The names of some individuals have been fictionalized to protect their privacy. These names are indicated by an asterisk (*) the first time they appear.

The Haunted
North

GHOST ISLAND

The heavily overcast sky draped the fabled 17,000-acre Chippewa Flowage wilderness waterways in a gloom that seemed unusually appropriate for this brisk October afternoon. A cold front had slipped through the region, leaving a stiff breeze rustling through the lofty second-growth birch and pines on the 140 islands in the Flowage and a fine mist roiling across the open water. Off an island near a spit of land called Sliver's Point, the two anglers sat in their fishing boat debating the best way to find a few of the Flowage's fabled muskies. Another island lay across the channel from them. The channel ranged in breadth from a few yards to the width of a football field.

On this day, veteran fishing guide Al Denninger told his client that the surest method of catching fish was one devised by legendary musky fisherman Tony Rizzo. Denninger said they'd pull up to shore on the closer island, near Sliver's Point, lay out their lines with hook-rigged suckers, set them up along the water's edge, and open the spools. They'd have three rods to a man, then sit back and let the suckers do the work of luring the elusive muskies. Not only would that give them the best chances for a fish, but the best odds for a big fish, Denninger maintained, joking that it was angling the "lazy way."

"But it's a good way to fall-fish," Denninger says of Rizzo's technique, which he often uses in September and October. "The bait's not moving, it's just sitting there, so that's the right speed."

The men pulled the boat up on the sandy shore, put out the rods and lines, and unfolded a couple of lawn chairs. Then it was just sit and wait.

"You check the lines every so often and listen for the clickers," Denninger says. "You're just killing time until something happens."

Directly across the water from the men was the island whose southernmost point, where the channel narrows, was only some eight to ten yards from the tip of the island on which they now sat. The channel is so shallow off the isles' points that during dry spells there's barely a foot or two of actual water separating the landmasses. A sand-and-gravel bar is frequently visible in the shallows.

As the men quietly talked fishing and listened for a hit on their lines, their gazes ranged across the pristine waters. Only nature interrupted their reverie, the occasional cry of a loon or gull and the gently lapping waves of the pristine waters against the shore.

Suddenly, Al Denninger saw his friend's face go pasty white and his eyes widen. He was looking off toward the far island.

"What's that?" his friend stammered.

Denninger turned to look, expecting to see an animal swimming in the water, or maybe a loon.

"No, no! That, up there!" the man said pointing down the distant shore, where the channel was widest, about a hundred yards away.

Denninger followed the man's gaze.

A floating, white, bulbous form was clearly visible against the tree line along the shore, about ten feet in the air. It appeared to be emerging through the trees, yet was not changing form or shape as it moved. The object stopped at the water's edge.

"It had been misting off and on during the day," Denninger remembers. "That's what I thought it was at first. But anything going through trees would dissipate. There wasn't any darkness to it, or any shadow. There wasn't any sun to cast shadows. It looked like it had shoulders and it was tapered on both ends. You can't see the right shoulder; it had a gap there."

Denninger was right. Clouds, smoke, fog, or steam weren't causing what he saw that afternoon. Because what astounded him the most, and what he noticed more than anything else, is that the mysterious shape moved ... against the wind.

What Al Denninger and his companion didn't know at the time is that the island on which the strange apparition materialized has a history of peculiar and unexplainable phenomena so pervasive that the owners of a nearby lodge have given it a name that speaks to its unsettling legacy: Ghost Island.

Barb and Bill McMahon have lived on the Chippewa Flowage for over thirty years and owned Golden Fawn Lodge all that time. Their home and resort is in a cove within eyesight of Ghost Island a few hundred yards across the water.

Barb says: "We named it Ghost Island specifically because of the unusual things that have happened there. We had guests who would ask if there were cottages on that island, or if someone lived on it. They'd say they heard noises, sounds. No one would ever tell me what they heard, though, just odd sounds."

Now, the name Ghost Island cannot be found on any official topographic map because very few of the seven score islands in the Flowage have formal designations. Most are known locally by geographic or historical landmarks, such as Big Timber Island or Darrow Island. Sometimes resort owners give islands their own names, to help locate them for vacationers.

The islands are actually high ground remaining from the flooding when Northern States Power Company built a dam in 1923 on the Chippewa River at Winter, Wisconsin. The river was joined with ten large, existing lakes in the overflow to form the thousands of acres of interconnected waterways and island wilderness known today as the Chippewa Flowage, one of the nation's premier vacation and fishing destinations. Off the water, the land has been reforested with second-growth pines, oak, birch, and maple trees to cover the scars that remained from the logging that laid waste to the forest more than a century ago.

When their guests' reports about the nearby island started surfacing in the early 1970s, the McMahons first attributed their uneasiness to the sounds of nature perhaps unfamiliar to "city people." What little information Barb could draw from guests did sound as if they were describing animal sounds. Further, the McMahons knew the island had no cabins, camping areas, or other permanent or temporary human habitat. The odd fall hunter occasionally might look for deer, or a fisherman might temporarily beach his boat at the shore, but no one would have any business on the island for more than a few minutes or hours.

"That's why it was always unusual when people reported hearing things," Barb says. "There is no camping there, officially or unofficially. There aren't more than eighteen camping spots on the entire Flowage. There are a few day-camp sites, or you can cook out in a clearing, but there's no tent camping."

Could it simply be that natural causes were at play, or that hikers or campers were on the island? It's possible, but Barb eventually concluded that, just maybe, something more disturbing was at play here.

The McMahons first labeled the place Ghost Island on their resort brochure in the 1970s as a kind of joke. But then the teasing tones faded in the face of those persistent and baffling questions about the island, queries that came their way, guest after guest, year after year. An occasional puzzled guest or two, she could understand; the sudden cry of a loon can startle almost anyone. But when it became a half-dozen or dozen times each season that vacationers tracked her down to ask if someone lived on that island, well, Barb started seeking more detailed information.

"I asked if they had heard people, but they didn't say they ever heard voices, or singing or laughing or humming. They just heard strange noises. I always thought it was unusual that people would not describe for me what they heard, but then again people perhaps don't like to, because they don't want someone to think they're peculiar or hearing things, or to be told it was all in their imagination."

The McMahons' resort stretches across several hundred yards of waterfront acreage on a wide, quiet bay. Vacationers staying in the cabins farthest away from the main lodge to the southeast, and thus closest to Ghost Island, were often those who most frequently made comments or asked about the island.

But then any doubts about the veracity of their guests' reports ended when Barb's husband, Bill McMahon, experienced firsthand the ominous atmosphere of Ghost Island.

"There is an inlet over there where it's nice and quiet to fish," Barb says. "But my husband was uncomfortable there and he didn't know why. He would weigh anchor and leave. And that's what happened to other people."

Barb says her husband is a veteran outdoorsman who knows the Flowage like the back of his right hand; he is not easily intimidated by the loneliness inherent in wilderness living, nor has he any similar feeling about any other location in the Flowage. She says her husband has not fished near Ghost Island in years.

"He said the hairs on the back of his neck would just raise right up when he was by that island. He felt extremely uncomfortable. Sometimes he thought he was being silly, so he'd go back again. He went several times, but he stopped. He said, why go and stay only fifteen minutes? He said it was like someone is there on the island watching him ..."

Or some thing?

But knowledge of this place called Ghost Island did not come Al Denninger's way for some time. Although he had guided fishermen and hunters for nearly two decades, he had never heard the island on which he was watching the floating entity referred to as Ghost Island.

Denninger and his client were transfixed by what they were watching. Nothing in Denninger's experience had prepared him for this, and from his background it's safe to say that he is a man prepared for almost anything. Although he was an old hand at the Flowage, guiding had been a sideline.

Until his retirement in 2001, Denninger was a professional Milwaukee firefighter. He had seen nearly everything a firefighter could witness in his three decades in one of the world's most dangerous occupations. He is not a man to be trifled with, nor someone who seems even remotely capable of being frightened.

"To me, it was just interesting," Denninger says of the mysterious form. "I knew that it was something that didn't belong there. It was totally foreign, strange; I've never seen anything like that. I wasn't scared, but I did get more excited as I wondered what it was."

His client was clearly the more upset. He wanted to pull up their lines and get away from the area as soon as possible. "He was like, 'Let's get the hell out of here!'" Denninger says. "He didn't like it. He was more freaked out than I was."

Yet, as the object continued to hover on the shoreline across the channel, the amiable Denninger, who bears a resemblance to film actor Roy Scheider, characteristically kept his wits about him and grabbed one of the three cameras he had in his boat, a Polaroid instant camera. Those who know him best joke that he is rarely without his cameras, and takes photographs of anything and everything. His wildlife and nature photographs are especially noteworthy. Normally he used the Polaroid to take quick snapshots of his clients with their catches, since the fish were generally caught and released. The resulting photos would turn up on resort bulletin boards or in a Sawyer County weekly newspaper.

But instead of a smiling fisherman with his catch, the picture Denninger captured on that day was of this extraordinary floating form that looks more than a little human-like. The soaring birch and pine trees in their early fall foliage along the shoreline of Ghost Island are clearly visible behind the figure.

He tried to take a second picture, but the shutter button stuck. He assumed the Polaroid was out of film, pulled the developing print out, and put the camera back down in the boat as he kept an eye on the figure. In retrospect, Denninger wishes he'd taken out either his video camera to tape the figure's movements or the 35mm camera to fire off more shots, but he wasn't thinking of that at the time. Between keeping the object under observation and trying to figure out what was causing the phenomenon, the men were enthralled and puzzled.

"It sat there for a couple of minutes," Denninger remembers. "And then it slowly started to go to my right, its left. It went down the shoreline about fifty yards, hesitated there for a second or so, and then it went up in the air fairly slowly. It was a gray day and so it blended into the sky. It could have stayed up there for another two hours, but we couldn't see it at all."

Denninger estimates the object's height at anywhere from twelve to fifteen feet, based on the distance he was from the object. "It was big. You found yourself stepping back mentally" to keep it in perspective, he said. "You knew it wasn't right."

He even climbed into his boat and motored closer to Ghost Island, near where he estimated the object had appeared. There was no sign that anything had been in the area.

Despite his companion's unease, the two fished a short while longer before leaving the island for another spot some distance away, but neither place proved very good fishing.

"There was nothing happening there and so we left," Denninger says. He was working out of Indian Trails Resort, on Pokegama Lake, a few miles away, and that's where they headed.

Then there is the matter of the Polaroid camera.

It was not out of film.

"I thought I'd put another role of film in the camera," Denninger recalls. "I looked at the back (of the camera) and it says three. I had three pictures left! So I pushed the button on the camera and took a picture of the guy with me. It worked fine then and it's worked fine ever since. Now, I'm not an idiot. I wasn't so excited or scared that I was too stupid to push the button. So I've always wondered if that had anything to do with what we saw?"

The owner of Denninger's base of operations, Indian Trails Resort, one of the oldest in the region, is the noted Sawyer County historian and author, John Dettloff. He was the first person to whom Denninger showed the picture.

"He said this thing kind of rose up and disappeared," Dettloff recalls of the conversation he had with Denninger. "He asked me what the heck

Ghost Island

I thought it was. He didn't come in and say, 'I took a picture of a ghost.' We were all baffled. It has very defined edges on the sides and the top. It almost looks like the shoulders, the torso of a figure. But it was huge, about ten feet tall when you compare it to the trees. For quite awhile we just talked about the picture as odd."

Dettloff later took a boat himself to Ghost Island and walked around but didn't find anything that would point to the source of the figure Denninger saw. "Many people thought it was smoke from a fire, but there were no fire signs anywhere. Some leaves I picked up looked a little odd, but I couldn't come to any conclusions. I was looking for some clue, something different. There was nothing I could say for sure" that could have been the cause of what Denninger had witnessed.

Dettloff explains that everyone who lives, works, or vacations on the Flowage is used to seeing fog, smoke, or low-lying clouds. But he says he doesn't think the photograph is of any of those natural phenomena.

"You might see at ten different places on a distant shoreline a bunch of vapory clouds or fog, but it has a different type of look to it than what's in the picture," he adds.

The resort owner has known Denninger for a quarter of a century and believes in the photograph's authenticity. Since it's a Polaroid, there is no possibility of tampering with a negative. Besides, both men saw the object before the photo was taken.

"It's something we can't explain. What would cause Al's client to have his blood run cold and for Al to even take the time to photograph it?"

The photograph and Denninger's experience were topics of conversation around Indian Trails Resort for weeks, but didn't spread much farther until John Dettloff visited Golden Fawn Lodge and the McMahons some time later.

"I asked [Barb] if she'd ever seen anything strange on the island across the lake," Dettloff said.

"Which island?" she replied.

Dettloff pointed to a map of the Flowage and the island across the bay from the McMahons' lodge.

"Oh," Barb nodded. "You mean Ghost Island."

Dettloff could barely conceal his surprise.

He or members of his family have owned the 65-year-old Indian Trails Resort since 1972 and he has spent years studying the history of Sawyer

County and the Chippewa Flowage, yet he did not know that that particular island had been given any sort of name, official or unofficial. To him, it was just another of the scores of uninhabited and unnamed islands in the region. It lies on the other side of the Flowage from Dettloff's home.

"Why do you call it that?" the astonished Dettloff asked Barb McMahon.

She then told of the stories of strange sounds she had been hearing for decades about the island. It just seems like a haunted place, she told him. She even showed him a register the family kept of the reports of unusual activity on the island, a sort of family ghost register.

When Dettloff related the McMahons' story to Al Denninger, he, too, was amazed and later visited with Barb and her husband to learn firsthand what they knew about Ghost Island.

"When I heard the story, I was pretty skeptical," Barb recalls. "But when I saw the picture, well, it is unexplained. What's odd is that there was no bottom [to the figure]. And if it was smoke or exhaust or a campfire, it would change shape."

Denninger emphasized to her that the figure kept the same shape the entire time he watched it along the shoreline.

As one of the most knowledgeable local historians in the region, Dettloff says there is little exceptional in the history of what he now knew as Ghost Island. As high ground before the 1923 flooding, the island was actually just another wilderness tract close to the Chippewa River as it flowed through Sawyer County. As far as he can determine, there were no permanent settlements at that particular locale, but he does point to two interesting historical facts that make the argument for a haunting there intriguing.

The pioneer thoroughfare known as the Chippewa River Road between Eau Claire and Chippewa Falls to the south and Hayward to the north was built in 1884, and followed, as its name suggests, the Chippewa River nearly all the way. A section of the road cut directly across Ghost Island.

Although the highway was rerouted when the Flowage was created, for nearly forty years travelers by foot, by horse, by wagon, and finally by automobile traveled that historic route.

Could some foul event on that old roadway have released the ghosts of today?

A second possibility links Ghost Island with the Ojibway people, the historic Native American inhabitants of the region. The vast Lac Courte

Ghost Island

Oreilles Reservation, based near the community of Reserve, is intertwined with the Flowage on its western and southern edges.

Dettloff thinks it's not inconceivable that there could be Native American burial grounds on the island.

"Many burial grounds are kept quiet by the tribe. And even they don't know now where many of them are located," Dettloff reveals. The old high ground areas, now the islands of the Flowage, were commonly used for Native American interments in centuries past. To protect the sites from the encroaching white settlers, or even other tribes, the Ojibway seldom marked the sites or disclosed their locations.

Despite all the speculation and discussion, only one firm conclusion about Al Denninger's photograph and Ghost Island has been established.

There was something hanging in the air on Ghost Island, the Polaroid photograph establishes that fact, but what it was and why it was there continues to puzzle. Explanations that attribute the phenomenon to natural causes seem inadequate. Yet are we to assume its source is supernatural?

Most everyone connected to the sighting takes a cautious approach in answering that question.

The journalist and photographer who initially broke the story, Kathy Olson, of Stone Lake, keeps her reportorial neutrality, yet she agrees that the source, Al Denninger, and the photograph provide rather convincing evidence of something at least . . . unnatural.

"Skeptics will say it was a cloud formation or fog and I will never convince them otherwise," Olson says. "But I think there are a lot of things that can't be explained away. This may be one of them. A ghost? I don't know. A presence? An entity from another dimension? I don't know how to explain it."

For his part, historian John Dettloff takes a matter-of-fact approach.

"The picture tells the whole story. It's a Polaroid. Whatever is on that picture was there. It's something we can't explain. It has nothing to do with Al's character. Where did the picture come from? Al didn't make a lot of judgments about it, he just showed it to people."

As for Al Denninger, he doesn't talk much about the story anymore. He's had a professional photographer look at the photograph. The expert said it was impossible to manipulate a Polaroid photo, as there is no negative.

Denninger even found himself guiding a psychic who had heard about the ghost photo and wanted to visit the island. "He hired me for two days. But he went onto the island and said he felt nothing. That didn't mean nothing ever happened there, but there was nothing there now," Denninger remembers. The psychic told him the object was "something from beyond," but didn't elaborate.

Denninger remains nonchalant, but still puzzled. What he told reporter Kathy Olson at the time remains true to this day.

"I do believe in ghosts. But I never gave it much thought before that. I was simply totally intrigued, totally in awe of what I was seeing, and I absolutely believe that we're not alone in the universe."

He's never seen anything more on or around Ghost Island. But he would sure like to.

Perhaps Barb McMahon has the most interesting perspective on Ghost Island and its reputation for unnerving the most veteran of wilderness folk.

"This goes back to people asking about that island. Sometimes you talk yourself out of something. You think that it must have been your imagination. That's why people will ask those questions but won't tell you what they've heard. Or what they have felt. I'll bet there are many people who have been there [Ghost Island] and, not because they're not catching fish, but for whatever reason one person says to the other, let's try someplace else. And they won't give an explanation. But they have this discomfort, this eerie sensation. This unexplained sense that someone is watching them, someone they can't see."

It is, she says, a fear of . . . the unknown.

THE LYNCH AFFAIR

The time is shortly before noon on a sunny day in early December 1871. The place is the 160-acre homestead of Richard Lynch, near Hatchville in southeastern St. Croix County. One of the hired men, young Jim Snodie, is raising his broadax for another swing at a chunk of downed timber that he will shape into one more railroad tie. His boss will sell the ties to the train lines building roadbeds throughout the region for the burgeoning passenger and freight service between Chicago and the Northwest.

Although he is still a teenager, Snodie is a powerfully built young man with considerable experience in cutting and shaping ties for other farmers in the area. The ties are made from the trees cut clear to make way for settlers' cabins and farm fields. They are a good source of quick income for the farmers and local woodsmen.

Richard Lynch has hired Snodie and several other men to clear a portion of the heavy stand of timber on his farm. He is working in a clearing some 40 yards behind Lynch's two-story log house.

On this swing, however, he stops abruptly when he hears the welcoming clang of Mrs. Lynch's dinner bell coming from the back porch. Snodie drives the broadax's blade deep into a white pine stump, turns and runs for the kitchen door, his thoughts fastening around the pleasure of a few minutes of rest and a hot meal.

But as he reaches for the door latch, "Thwack!" his broadax embeds itself blade-first in the doorframe just inches from his outstretched hand.

He whirls around to confront whoever has thrown the ax with such powerful force and accuracy. Everyone else appears to be already in the house or working elsewhere on the spread.

Snodie frowns as he grabs the ax with both hands and pulls it out. A few feet away from the porch is another pine stump into which he sinks the ax with all his strength. He pulls a bit on the handle to make sure the blade is firmly embedded before he turns and heads again for the kitchen door.

"Whooshh! Thump!!"

The lethal ax flies past his left ear and bites deeply into the door-jamb. Again the young woodsman looks around for the perpetrator, but again no one is within sight.

Thoroughly perplexed, puzzled and not a little frightened, the brawny teenager yanks the ax from the frame, which it has nearly split in half, hefts it over his shoulder and treads warily back to the clearing. He doesn't know what is going on or why he's being attacked, but clearly it seems to him that some force does not want him to go inside that house. And he's not about to push his luck.

The flying broadax that nearly ended Jim Snodie's young life on that day proved to be among the first in a series of bizarre ordeals that some called the work of poltergeists or spirits. Strange events would happen through most of the 1870s at the Lynch farm, about 13 miles west of Menomonie, in St. Croix County's Cady Township. So notorious and widespread became the reports that visitors by the hundreds from the United States and abroad and newspaper reporters from all over the country descended on this little homestead tucked away in the Big Woods of Wisconsin.

And what exactly did the sightseers and journalists witness?

A Menomonie newspaper editor, R. J. "Rock" Flint, would later describe some of the events as "... chairs jumping to the ceiling and then falling to the floor with terrible force, crockery and tinware flying across the room like lightning, propelled by some invisible agency. Bullets of wood, pieces of board, axes, handspikes, etc., etc., hurled through the air by unseen hands."

Cooking utensils were said to have hurtled across the kitchen, furniture rearranged itself into piles, and bolts of cloth were mysteriously cut into patterns...or slashed to shreds. On another occasion a pair of shears hovered in mid-air above a quilt before veering downward to cut it to pieces.

Whatever—or whoever—was responsible for the events created one of the most sensational "hauntings" ever reported in Wisconsin.

One Spiritualist believed as many as seven spirits were loose on the place, while editor Flint wrote in the *Dunn County News* that some people thought it was the work of 'Auld Cloatie,' an obsolete term for the devil.

Flint wrote on September 13, 1873, that the problem was "a conundrum we cannot answer. It may be a spirit, animal magnetism, odylic force, witchcraft, or the devil, for naught we know. We believe the

The Lynch Affair

Lynches are honest and are not practicing deception."

Were the Lynches honest and guileless victims of some demonic force, or were family members, as some observers suggested, at least partly responsible for the widespread commotion?

Not much was or is known about the family's background, nor why they left Indiana for the harsh Wisconsin wilderness, so such a question is difficult to answer—especially now from a distance of nearly a century and a half.

Richard Lynch, his second wife, Elizabeth, and five children—three boys and two girls—moved to Cady Township in May 1871 from Marshall County, Indiana. By August of that year, Richard had built, with the help of several area neighbors, a two-story log house in the midst of the forest that stretched for miles in any direction, broken only here and there by settler's cabins with their few acres of planted crops. The Lynch homestead was in Section 36 of Cady Township.

Rumors about the first Mrs. Lynch circulated soon after the family's arrival. Some said she had lost the thumb and forefinger of her right hand in an accident and died from the infection. Another tale had it that she'd been murdered, but details were sketchy.

When the family arrived in Wisconsin, Elizabeth Lynch was barely out of her twenties, scarcely a decade older than her stepson, 20-year-old Alfred, who was away working on another neighborhood farm during most of the "troubles" at his family's farm. The children who lived at home included David, seventeen; Mary, ten; Georgie, seven; and Lucinda, nicknamed Rena, age two. She was the only child Richard and Elizabeth had together.

Most contemporary reports about the Lynch haunting assert that all was serene in the household for the first six months they lived in their relatively spacious cabin. Later, however, a Minnesota newspaper reporter would claim Elizabeth Lynch had grown unhappier by the month on the Wisconsin frontier, and that the alleged ghosts or spirits were nothing more than pranks instigated by her and ten-year-old Mary to convince Richard to move back to Indiana.

Whatever the case, the series of intriguing, albeit sporadic, episodes eventually touched the lives of not only the Lynch family but neighbors, volunteer "investigators" of the paranormal, newspaper reporters, and the simply curious.

It is not entirely clear at what point the family problems became public, nor is it entirely possible to piece together a consistent chronology of what is alleged to have occurred. The public record is sparse and, of course, no one is alive today who remembers the events.

Apparently, Richard and perhaps Elizabeth first thought it was nothing more than prankish behavior by one or more of the children. All of them denied knowledge of the mischief, but Georgie, who had been caught in a number of fairly typical childish highjinks, was sometimes spanked when household items went missing. For instance, when Mrs. Lynch put down a utensil while preparing a meal, she'd find it had vanished if she became occupied with another chore. She also began missing dresses. Some were found rolled up and stuffed into odd nooks and crannies; others had been cut to shreds, suitable only for the ragbag. Two holes were cut in a feather bed. Dishes and pans disappeared.

That month of December 1871, however, seems to be close to the beginning of the Lynch family affair, although much of what happened that month and over the course of the next year or two, before stories began appearing in the newspapers, seems to be conjecture and second-hand information.

One of the few eyewitnesses who left a record was that young hired man, Jim Snodie, who spoke in detail about what he termed the "happenings" in 1937 to Dick Owens, his grandnephew. Owens made a careful record of his interview with Snodie and, although nearly 60 years had passed since Snodie worked for the Lynches, his memory seemed undiminished, even though some of what he alleges seems astonishing.

On the same day Snodie was attacked by the broadax, he told Owens, Elizabeth Lynch hosted a quilting bee for several local farm women. The women were sitting in a circle admiring their handiwork when a pair of shears, which had been used to cut the cloth squares, leaped into the air and attacked the quilt, slashing it to ribbons.

As the neighbor women watched in disbelief, Elizabeth screamed, bringing her husband on the run. He got to the room in time to see the shears ripping up the last of the quilt before falling to the floor. Understandably, the women gathered up their belongings and left.

Snodie said the Lynches were "highly disturbed" as they grimly picked up the pieces of quilt and put them in an old carpetbag.

Many of those early episodes in late 1871 and early 1872 seemed to center upon cloth, quilts, or clothing.

Once after Richard Lynch had returned home from town with dress goods for his wife, she put the material away in the bedroom. Several days later when she went for it, the cloth was gone. They found it in the barn, rolled into a bundle with the shears inside. From the cloth had been cut the skirt and sleeves for a dress to fit ten-year-old Mary.

A second bolt of clothing material also vanished, only to be discovered weeks later rolled into a hanging wall map Richard had in the house. A perfect bib-type apron had been cut out.

The family appeared to be successful for quite some time in keeping the turmoil within the family, a few hired men such as Snodie, and some neighbors. However, an afternoon of hay-cutting in August of 1873, some 18 months after Jim Snodie's run-in with the broadax, ended in several disturbances so astounding that they eventually attracted the attention of the regional press.

A neighbor, Frank Duffie, had volunteered to help Richard Lynch cut the hay. Side by side the men worked, swinging their scythes in the sun-washed field at the hem of the forest.

At about 4:00 P.M., Mrs. Lynch screamed from the house. The men raced into the cabin in time to see chairs jumping to the ceiling and crashing to the floor, tinware and cooking utensils flying across the kitchen and then, just outside beyond the open doorway, slabs of boards and scraps of iron sailing through the air.

Lynch and Duffie thought that somehow they could catch the culprit if they stationed themselves at two corners of the house so that together they had a full view of all sides of the house. Mrs. Lynch stood nearby.

They waited.

Suddenly, a large pine box near Duffie leaped into the air and landed ten feet away on the porch. An old horseshoe that had been hanging on a peg in the milk house arced through the air and came to rest beside the box. Instantly, a commotion rocked the empty house. Duffie and the Lynches ran back inside, but everything movable had been piled high into one corner.

Later that day, an ax that had been rammed into the end of a log struck the side of the cabin's doorway and bounced several feet into the front room. Mrs. Lynch took it to the milkhouse, wedged it inside a wooden crate and then finished the job by piling wood planks and a bag of salt on top. But no sooner had she returned to the house then the ax reappeared, this time clattering onto the porch. Her husband grabbed it, took it a short distance into the yard and pushed it inside a hollow log. There it remained—at least for the rest of that day.

Although a few neighbors had known of some of the earlier incidents and kept the news relatively quiet, gossip about the flying furniture and farm implements spread like a forest fire. Area newsmen began showing up on the Lynches doorstep to witness the supposed poltergeist's activities, then vied with one another in sensationally recounting what one reporter called "the most absurd capering of some supernatural agency."

Strangers' imaginations were then sparked by what they read. They converged by foot, by horse, by rumbling ox cart, winding their way through the nearly impenetrable forest.

One newsman estimated that more than 300 visitors had descended upon the Lynch family within a six-week period; another estimated it closer to a thousand visitors.

Meanwhile, Elizabeth Lynch had begun binding Georgie's hand and foot and tying him into a chair or to a cradle, still believing that he was somehow partly to blame. Even that didn't work. One day while Mrs. Lynch was washing clothes, Georgie sat tied to his cradle. His sister Mary watched him. Their mother turned from the washboard to put some wood into the stove. Turning back to the tub, she found her bowl of soft soap gone. She went after more and, upon her return, Georgie told her that the soap could be found under his head. Sure enough, when Elizabeth raised the child's head she found the soap. Georgie and Mary denied any responsibility.

It didn't seem to matter whether Georgie was bound or not. Often, while the child was confined, a teacup might fly to the floor and shatter, or a saucer would leap from the sideboard and land undamaged on the floor.

"There, mother! You see I didn't do that!" Georgie would shout.

On another day, Mrs. Lynch cooked a kettle of fresh squirrels for the family's hot midday meal. After cautioning Mary to watch the boiling pot, she took a pan to the milkhouse to get flour to make bread. She got the flour, sprinkled salt over it, then returned to the house. As she stepped through the doorway, she saw that the squirrel stew pot had disappeared from the stove. Mary claimed innocence. Mrs. Lynch put the pan of flour on the table, then she, Mary, and Georgie searched for

The Lynch Affair

the missing kettle.

After she had rummaged around a bedroom, Mrs. Lynch saw that the flour was gone. In a few moments, it was discovered under the stairway; again it was placed on the table. Mother and children then went up to the garret where they found the pot of squirrels sitting in the middle of the bed, a corner of a bedspread thrown over it. As Mrs. Lynch took off the spread, the contents steamed and bubbled as if it were being lifted off a hot stove.

Little Rena's beautiful hair was at the center of another incident in April of 1873, one that helped spread the family's notoriety to the farthest reaches of North America.

Elizabeth Lynch had called her children to an early lunch before she fed the hired men. George and Mary showed up, but not Rena. Her mother found her sitting in the front yard with her hands in her lap. The child's long hair, which had hung in golden ringlets, had been shorn from her head; chopped tufts of hair were all that remained of her waist-length tresses. A pair of scissors lay nearby, but not a strand of her hair was ever found. Understandably, two-year-old Rena could not explain what had happened.

The annoying pranks continued and the family's notoriety attracted attention.

Dunn County News publishers "Rock" Flint and E. M. Weber visited the Lynch home in September of 1873 and reported on their "investigation" in several articles reprinted from coast to coast.

The men arrived on a Saturday night that apparently passed uneventfully. On Sunday morning after breakfast, Flint and Weber went outside in order to give the family a chance to finish up their work. They were joined in their vigil by clerks from the nearby Knapp, Stout, and Company store: Messrs. Thompson, Kendall, Johnson, and Burch. The morning air was cool and the men built a fire at the edge of the woods, about 40 feet from the house.

They heard a commotion coming from the house. Someone shouted from inside that teacups were falling to the floor but not breaking.

Flint wrote that one man "who was near the door, stepped forward and picked up the cup, placed it on the table, took Georgie, who was in the room, by the hand, and started for the door. In a moment another cup sped to the floor and lay on its side, whirling with great rapidity. Thompson started for this one, also, and as he grabbed it, the cup moved away from him and passed under the table. He went around to the other side and caught it while it was whirling. This transpired while we were at the fire, and we relate it substantially as it was told us by several eyewitnesses."

Flint and Weber raced to the house hoping to watch this "spirit" at work. They stood in the doorway when, as they wrote,

"...with almost lightning swiftness an egg darted across the room, struck the corner of a box, and was smashed. Shortly, after, the potato masher, which stood on the dresser, went the same way with incredible speed, and landed in the corner 'kerslap.' In a little while a couple of pieces of broken crockery lying on the stove made a sudden change of pace and landed in the corner.

"These three things we saw distinctly, and others in the room saw them. Perhaps we were fooled by some trick of legerdemain. If so, who did it? The boy seven years old who sat at the table quietly eating his breakfast? The girl, ten years old, who stood nearby, wiping a dish? Mrs. Lynch, who was busy at work? Or Mr. Lynch, who was not in the house? It seems to us improbable, if not impossible."

Yet the "improbable, if not impossible" events increased daily. Shortly after Flint and Weber's visit, the Lynches hosted A.B. Finley, the Barron County school superintendent. He, too, stayed all night. As was not uncommon on the frontier, family and guest stayed in one room: Richard, Elizabeth, and Rena in one bed; Finley in a single bed across the room; and Mary and Georgie sleeping on the floor between the other beds. David was absent.

Soon after they had retired, Georgie complained of something pinching and scratching him. Finley took Georgie into his own bed, but still the child complained. He clamped the boy's hands in one of his own and put his other arm so tightly around him that Georgie could not move a muscle without detection. All was still. Suddenly Finley felt the bedclothes stirring. He swatted, he grabbed, and he caught—nothing. Finley left the next morning as baffled as he had been when he arrived.

Not so befuddled was a skeptical reporter from the *St. Paul Dispatch* who visited the Lynches on November 3rd and 4th, 1873. When curious scratching emitted from the children's bed during his own all-night vigil, he got up and held the hands of both children. The noises stopped immediately. The reporter spent 20 hours in the house. He went away persuaded that Mrs. Lynch and ten-year-old Mary, whom he called "strange and precocious," had duped people. He felt that Mrs. Lynch

The Lynch Affair

was bored and unhappy in her dreary, backwoods home and that, after her husband's refusal to sell the farm and move back east, she created her own excitement. And since the remote location of the house meant most visitors had to spend the night, the newsman said the Lynches were paid much more than a commercial hostelry would have been. The "haunting" was a moneymaking scheme, he argued in print.

The majority of observers, however, continued to believe that the Lynches would have relinquished almost anything to be rid of the manifestations, that they were victims rather than perpetrators.

Certainly there were enough outside observers that it seems unreasonable to assume family members, including a girl not yet in her teens, tricked each one. For instance, a Mr. Knight, who lived near Wilson, recorded more than 40 different occurrences during the few hours he was there.

Then one Ambrose Evans visited the Lynches. When breakfast was ready, he sat down at the table. Soon, the distinctive odor of kerosene filled the air. It seemed to be coming through an open bedroom door. Evans followed Mrs. Lynch into the room where, in the middle of the bed, lay an uncorked jug of kerosene. Nearly a gallon of it had emptied onto the bed, saturating the feather mattress and ruining the quilts.

Meanwhile, newspaper reporters continued to find their way to the isolated farm. When *Milwaukee News* reporter J. D. Goodrich arrived at the house for his own investigation, David and his father were working in a field while the younger children played in the yard. Goodrich was standing by the outside cellar door talking to Mrs. Lynch when a noise erupted from inside the house.

"There," Mrs. Lynch told the reporter, "you hear that, and you also see that none of the family are in the house."

Hurrying inside, Goodrich and his hostess found a dining room table tipped over.

By 8:30 A.M. the next morning, Goodrich was observing some very lively activity, as he wrote:

"One thing peculiar is that you never see a thing start, but the minute you turn your eyes the thing gets up and gets. Another peculiar feature is that where a thing strikes there it lays, neither rolls nor bounds. We took some of the same things and threw them a number of times, but they would bound or roll every time. We saw a piece of broken cup hit a little two-year-old girl on the back so hard she nearly cried. A raw potato hopped out of a dish near where we were and lit on the floor; and while we were watching a stove handle light in one place, a tin plate whisked by our head in another direction."

Newspapermen were not the only ones who wanted to discover the causes of the family's troubles. Ministers, spiritualists, and mediums were also unsuccessful, but they did offer some remarkable ideas.

The Rev. John Barker, who lived on Cady Creek in Pierce County, said the devil himself was at work in the Lynch household. Intent upon exorcising the demon, he approached the Lynch house with Bible and prayer book in hand. He put the books in a handkerchief, tied its ends together and placed the little package on the staircase. The Rev. Barker then challenged the demons to remove it.

They did ... when Rev. Barker wasn't looking. Both books were later discovered on a bed with every page torn out. The handkerchief was located in a barrel of feathers.

The purported psychics and clairvoyants weren't any more successful than the Rev. Barker.

One Saturday afternoon a seer named Mellon, from the tiny community of Rock Elm, visited the Lynches. He saw nothing that day of an otherworldly nature. The next day he had better luck. He said the spirit of Richard Lynch's first wife was in the house...with six other spirits! It was this group responsible for all the turmoil.

When Lynch asked why so many household items had been destroyed, Mellon said that it was to open the minds of the Lynch family and others in the community to "the truth of Spiritualism."

Richard Lynch grumbled that it seemed a needlessly disruptive and expensive way to gain converts.

By that time, a large group had gathered. One man asked Mellon if the spirits could throw things around as they had done previously. Yes, he said. Lynch then asked the spirits to move a cup from a shelf to the floor. The cup didn't move. The spirit, speaking through medium Mellon, apologized by saying it was alone and could not perform without the assistance of the other spirits.

And where were the other spirits? someone asked.

Gone to Knapp Station, the solitary spirit said, to attend a camp meeting. He could not predict when they'd return, and only grudgingly agreed to go after them.

Mellon then announced that the "spirit" had departed, presumably for Knapp Station.

"Humbug," muttered those in the crowd disappointed at not seeing an example of unearthly tomfoolery.

A few weeks later, another visiting clairvoyant, a Mrs. Carlton from River Falls, said she, too, saw seven spirits. However, she told the family to bar any more visitors and to hold séances among themselves, during which a family member acting as the medium would solve the mystery.

Though skeptical, Richard Lynch gave it a try. Reports were that during several family circles the table around which they sat moved about, but all attempts at questioning the circling "spirits" were fruitless. The family gave up spiritualism in disgust.

The personal recollections of Jim Snodie include two additional and quite astonishing episodes which, if they are to be believed, make the Lynch affair far more sinister than the relatively innocuous tricks perpetrated by a frustrated housewife in complicity with one or more of her children.

In the first, the Lynches almost lost their house in a deadly roof fire. The incident began one midday shortly after Snodie had seated himself at the Lynch's table for dinner.

"We heard an eerie, high-pitched noise, similar to a pig's squeal, coming from somewhere upstairs," Snodie recalled in the 1937 interview. "Mr. Lynch left the table in a hurry and ran for the stairs. We could hear him walking around from room to room, asking in a loud voice, 'Who is there?' The house was otherwise quiet. He returned to the table, shaking his head but saying nothing."

Lynch and the hired men resumed eating. The squeal again came from upstairs.

"Naturally, we all looked upward. It was then we saw a piece of white paper floating down from the ceiling. The boss made a grab for it and caught it before it could hit the floor. He read it out loud to all of us."

Snodie remembered the words Lynch read aloud:

Everybody leave the house at once. All the women line up on the west side of the house and all the men line up on the east side. Hurry, for if you don't, the house will burn down.

Richard Lynch told everyone to settle down, finish their meals, and get back to work. Just then there was a loud noise from the roof.

"The smell of wood smoke drifted into the room from a partly opened window," Snodie said. "(Lynch) rushed outside and then hollered that there was a fire on the roof. We all jumped up and ran out. Sure enough, the shake roof was blazing away, the flames at least two or three feet high. Mr. Lynch lined all of us men up on the east side of the house and the women folk on the west side. He was trembling with fear when he joined us on the east side. At that time, the whole roof was covered with flames."

But Snodie said the fire quickly went out. Some few wisps of smoke drifted skyward, but they soon dissipated.

"The boss got a ladder from somewhere. He climbed onto the roof, examining the shakes as he went along. He said there wasn't one shake that was charred. No evidence of a fire was found anywhere on the roof. We were all pretty well spooked by then, I'll tell you."

The news accounts of the Lynch haunting quite naturally brought strangers knocking at the Lynches door. Some came from as far away as Norway, Sweden, France, Germany, and England; all were attracted by the prospect of seeing "spirits" at work. But many of them were far from welcome, as with a shocking incident Jim Snodie witnessed involving two men from Albany, New York.

"We were getting ready to go back to work after lunch" Snodie said. "A loud knocking came at the door. Mr. Lynch jerked the door open. Two men appeared in the doorway. One asked if they could come in. He said he and his friend had come all the way from Albany, New York, to watch the 'spooks' at work."

Lynch refused, Snodie said, claiming the hired men were going back to work and nobody would be home. But both men crowded into the room and slammed the door shut.

"Almost simultaneously someone shouted, 'Here comes a note!' And, sure enough, down from the ceiling fluttered a piece of white paper," Snodie said. "Mr. Lynch ignored the note and grabbed the door latch intending to physically eject the men. He tugged and tugged at the door but could not get it to budge. He then stooped and picked up the note. It stated that the men were not welcome, and should state their business immediately."

One of the men — Snodie called him "Mr. Loudmouth," because neither man introduced himself and this one seemed to do all the talking — said

The Lynch Affair

they'd come to identify the culprit behind the "foolishness" and report that person to the "authorities." He boasted that neither of them was afraid of any unseen force and that whatever was responsible should show itself.

At that moment, another note floated down from the ceiling, Snodie said. This one said the men should go up to the bedroom at the top of the stairs at 1:15 P.M. that afternoon. Everyone else was to remain downstairs.

At the appointed time, the visitor who'd been doing all the boasting headed for the steps. His friend declined to accompany him. With a nervous laugh, "Mr. Loudmouth" headed for the bedroom. The men downstairs heard him slam the door.

Minutes passed. Finally, Richard Lynch said he would see what was going on. He didn't appear to be in any hurry as he climbed the steps to investigate the problem, Snodie recalled.

Lynch opened the door. He didn't go in.

"He's dead," Lynch called down to the men.

Snodie said no one moved for several seconds, then each man climbed the stairs to see for himself. Just inside the bedroom door was the body of the boastful visitor.

"I think he died of pure fright," Snodie said. "All the men wished to God they had never laid eyes on such a sight."

The hired men filed out to their jobs. The Albany man's body was loaded onto the light livery wagon in which the visitors had arrived and taken to Menomonie.

In one regard, Elizabeth Lynch did have her way in the end. Her husband came to regret his decision to leave Indiana. Whether it was the death of the visitor from Albany, the roof fire, a survey of his property losses—smashed furniture, broken dishes, mangled silverware, shattered mirrors and clocks, shredded clothing—or the continual disruption of strangers and nosy newsmen banging on his door, Lynch decided to make a bold decision.

He would split up the family. Young Georgie and Mary were bundled off to the McMahans, neighbors living a mile away. Though it is not clear why Elizabeth Lynch would ever agree to have two of her stepchildren moved to a neighbor's house. But peace apparently settled upon the Lynch household and all of Cady Township.

What are we to make of all this?

According to Jim Snodie, Richard Lynch was a stern and formal employer who insisted upon being called "Mr. Lynch."

"He commanded respect and since he was a big man, nobody argued with him about his request," Snodie said. "He seemed to lack a sense of humor."

If that is the case, perhaps reporters were right when they speculated that Elizabeth Lynch was retaliating against her strong-willed and much older husband for his refusal to sell the farm and move back to Indiana. She could easily have enlisted Mary's help in performing some of the "mysterious" feats. Much of what was reported was simply missing household items or petty mischief. She could have encouraged the children to hide the utensils, pots and pans, or throw objects when adults weren't looking or to cut up clothing material.

Yet, there are the other, far more disturbing events—the cruel shearing of little Rena's beautiful hair, the roof fire, the near fatal ax attacks and the death of the visitor from Albany. Unless we are to dismiss Jim Snodie's memory of those years, or to assume that Elizabeth Lynch conspired with her children to brutalize her own daughter, to commit arson, and to murder, the Lynch affair leaves many unanswered questions.

The fact that all disturbances ceased after the two youngest children were removed doesn't necessarily prove they had anything to do with it, at least not on a conscious level. Parapsychologists say that moving objects are often associated with the presence of young children and, more frequently, by teenagers. The only teenager, 17-year-old David Lynch, is rarely mentioned in contemporary accounts; he had possibly been "hired out" to nearby farmers.

The Lynch house and most of the Big Woods in Cady Township vanished long ago. A county road is said to cross where the house once stood. Lush farm fields stretch to the horizon, while silos dwarf the scattered, white clapboard farmhouses. The once-thriving village of Hatchville is a forgotten memory. The Lynch family left the region, presumably headed back to Indiana and a quieter lifestyle. There is little to remind the visitor of the remarkable story of Richard and Elizabeth Lynch, or of those few years in the 19th century when this little corner of Wisconsin drew international attention to a story that can still tantalize and mystify.

CONFIRMATION

All the little boy was thinking about was that he had to go to the bathroom. He saw that the house was dark of course, well past midnight, and the short walk from his bedroom down the carpeted hallway and around the corner to the bathroom was one he had made many, many times in his 13 years. No big deal he thought, so he jumped out of bed and headed toward the door. Since his family had the tradition of sleeping with their bedroom doors open, he could head right on down the hallway and past where his parents, brother, and sister lay sleeping in the other three bedrooms which opened off the upper hallway of this fairly typical, split-level 1950s-era home.

But the boy never made it. He got the shock of his young life.

An apparition hovered in the hallway less than ten feet away from where he stopped cold in the doorway of his bedroom.

"It was floating about one or two feet off the ground," he says today, nearly 30 years later. "It was white and transparent. I could see a head with hair. I think I even saw glasses on it, but the face was completely blank. As much as I could see, it looked female. It had a maternal bliss, a kindness about it."

The body of the form was a pale, billowing mass that seemed to undulate as if a gentle breeze swept down the hallway. No legs or feet extended from below the form.

"Where the arms would be there was a bit of a bulge, like its arms were crossed or it was holding flowers or something. But I couldn't see its arms. It seemed to be looking in my direction, looking at me. I didn't sense any hostility. It didn't move toward me or away from me, it just stayed where it was."

The boy, too, stayed where he was. He could not think of what to do. What he wanted to do, of course, was get to the bathroom, but to do that he needed to get past this thing which filled up most of the hallway. The boy really, really did not want to go down there.

"It looked too much like a human figure," he says. "I remember seeing moonlight coming in from one side of the hallway, and I remember wondering if that could be moonlight bouncing off the mirror at the end of the hallway and coming back and creating a reflection. But I looked at it and looked at it and decided that, no, that was not possible. It couldn't be a reflection off the mirror because it wouldn't look like that. That's when I decided I'd have to stay in the bedroom for the night. I dropped to the floor, stretched my arm out and closed the door. I went back to bed and stayed there."

Suddenly a young boy's physiological needs were of far less urgency than trying to figure out what in heaven's name loitered in the hallway just beyond his now firmly closed bedroom door.

It wouldn't be until much, much later that an answer came. Long after he'd left that house in which he grew up, long after he had left the town of his youth and gone on to make his way in the world. It would only be then, decades later, that he would realize the figure he saw on that night had probably been his own grandmother looking down on him, comforting him, and saying good-bye to him.

The young boy's name is Tom Blair* and the small Wisconsin community in which he grew up and where his parents still live in that split-level house provided him with a fairly typical 1960s and 1970s childhood. He attended public school there and then went off to the university in Madison, from which he graduated Phi Beta Kappa in 1983 with a double major in German and geography.

Now at this point that youthful encounter with what some readers would dismiss as a figment of teenage imagination or a particularly disturbing dream might be expected to have been forgotten, or even laughed at by young Tom as he entered adulthood and put away the fantasies and nightmares of childhood. That would be the natural reaction to a story like this, but Tom Blair is no ordinary witness to ghostly encounters, nor did he ever forget what he saw on that night so long ago.

Dr. Tom Blair is a scientist. Specifically, a soil biochemist with the advanced degrees, journal articles, book chapters, and research-in-progress to satisfy even the most jaded of observers. After finishing his degree at the University of Wisconsin–Madison, Blair went off to a University of California campus where he received his master's degree in geography and, in 1993, a Ph.D. in soil science. His doctoral dissertation was titled, "The Effects of Soil Moisture and Soil Organic Matter on

Confirmation

Potassium Availability in a Calcareous Vermiculitic Soil."

His curriculum vitae lists 19 referred journal articles, 17 book chapters and published proceedings, and five manuscripts either submitted or in preparation.

He worked for eight years as a consultant and visiting scientist for an international rice research institute in the Philippines before taking his current position in Iowa as a soil scientist for the federal government. He has plans for 15 to 20 journal papers based on his research in the Philippines, including one that will be submitted to the journal SCIENCE.

Blair's formal education and fidelity to the scientific method make him a particularly distinctive observer of supernatural matters. But that doesn't mean he is entirely understanding even now of his experience three decades ago. It is an event, one suspects, which will stay with him until the end of his days.

"I didn't tell anybody about this" he says of that floating figure in the familiar hallway of his comfortable home. "Being a bit of a scientist even then, I suppose, I knew I couldn't explain it. I wasn't sure what it was. And of course you don't want to be laughed at for seeing something that other people wouldn't understand. So I filed the experience away, sort of put it under my 'not explained' file hoping that some day I would be able to explain it first to my own satisfaction, and then to other people."

He knew full well that he had not imagined the entire incident, and yet didn't know what it was he had seen.

"When I woke up in the middle of the night, I wasn't having bad dreams. I'd never had any ghostly experiences, I hadn't seen a scary movie the night before. I just needed to get to the bathroom. That's all I was thinking about."

What he eventually yearned for, Blair says, was some outside corroboration that this sort of vision was possible. Even though he trusted his own eyesight, the doubter in him kept him somewhat doubtful.

"I needed confirmation and replication before I would believe it myself. And I didn't want to discuss it unless I had adequate confidence in it," he notes.

Blair didn't know that the vaporous woman in white would linger in his mind's "unexplained file" for nearly 30 years, that it would be there tugging at the back of his mind. He didn't know that it wouldn't be until he took a research position on the other side of the globe that he would find that what he saw in a small town Wisconsin was remarkably similar to experiences people had in the Philippines and throughout Asia.

She is known as the white lady and is amazingly similar to what Blair saw: billowing figures with absent or indistinct arms and legs; and they tend to inhabit a certain geographic area.

"Shortly after I moved to the Philippines, I began meeting people who would tell me stories about the white ladies they encountered. I asked what these ladies looked like and my friends gave me the exact same vision, the same description—of something floating off the ground, a white, transparent being and usually a female. You could see a head but no face. That was the first time I felt that I had some explanation for what I saw. After not thinking about my own experience for quite some time, I began comparing their observations with my own observations and I saw that we were really describing the same type of being, the same appearance."

Blair said a Filipino friend attended a school in which a stairwell was reputedly haunted. Several teachers were said to have died there. Blair's friend was running up those stairs one morning when she saw a white lady hovering near a landing.

"As in my case," he says, "the white lady there seemed to be looking at my friend with a benevolent air, maybe 'kind' is the right word. Like an older lady would have for a younger child."

The idea of a warm and caring, a motherly being keeping watch over a family or a place she loved also helped Blair identify who his "own" white lady might have been.

"I hadn't thought about that (the identify of the ghost) for many years. I just thought it was a figure. But then in the last couple of years I began to think about it. And I realized that the figure matched quite closely my mother's mother, my grandmother. She was a relatively large lady and this figure I saw in the hallway was not a thin being at all. My memories of my grandmother are quite distant, but she had hair like the figure did and she wore glasses. My grandmother died in February of 1970, so I would have been about 12 years old, which was right around the time of this encounter. I just can't say for sure, but my best guess is that it was my grandmother."

Since Blair cannot date the specific moment when he saw the ghost, he isn't certain if his grandmother was still alive. "That's quite unfortu-

Confirmation

nate but it was probably within a year one way or another, but I don't know which one came first," he acknowledges, adding that his grandmother lived her final years in a nursing home in his hometown.

"I don't really remember her well. My memories of her are as an older lady, but from what I hear from older relatives is that she was a very kind human being, very people oriented very devoted to her family. My mother is the same way, her life really is her children."

While he was not unusually close to his grandmother, Blair says his family was quite close, usually spending any holidays with his mother's family rather than his father's.

Why was it that a young Tom Blair was the one chosen to be seen by his grandmother and not his own mother or another member of the family?

"I don't know," he concedes. "My mother was the baby of her family. I think she was quite close to my grandmother. It could have been that (my grandmother) was trying to get close to my mother, not necessarily to me, and I just happened to be there at the time."

But Blair believes it may be something more, something almost intangible—his willingness to look at the world in new and different ways.

"Throughout my life I've had, every once in awhile, a very brief experience that I think could be related to my mind being relatively active. Suddenly thinking of somebody while I'm walking down the street, for instance, and then a few seconds later that person drives past and honks his horn at me. I talk to anyone, I listen to anybody's opinion, and I don't assume anyone is wrong until they're proven wrong. So I guess I might have been a receptive audience for this vision on this occasion."

He has never told his parents about the apparition, although he recently related the story to his brother and sister. Both of his siblings said they had not had any similar sorts of experiences, yet they were quite accepting of their brother's experience.

While he worked for eight years in the Philippines, Tom Blair traveled widely throughout Asia and came to some conclusions about the appearance of apparitions in the United States and other cultures.

"The countries I've lived in and traveled through are slower than our culture is. We're by far the fastest paced country I've ever lived in. We don't have time to slow down and open ourselves up I would say. The thoughts of people in Asian culture are more toward people, their families, their relatives, their neighbors, whereas we spend more of our time

Haunted Wisconsin

focusing on work production, on buying things that we think we need for our lifestyles. We're more work and progress oriented. This would just be a guess, but maybe these (spirits) are more likely to appear to people who are more liable to see them, to be where they have a receptive audience you might say. These things do appear in our country, there are reports of them, but perhaps they are just not as common."

Blair, of course, cannot remember the precise date of his ghostly encounter and thus doesn't know if his grandmother had passed on. However, the fact that she may still have been living does not necessarily rule her out as the ghostly figure.

Blair cites as an Asian example appearances of a person countless miles away from where he or she actually lives. The spirit looks like the real person, they let themselves be seen by somebody they know, perhaps they'll even speak, but it's someone who shouldn't be where they're being viewed. Perhaps the person is from a different part of one's life, childhood for instance, or lives in a different country or even on a different continent.

"If you see them in passing that's a sign that they are going to die soon," Blair says of this type of apparition. "Two Nepalese friends told me in separate conversations that that's quite well-known in Nepal, that if you see somebody out of place, that means they're going to die soon."

A close Filipino friend related a personal experience to Blair about just such an unsettling encounter.

"On the same day her brother died in one town he appeared to a close friend on the street in another city," Blair recalls. "He also appeared to his aunt in the town where the family formerly lived. The aunt reportedly saw him walking down the street. He looked completely normal. They even stopped and talked. My friend's brother told his aunt he was staying with his grandmother. It was a normal conversation. Then later that day, the aunt went to the grandmother's house to look for that young man. His grandmother said he wasn't staying there and then they got into a big argument. My friend then arrived on the bus to tell her aunt and her grandmother that her brother had died earlier that day."

The openness with which Tom Blair approaches the possibility of spectral beings existing outside our present understanding of the physical universe is at once both startling and understandable. Surprising because the words are spoken by a man of science yet reasonable because he is an eyewitness who does not ignore what his eyes and his brain tell him about that night years ago.

"While I view myself as relatively creative and open-minded, I try to simultaneously maintain serious, rigorous standards in my activities," he says, pointing to his extensive resume and list of publications. "In general I try to thoroughly test new ideas before discussing or publishing them and to maintain a reliable reputation."

He is expansive when defending his role, as a scientist, against the inquisitiveness about the sort of paranormal experiences skeptics say is not possible.

"One has to recognize what we understand and what we don't understand. Just because we don't understand something doesn't mean it's wrong. That's a common mistake even among scientists who say that if you can't prove something conclusively then your whole idea is wrong. That's simply not true. Sometimes we have to recognize the limits of our technology, the limits of our understanding and say well, something happened, I saw it, I know it happened, and if I can't explain it, that doesn't mean it didn't happen. That means we need to learn more, that there are parts of our universe we may never understand. We have to recognize that. These appearances, these beings we see, ghosts, fit into the idea that we have spirits inside of ourselves, that we have a soul. It's been said many times before that when you die, your soul may linger on and perhaps that becomes what we call a ghost. I think when you consider the fact that so many countries around the world with so many religions all report ghosts that (the soul) may be part of us. When you're born you have a spirit inside of you. Who knows where it comes from or what it is or what happens to it after you die, but given the fact that these same experiences keep happening to people all around the world means that it's a part of us. I guess for critics who say you can't explain it, well that doesn't mean it's wrong, just that we don't know enough right now."

As befits a scientist, Tom Blair's voice is even and his manner is deliberative when he talks about the prospect that mortals coexist with revenants of the dead. He can calmly reconcile his scientific knowledge with what he clearly understands is beyond the ken of most of us—that someday we may see beyond our corporeal selves.

"My research has often been described as new ideas; I have a different way of looking at things," he says. "I guess I am going into such new areas with my work that I can't prove conclusively what I think is going on, but the evidence sure looks like it. It's the same as these ghost stories—you can't prove it conclusively, but it sure looks like it."

With Tom Blair there is every indication that he will continue examining the evidence of apparitions until he is satisfied that they do—or do not—exist in this world or in any other.

THE PAULDING LIGHT: MYSTERY SOLVED?

Ezra Zeitler first heard about the North Woods legend of the Paulding Light when he was a student at Lakeland Union High School, Minocqua, in the late 1990s. "On Monday mornings students would come back and say they had seen the Paulding Light over the weekend and it was real scary and mysterious," Zeitler said.

Despite the captivating stories, he didn't make the 120-mile round trip to the Paulding area, in the Upper Peninsula of Michigan, until 2000.

His younger brother, Micah Zeitler, heard similar stories after his family moved to Mercer from Minocqua.

"There's not much to do in Mercer, so we'd all go see the light. I was guaranteed to see it so that's the only reason I went," Micah said. He was impressed with what he saw and heard, including the legend that the light was produced by the spirit of a dead trainman. "I told everyone I'd seen a ghost."

Micah and Ezra, however, eventually went one step further and, with their university geography professor, set off to uncover the truth about the light. Their results may once and for all explain the origins of this particular mystery light, at least for those willing to accept something less than a paranormal explanation.

The Zeitler brothers certainly are not alone with their interest in what has alternately been called the Paulding Light, the Watersmeet Light, the Dog Meadow Light or, simply, the Mystery Light. For decades, thousands of visitors have made the nightly trek north out of Eagle River, Wisconsin, on U.S. 45, through Watersmeet, Michigan, to a point about a dozen miles north of the Wisconsin state line.

The visitor turns off on an old gravel road about four miles north of Watersmeet, drives up the hill and parks. If it's a "good" night, a dim, glowing orb of white light will appear in the far distance. The light may vanish for a period of time, only to reappear moments later. Sometimes other lights appear with it. During winter and early spring, the light may appear only infrequently.

Haunted Wisconsin

Theories abound as to what causes the light. Some believe it must be supernatural. To these folks, the light glows from the lantern of a long-dead trainman, or a slain dogsled musher. Some have even attributed it to UFOs draining energy from nearby power lines.

More earth-bound observers claim the light might be produced by methane gas escaping from a fissure in the earth. Others say the phenomenon is nothing more than the reflection of lights from boats on Lake Superior or cars on a distant highway.

Tourism officials quickly recognized the lure of the light. One vacation brochure calls it the Watersmeet Mystery Light and includes it in the same sentence as a local trout hatchery. Another brochure listing "Things To Do" in the Watersmeet region gives the phenomenon its own paragraph:

"The 'Light' appears almost every night after dark on a lonely old gravel road and has defied explanation for years. It appears to arise from the horizon, glows like a beacon, splits, changes color and mysteriously disappears as quickly as it came."

But how did the legend of the Paulding Light come to be, and what will one see in that pocket of Wisconsin/Michigan wilderness?

Despite the insistence of some locals—and tourism promoters—the "mystery" of the light is usually traced no farther back than to the mid 1960s when a carload of teenagers stopped one clear evening on that gravel road near the swampy area known as Dog Meadow. Suddenly, the teens claimed, brightness filled the car's interior and lit the power lines paralleling the road. They were so frightened they fled back to town and reportedly told their yarn to the sheriff.

One of the earliest documented sightings came in the late 1970s. Two Wisconsin men, Harold Nowak and Elmer Lenz, told a newspaper reporter that they parked their car on the gravel road and the light appeared in the distance—a bright spotlight shining directly at them. The light moved closer, backed away, and even appeared at an angle from time to time. Lenz grew up near a rail yard and he said the light looked just like a locomotive headlamp.

The men said a smaller light appeared below and slightly to the right of the large, white light. "The two, at times, seemed to move together, then part, one or the other disappearing, then showing again," Lenz said. The smaller light was red, though they claim to have also seen a green light.

Their description fit with one of the legends of the origin of the

The Paulding Light: Mystery Solved?

Paulding Light, that one night in the early 20th century a railroad switch-man with lantern in hand was crushed to death between two cars while attempting to signal the train's engineers. Another tale holds that a train-man was murdered along the old railroad grade where the light appears.

A third account claims that a mail carrier and his sled dogs were mysteriously slain in the early 1800s at Dog Meadow, below the vantage point from which the light can best be seen. The modern road through the region was built on the Civil War–era military road from Fort Howard in Green Bay to Fort Wilkins at Copper Harbor. Federal troops during the war guarded copper supplies moving along the road. But much earlier, men with teams of sled dogs delivering the mail to isolated communities used the old trail. The light, it is said, is the lantern held by the mail messenger looking for the men who murdered him.

Harold Nowak and Elmer Lenz were skeptical of supernatural explanations. They bravely got out of their car and walked toward the light. But as they approached, it seemed to disappear down over the next rise, but continued to cast a bright glow in the sky.

After a half-mile, and finding nothing that might explain the mystery, the pair turned around. As they walked back, the lights reappeared over the rise. When they got back to their car, other observers at the site told them that in the men's absence they'd seen a large red light above a small white one in the middle of the road a block ahead of them. If the reports were accurate, the lights would have been between Lenz and Nowak and their car.

The men drove ahead for some distance, parked, and shut off their car lights. The mysterious light reappeared with a smaller one beneath it shining down the middle of the road. A minute later, the larger light van-ished, and the smaller light, Lenz said, "seemed to touch down and burst into three" orbs. The outer two lights disappeared, but the third remained about 200 feet away. Nowak snapped on his headlights but the light in the road didn't move. Minutes later, the men claimed this single light rose in the air four or five feet and vanished.

Several years after Lenz and Nowak, *Milwaukee Journal Sentinel* reporter Harry S. Pease described what he saw for the newspaper's defunct *Insight Magazine*: "We had chosen the hill above Dog Meadow because it's easiest to find in the dark. You just drive north from Watersmeet on (U.S.) 45 about four miles, turn left onto the town road and stop on the high ground. Our eyes and ears sharpened with the passage of the minutes. We could hear cars a long way away on the highway. We could see a dimness—not so much a bigger as a less dark V— as we looked ahead down the road and the power line that ran beside it. Then we saw the light. Right ahead of us, it began as a diffuse glow and then condensed into a hard knot of brilliant white. You had the feeling that maybe it was moving, but you couldn't be sure you weren't moving your head instead. It could have been big and distant or small and close. There was no way to tell. The silence remained unbroken."

The appearance of so-called mystery lights is not an uncommon phenomenon. In states as diverse as North Carolina, Missouri, Texas, and Colorado, dancing, pulsating, or glowing spheres of light have been described by thousands of witnesses. While supernatural explanations are often the most unusual reasons given for these lights' existence—and more often than not involve murdered train engineers or mysterious UFOs—many scientists have taken an interest in the lights.

Some research indicates, for instance, that mystery lights are more likely to occur in regions where earthquakes may occur, or where unknown faults in the earth could trigger visible atmospheric lights when escaping gases, such as methane, mix with oxygen. Another scientific explanation holds that the shifting and grinding of rocks deep below the earth's crust generates electrical charges in the atmosphere. The shifting charges can make any light produced to seem to act in an "intelligent" fashion. This explanation has been used to explain the Hornet Spook Light in Missouri, since it appears near the famous New Madrid earthquake fault line.

However, the Paulding Light may be the result of much more mundane activity. It's an explanation that has been offered by many observers, including reporter Harry Pease 20 years ago, but one that seems to be disregarded by those who want to believe there is some supernatural or extraterrestrial "intelligence" behind this light. Or those who think unsolved mysteries are good for tourism.

Micah and Ezra Zeitler both studied geography while attending the University of Wisconsin–River Falls. It was there that the two met Geography Professor Don Petzold, and told him about the light. He became intrigued with the mystery.

"When Micah came back from his first experience (of seeing the light),

The Paulding Light: Mystery Solved?

I was immediately skeptical. I started asking him questions," Petzold recalled. "Were these lights seen before cars were around? Before the highway was built? When was the first viewing made? I found out someone said it dated back to Indian times, but of course it wouldn't be associated with the ghost of a wrecked train because there weren't any trains there either. And who could document that it dates back that long? I was determined at some point to see the light."

So with Micah and Ezra Zeitler and a set of good topographic maps, Petzold set off for the Upper Peninsula in 2000 to answer those questions and solve for himself the riddle of the Paulding Light.

The three men drove to the site on a summer Saturday night. "When we pulled up, there were about ten or fifteen other vehicles there," Ezra remembered.

The three men took out a pair of binoculars and walked over to a fence, near where the gravel road ended. Petzold and the Zeitlers noticed that a power line right-of-way extends in the northerly direction from which the light appears. Then they saw the light itself.

"It was in the right-of-way," Ezra said. "It did look like it was hovering around. A red light appeared. I can't remember if I could identify them as moving up and down, but it looked as if they were hovering."

Complete darkness had not fallen so the men could detect the skyline in the distance. It didn't take them long to realize what they were looking at.

Car lights.

"I could tell they were headlights of cars, taillights of cars," Ezra said. "After that we kept passing the binoculars among us. Each of us agreed."

It was not as easy to accurately pinpoint the distance of the light.

"We had a gazetteer with us," Ezra said. "We figured it was probably U.S. 45 that had the traffic on it because there aren't many other roads around that would have so much traffic."

Because the lights were appearing from miles and miles in the distance, the highway itself was not visible.

"There's a straight line of sight right down the cut for the power line," Petzold said. "The highway is really straight, with one short exception. So, we thought the light appearing must have had something to do with cars coming up and over this hill that's about a mile beyond Paulding, but that's a distance of about seven miles from the viewpoint. The white light does appear as one large light, but over a seven-mile distance the headlights converge because of refraction and temperature differences in the atmosphere to look like one, large light. Then as the cars come down the hill, it gives the appearance of coming closer to you, but then all of a sudden it disappears at one point. But that's when the light dips below the trees or some lower elevation. As a climatologist, I attribute the movement of the lights to refraction in the lower part of the atmosphere. I think it would really be quite different if the car lights producing this effect would be closer."

The red lights, Petzold said, are occasional taillights going north up the grade outside Paulding, known locally as Cemetery Hill. "Sometimes you can see the red lights when the white lights are there and approaching and other times you see the red lights alone. And there are two red lights. We looked through the binoculars and you could see the two red lights."

To confirm their theory, Petzold and the Zeitlers got back in their car and headed north on U.S. 45. "On the other side of Paulding," Ezra said, "the highway goes up a gradual incline on a long, straight hill. Toward the top of the hill I could see in my rearview mirror the headlights of the cars that were stopping at the viewing point. That's when we really knew that seeing the Paulding Light was not a real mystery."

Ezra even flashed an S-O-S with his lights, but didn't get anything in reply from drivers who had pulled off the gravel road to watch the "mystery" light, which at this point was being produced by three geographers.

The trio headed back to the viewing area to let people know of their discovery. The response was less than enthusiastic.

Micah Zeitler: "There was a local guy who said Ripley's Believe It Or Not has been there and it's been on Unsolved Mysteries. I asked him if he'd ever gone seven miles up on U.S. 45, on that long, gradual hill. I told him those are car lights. He didn't believe me."

Petzold was amazed at the man's reaction. "He was really quite adamant. He said he saw them every night. Apparently he has been there several times or at least on a regular basis to check out the lights. He was certainly a believer and whatever we said would not sway his beliefs at all."

Not everyone watching the lights that night was such a true believer. As Micah was telling the local man about their discovery, another observer leaned in to Ezra and asked, "Is that true?" When Ezra allowed that it was, the tourist turned to his buddy and said, "You owe me ten bucks!"

Petzold said an understanding of the Paulding Light was not difficult to arrive at.

The Paulding Light: Mystery Solved?

"I said we can't possibly be the first people to have looked at a scale map and said, 'Ah, ha! This is a pretty straight road and there is this gradual incline ...' It would be neat to stop traffic for a period of time and go up there with headlights and flash a signal," Petzold said. He dismissed out of hand the idea of the lights coming from ships on Lake Superior. "I don't understand how this could be envisioned. It's not physically possible."

There is an equally simple explanation for the light's supposed irregularity—uneven traffic flow in one of the more isolated regions of the United States. Micah Zeitler first visited Paulding on a late Thursday night in early spring "It took 15 or 20 minutes for the light to come out," he said. "Now I know why." There's not much late-night traffic on any Upper Peninsula highway during the early spring. But it's a different story on a Saturday night during the height of tourist season.

Another reason people who have seen the lights may not consider Highway 45 as part of the answer is that motorists must turn left off the highway, which seems to mean they would be looking west to the lights and into the wilderness. In reality, the gravel road veers around so that one is looking north toward U.S. 45. The long hill north of Paulding is at Maple Hill Cemetery, over ten miles from where the Zeitlers, Petzold, and countless others watch the lights. The cemetery is at 1,315 feet above sea level, while Paulding, south of it, is in a depression. Thus, observers pick up the lights going up or down Cemetery Hill and then lose them as cars descend into Paulding. The village itself emits a soft glow in the sky that may account for some reports that the bright lights are followed by a radiance as they disappear from view.

The rational explanation Petzold offers does not diminish his fascination with the Paulding Light.

"There is this incredible combination of topography, geography, the alignment of the highway, and this power line. I suppose it could be reproduced somewhere else, but I don't know. This would not happen if it were a much shorter distance because then you would be able to separate the two headlights easily. But seven miles is a long distance for light to travel in a straight line, over terrain of forest and hills. It's just the right combination of natural and manmade effects."

Since his visit to Paulding, Petzold has tried to find a duplicate convergence of lights over a great distance. "I haven't seen it yet, but it's in my mind fairly constantly to check that out. It's not often that you can see traffic for seven miles."

Petzold found the light "mesmerizing," even during a second visit later on. Even a professional scientist can understand those who prefer supernatural scenarios in explaining the light.

"It was right at the point of sunset and we were able to see it, but not as distinctly because there was still some daylight. It was also a rainy day. If you stare at (the light), you can imagine that, well, here comes the train and there's the conductor with his red lantern trying to flag it down before it crashes again. You can believe that if you want. Because that's exactly what you see ... in a sense," he said.

Logical explanations will not deter those who prefer to believe otherwise. Even the government has gotten into the act by erecting a sign on U.S. 45 giving the "history" of the Paulding Light. Tourism officials have found the light to be good local entertainment. On a warm weekend summer night it is not unusual for several dozen people, some sitting in lawn chairs with camcorders at the ready, to watch the lights appear and disappear.

Ezra Zeitler takes college buddies to see the light. "If they want to go there, I'll take them. I won't tell them anything. I want to see their reaction."

Micah Zeitler noted that a campground has been built near the best viewing point. He said the camp was probably built after someone "saw the light."

But another observer pointed out that if one turns west on the county road before the mystery light, he will pass another geographic landmark. Sucker Lake.

DO NOT DISTURB

Old Teddy King grunted and sweated as he dug into the Knapp cemetery plot holding his mother's coffin. With each swing of his shovel, Teddy slowly cleared away nearly 30 years of dirt and stone so that he could move his mother's remains to another graveyard nearby.

The year was 1936. Late August. St. Croix County officials had ordered the graves moved. A new road was going to be built and the county needed the cemetery as part of the right-of-way. Most of the remains had been transferred earlier in the month. Mrs. King was the last one to leave.

The old man wrestled the decaying casket into a makeshift wheelbarrow and set off down the country road.

Now, watching all this was Lloyd Owens, a young man who was working for his room and board that summer at the Al Larson farm, just crossways from the cemetery. Curiosity is a compelling affliction of the young. That's what persuaded Lloyd to cross the road to Mrs. King's empty grave. He shivered as he looked down into the damp hole. As he poked around in the fresh dirt with the toe of his boot, something shiny caught his eye. Lloyd picked it up, cleaned it off, and held it up to the fading sunlight. It was a pink, glass handle.

Maybe it came off Mrs. King's coffin, he thought. I'll just give it to Mr. King, next time I see him in town.

He stuffed the object in the pocket of his bib overalls and trotted back to the Larson house and on up to his room where he put the handle on his dresser top. Then he went off to the barn and evening chores.

Lloyd didn't sleep well that night. Although houses were often sweltering during those summer nights before air conditioning, his room seemed abnormally cool, yet twice he found his sheets and bedspread on the floor.

Early the next morning, the boy got up quickly, dressed, and was about to leave the room when the dim morning light glinted off something on the floor. The pink glass handle was leaning upright against the bedroom door. He carefully picked it up, put it back on the dresser and hurried out the door without so much as a backward glance.

The day passed, evening chores were completed and Lloyd again climbed those stairs to his room, this time a little more slowly than usual. He couldn't get that odd morning incident out of his head.

Lloyd pushed the door open but, as it moved, something scraped across the floor. He struck a match and lit the carbide lamp on the wall just inside the doorway. The pink glass handle lay on the hardwood floor, tight against the bottom of the door.

Lloyd snatched up the handle and again put it back on the dresser, just where he was certain he had left it that morning. A cold breeze blew through the room. The carbide lamp flickered. Lloyd did not close his eyes that night.

Just after dawn, Lloyd packed his small suitcase and left the Larson farm for his own home not far away.

"He asked me if I would take his place," remembered his older brother, Dick Owens. "He said he was very tired from the heavy work schedule and really needed a few days rest."

Dick was only too happy to oblige. Several times in the past, he had helped out at the Larsons, and even replaced his brother when the younger boy wanted some time off. The depression years made good jobs and ample food hard to come by, and Al Larson was good to his hired help and his wife served wonderful meals. Lloyd did not tell his brother anything more than that he needed some "rest."

"I moved into Lloyd's room that same morning," Dick said. "But I nearly stepped on something in the doorway. I picked it up. It was a glass handle of some sort."

Dick put it on the dresser and unpacked his clothes. He was hanging some shirts in the closet when he felt a slight breath of wind stir the air.

A full day of farm chores nearly erased Dick's memory of that morning's incident. By nightfall he was more than ready for a good night's sleep.

"I lit the old carbide lamp," Dick said. "That's when a breeze seemed to blow from the window on the other side of the bed. It was strong enough to make the gas flame flicker. I stepped around the bed to close the window, but it wasn't open."

The gas flame steadied and the coolness subsided. Dick relaxed.

"But that's when I noticed the glass handle in the doorway. I must have stepped over it," he said.

Do Not Disturb

Dick again picked up the handle and put it back on the dresser. He climbed into bed and fell asleep, but awoke only a few hours later with a chill. "I reached for the covers but they weren't there. I jumped out of bed and found them in a heap on the floor. Well, I flung them on the bed and climbed under them."

Morning did not come soon enough. Several times Dick woke up feeling an iciness swirling around him. He pulled the blankets over his head and half-dozed for the rest of the night.

The alarm clock rang precisely at 5:00 A.M. Dick's responsibility was to milk at least ten of the dairy farm's twenty cows before Al Larson got to the barn. As he swung his feet out of bed, his right foot landed on something sharp. He looked down. The glass handle was on the floor. He tossed it back on the dresser top.

"I admit to being the most frightened teenager in the county at that time," Dick remembered.

It would be another two days—and nights—before Lloyd returned to take back his old job. "It was only then that I learned of the origin of that handle," Dick said. He in turn told Lloyd about his own troubling nights. "Lloyd felt badly for not telling me. I accepted his apology, but I was still upset."

That's when both boys decided the wisest course of action was to return the glass handle to the graveyard. Lloyd ran upstairs to find the handle outside his open bedroom door ... on the floor at the head of the staircase.

"We ran to the cemetery," Dick said. "Lloyd pitched it as close as he could to the gravesite where he'd found it. We both turned and raced back to the farmhouse. I packed my clothes and wished him luck."

Lloyd told his older brother that he was never troubled again by cold gusts, the loss of his bedding, or traveling casket handles.

Dick was content to leave this brush with the hereafter behind him. "I didn't offer to spend another night there just to find out if Lloyd was telling me the truth."

A FLAME IN THE WINDOW

Joan Lecher was afraid of the dark. She slept with the lights burning. But when Joan moved her family into a house she said was haunted, for the first time in her life she wasn't afraid.

"When I'm alone I feel content and at ease," she said of the tall house painted white on the north side of Wisconsin Rapids built before the Civil War. It is a sturdy, comfortable dwelling, spacious enough even for Joan's large family of six children.

It was Christmas 1973, Joan remembers, when the idea first presented itself that another boarder shared her house. Joan and her former husband were sitting on the living room couch when she caught sight of a shadow passing by. Out of the corner of her eye, she saw it go into the kitchen. Incredibly, she wasn't alarmed. Then. But five minutes later a second shadow seemed to flit by. Her husband saw it, too. The couple got up and walked into the kitchen and then looked in the combination den and laundry room behind the kitchen. They checked the doors and windows. Closed and locked. They had no idea what they had seen.

A few days later, Joan's daughter, Kathy, stood in the kitchen combing her hair in front of a large, old-fashioned mirror. An elderly man's face appeared as a reflection in the glass from just behind her shoulder, staring intently at her face. She spun around but found her herself quite alone in the room.

During that same holiday period, a young girl temporarily living with the Lechers was staying in the room off the kitchen. She was asleep one night when she woke with a start. An old man stood in the doorway watching her. It was no one she had seen before. Too frightened to scream, she pulled the covers up over her face and hoped he'd go away. He did.

Later, when the two girls compared notes, they discovered striking similarities between the two figures.

In an attempt to discover the identity of the apparition, the Lecher children and several friends gathered around the kitchen table for a

A Flame in the Window

séance. Someone asked the "ghost," if present, to manifest itself in some way. A coffee cup slowly rose in the air. The amateur psychics tumbled out of the room.

On another night, the intrepid gang gathered again. Nothing happened, though several of the youngsters claimed to have heard sounds like the sawing of wood coming from the attic. Joan had begun remodeling the old house. She thinks perhaps the ghost—whoever it was—might have been helping, although no evidence of its handiwork was ever found.

Sometimes months or years would pass by without any additional evidence of a haunting. Then, suddenly, there would be a new reminder that the family was not alone. That's what happened to Joan's 18-year-old son, Lance, one night as he babysat his younger brother. He heard distinct footsteps upstairs; someone was striding back and forth in the hallway and through the bedrooms. Lance was certain that someone, somehow, had broken into the house. When his older brother, Kim, arrived home shortly thereafter, he went upstairs to investigate. No one was there and nothing had been disturbed. Little Joe had slept downstairs all through the excitement.

The footsteps persisted. Joan heard them, too. On at least one occasion, the footsteps came from a room in which several mattresses covered the floorboards!

"Somebody's here keeping an eye on me," Joan remembers thinking, adding that the footfalls became such a routine in the house she no longer investigated the noises. Through the family's personal and professional turmoil, she thought the friendly spirit was taking care of her. On one winter's evening, Joan sat in an archway between the living room and the kitchen. She faced the tall, low-silled living room windows that looked out upon the street. In the bottom left-hand corner of one window a small flame suddenly appeared, a bright, single image that glowed for several seconds. The flame was pure white.

Joan particularly sensed the mysterious resident when she was troubled. Her children took to calling the ghost H.B., the initials of a previous owner of the house, an old bachelor who had been found dead in bed, apparently of a heart attack. Yet Joan had first seen two shadows. H.B. did take care of his invalid mother in the house before she had to enter a nursing home.

For her part, Joan Lecher believes her own senses and the eyes and ears of her children, yet she can offer no rational explanation. She hopes one day to learn the identity of her ghost—or ghosts. Meanwhile, she knew that whoever or whatever watched over her and her family was there for protection against the vagaries of life.

THE PARKER HOUSE POLTERGEIST

The century-old mansion stands prominently on Maple Street in River Falls, Wisconsin. The four-square dwelling is painted green and is a bit shabby today, but its once gracious appearance can be detected in its sheer size and in the unusual roof slanting dramatically upward to a cupola resting like a wooden crown upon its peak.

Early Wisconsin lieutenant governor Colonel Charles Parker built the home for his family. Through the decades the house has undergone many renovations and purposes—a single-family home, a duplex, and now small apartments and sleeping rooms.

Early in the 1970s, Tim Early and his then-wife, Alice, bought the house, planning to rent out the second floor and then remodel the downstairs portion for their own family, which at that time included their daughter, Jessica. Tim's family has been prominent in River Falls through the years; his father was once a Wisconsin state senator.

Shortly after the Earlys moved in to what has been called the Parker mansion ever since it was built, they had the sense there was at least one other, albeit unseen, occupant.

"It was like someone was with us," Tim recalls of those early months in the house. "You know how someone can sneak up on you and, although you don't hear them or see them, you know that someone is there? Well, it was that kind of an experience."

Both Tim and Alice thought it might have been a ghostly presence, though neither one ever saw an entity of any sort. Instead, there was some mischievous business—doors opened for no apparent reason, lights suddenly blinked on, little Jessica's rubber ball inexplicably rolled across the room, the volume of a stereo suddenly increased.

Neither parent ever discussed the odd events with two-year-old Jessica, yet on more than one occasion the little girl came running out of her bedroom at night because something had frightened her. She could never put into words what had scared her, but her parents didn't think it was her imagination at play. Later, Tim learned that a friend of his had sensed a presence in the same room when he had been a renter there as a college student at the local university some years before. The entire house had been subdivided into several apartments and sleeping rooms at that period. The man often joked with his friends about his "third roommate."

The unexplained incidents increased when the Earlys started a major remodeling project on the first floor. The two largest rooms on that floor were a living room and dining room separated by a pair of the mansion's original French doors. Draperies had also been hung to cover the archway, since both rooms had once been used as sleeping quarters by earlier tenants.

Tim Early remembers one day in particular. "We were remodeling what was going to be our living room. The evening we completed the work I was sitting in the dining room with Jessica. Alice was in the kitchen. At the same time the light went off in the empty living room and the French doors between the rooms opened. I called (out to) Alice and about the same time, the screen door on the front porch opened and closed."

There was no breeze that night. Alice Early assumed that their "friend" had left the house and for a very specific reason. She thought it was because they had remodeled the main room and were going to make use of it. Another dweller would simply have made the place too crowded.

Any old house has a varied and sometimes obscure history. The Earlys researched the history of their home but couldn't establish any link between the haunting and any former owners or occupants. Their experiences did prompt a continuing interest in psychic phenomena. On one occasion, an English exchange student told them the rounded walls found in some parts of the house were designed to foil evil spirits—they couldn't find a corner to hide in!

The Earlys did try to find out more about the source of the mysterious happenings when they asked a psychic from southern Wisconsin to hold a séance in the house.

The psychic found two presences in the house, a negative entity and a "friendly" spirit, which is the one Tim and Alice had encountered. The psychic did not want to dwell on the negative presence but instead described the pleasant spirit she could "see" as a gentleman sitting in a rocker on the long-vanished side porch, stroking a cat and gazing off into the distance. He seemed to very attached to the cat, the psychic said. Tim Early thought the man was probably looking off toward the street that was blocked in the

The Parker House Poltergeist

1970s by a large corner house. The psychic could not get any better mental picture of the negative specter and they all left it at that.

"There is definitely a (friendly) spirit in that house," the psychic said. "This was his house at one time. I don't think he'd do anything negative. If the spirits (who live in a house) are friendly, they were very happy."

The Early family moved away from Maple Street many years ago. Occasional rumors still circulate about odd events in the old mansion. Neither Tim or Alice would be surprised—they've never forgotten their years in a haunted house.

THERE GOES MAMIE!

Grandmothers come in all sizes, all shapes, and all dispositions. But they all have one thing in common – grandmothers want to be remembered by their families. One way in which they can be certain they're not forgotten is by coming back—after death—to check up on their loved ones.

Grandma Mamie did that.

On a crisp, fall night in 1962, Pat Orcutt, of Whiting, Wisconsin, curled up in bed with the novel she was reading. About 10:00 P.M. she happened to glance up from the pages. Her grandmother was standing beside the bed. Nothing odd about that, except that Grandma Mamie had been dead for years and was buried in Elmira, New York.

The apparition was that of a young woman dressed in the clothing of the turn of the century.

Oddly enough, Pat recognized her immediately. A "feeling of warmth and benevolence" warmed the room as the ghost smiled down at Pat and nodded. Pat called out to her husband, but the ghost vanished before he came into the room. He argued that she had been dreaming. She insisted she had not. Suddenly all the window shades in the room snapped up simultaneously and noisily.

"Well, there goes Mamie," her husband chuckled, remembering that his wife's grandmother had been a bit mischievous with a colorful personality. He thought Pat had perhaps not been dreaming.

Pat believes her grandmother materialized at that moment to "see" her first great-grandson, Pat's baby, who had been born recently. An earlier miscarriage had caused her grandmother deep concern. She herself had cared for Pat as an infant and Mamie remained close to Pat's family through the years.

Mamie didn't return again until 1976, when the Orcutts were living in Wisconsin Rapids. Pat had painstakingly transformed a den wall into a sort of family museum, with old wedding licenses and ancestors' portraits in an assortment of frames. One day Pat found a frame containing pictures of Mamie, her husband, and Pat's father's parents, her paternal grandparents, face down on the floor. The glass was not broken and the hanger was still attached in the plaster wall.

Pat rehung the picture but several days later found it again face down on the floor. This time the hook had come out of the wall. She found a sturdier hanger and put the picture back up.

But the picture and its hanger continued to fall. Sometimes it was on the floor early in the morning; at other times, Pat found it there after coming home from shopping.

Pat's husband thought the picture either fell because of some vibrations or that one of the family's cats knocked it down. Yet, Mamie's picture was the only one of the many wall hangings disturbed.

One of the Orcutt sons had a different opinion.

Shrugging his shoulders, he suggested to his mother that Grandma Mamie had come back because she didn't like being in the same frame as her in-laws!

For some time the family joked about that possibility, but soon Pat realized her son may have been on to something. She discovered the picture was staying in place.

When Pat's parents came to visit, she told them about the falling picture.

Her mother offered another explanation.

She said that in her later years Grandma Mamie set out to destroy all photographs of herself. She had thrown away every photograph that she could find, and even cut her own image out of all the group pictures in the family albums. Pat had never known about this peculiarity; her mother thought it was due to senility.

Pat had no idea if Grandma Mamie really was continuing her crusade to erase photographic proof of her existence even after death. Perhaps she was and perhaps she eventually gave up. Grandma Mamie has not been heard from since.

UNCLE OTTO

A ghost can make itself known in a number of ways. The poltergeist, or "noisy ghost" to translate from the original German, allows its presence known through calamitous behavior—flying dishes, overturned furniture, or clattering footfalls on the stairway.

The origin of the poltergeist can be similar to that of most supernatural beings. When a person dies, so many experts speculate, an imprint much like that of a photographic negative is left behind. That imprint may take on physical properties and become a force of its own. If that negative behavior is powerful enough, the poltergeist, or in some cases an apparition, manifests itself to onlookers. Thus, we might find ghosts haunting homes to which they had a strong emotional or physical attachment during life.

The ghost of Otto Wolf* in Prescott, Wisconsin, was just that sort of poltergeist. In life, Otto had been a kindly man, blind since childhood. He lived in a rambling two-story house on Walnut Street with his brother and sister-in-law, Carl and Marian Wolf, and their son, George.

Uncle Otto, as he was called by one and all, including his own brother, had attended college and traveled to many parts of the world. But in his later years his blindness and frail health forced him to not venture far from his modest room on the second floor of the Wolf house. His very favorite pastime was to sit in an old wooden rocker as he quietly sang the German folk ballads he'd learned as a child.

Carl and Marian Wolf bought the house in 1930, shortly after they'd married. Carl was a businessman and local politician. His wife worked as a registered nurse at the local hospital. Otto moved in with his brother in 1932 and remained with the family until his death.

In 1960, two years after Otto Wolf passed away, the first in a series of bizarre and frightening events eventually convinced the Wolfs that the kindly old man's ghost had returned to the family he had loved so much in life.

George Wolf was a young adult in that summer of 1960 when Uncle Otto first let his presence be known. Late one humid August night, as George lay awake listening to the usual symphony of tree frogs and

54

Uncle Otto

crickets coming through his open bedroom window, the nightly chorus was joined by a new sound. He listened intently. What he heard made the small hairs on the back of his neck prickle. Slippered feet scuffed back and forth over the creaking floorboards of Otto's old room directly next to George's. He had gotten used to the man's nocturnal pacing when sleep eluded his blind uncle. The pace now was slow and steady just as it had always been.

George's curiosity got the best of him and he crept out of his room and down the hallway. He paused briefly, swallowed hard and opened the door to the closed room. He need not have worried. Nothing disturbed the gloomy quiet.

Maybe he imagined the entire episode, he thought, but not for long. At breakfast the next morning, Marian Wolf scolded George for pacing around Uncle Otto's room! George protested his innocence and insisted that the pacing was not his doing. At least he figured he did not imagine the whole episode. George's father had not heard the footsteps.

Nearly every night for days on end the footfalls came and went. George knew that somehow the old man was still in the house. Even though Marian had heard the footsteps, she still thought George was pulling some sort of prank. His parents scoffed at the idea of a ghost, but later events would convince them otherwise.

Surprisingly, George was not at all upset with the nocturnal ramblings. His uncle had been a kind and gentle soul during life, so he reckoned that the ghost, if indeed that is what it was, meant no harm to the family.

Nothing in Uncle Otto's room had been disturbed or changed since his death, including the old cane-bottomed rocker that had been his favorite resting spot. A few months after the pacing was first heard, George was walking down the upstairs hallway and noticed the door to his uncle's room was ajar. To his bewilderment the rocker was moving slowly as if someone had just gotten up. George checked the windows and doors but could find no significant movements of air—certainly nothing powerful enough to move the rocker. Yet George had seen it move. For many nights thereafter George heard the pacing from the next room during the night, followed by the soft creaking of the rocker. And each time that he entered the room, the rocker would be slowly moving.

George thought perhaps an errant squirrel or mouse, or one of the family's cats brushed against the rocker while escaping detection. He decided to play detective by scattering white flour on the floor around the rocker thinking a small animal would leave telltale footprints. His theory collapsed, however, when he rushed into the room after hearing the familiar creak but found no signs of either beast—or ghost—in the carpet of flour.

There are many cases of poltergeist activity in a home beset by crises such as an emotional trauma or sudden tragedy. The Wolf family soon discovered that Uncle Otto's appearance might have been a harbinger of sorrow.

Carl Wolf developed arteriosclerosis and diabetes that would cause his death at an early age. Within only a few years of Otto's death, his cherished family was experiencing hard times as a result of trying to cope with the financial drain of serious illness. When Marian Wolf subsequently developed rheumatoid arthritis and thus the family faced a double crisis, the poltergeist activity increased.

The winter of 1967–68 was particularly trying for the family financially, medically … and in the more erratic behavior of their nocturnal visitor. The nightly walks and the swaying rocker had become a part of the family's daily routine. Marian and George Wolf had long ago accepted the unnatural source of the activity.

As George looked back on the events of that time, he thinks Uncle Otto was trying to register his concern over the family's unhappiness. He knew the family was in trouble.

George had finished college and was looking for a job when he noticed that Otto's activities were increasing in intensity and duration. The footfalls could clearly be heard at all times of the day and night, quite unlike earlier years. Even Carl Wolf, nearly an invalid by this time and the last one to accept the presence of a ghost, admitted to his son that he often heard the noises when he shaved in a bathroom next to the haunted bedroom.

Then early one morning George was shaken out of bed by what sounded like a giant handball being batted against the wall in Uncle Otto's room. His parents had also heard the sound. Together they ran into the old bedroom but as usual nothing was found. Up until that time, the ghost had been almost gentle in his behavior, but this turn of events put the Wolfs somewhat on edge.

In December 1967 the family's financial plight worsened. They were

Uncle Otto

forced into bankruptcy and had to sell the house and many furnishings to pay debts. Uncle Otto's ghost was not pleased. The disturbances grew in severity, coming now from his old room and minutes later from other parts of the house.

Within a month as the family prepared to move to a smaller house, Uncle Otto tried to convince them otherwise in a most spectacular way. The family returned home after being away for an evening to find every light in the house turned on. Light even streamed through the window of a storage room in which all the electrical fixtures had been removed!

George quickly unlocked the front door and raced up the staircase. He opened the door to Uncle Otto's room. It was dark.

In that final winter of 1967–1968, and frequently before that time, the Wolfs' Siamese cats acted strangely when they were anywhere on the second floor. One cat had even been accidentally locked in Uncle Otto's bedroom overnight. The next morning, Marian Wolf found the cat crouched in the middle of the room with its fur sticking out. With a screech, it raced out of the door and never again ventured up the staircase.

Two cold spots in the house also mystified the Wolfs. One was in Uncle Otto's room and the other on a rear stairway. Passing through them was like walking into a crypt, George remembers.

A few weeks before the family moved out in early spring of 1968, George and his mother witnessed the most terrifying incident in their eight years of living with a ghost.

George was in his room reading. Midnight neared. The house, and most particularly Otto's bedroom, had been unusually quiet. Suddenly the roar of splintering wood shattered the stillness. George launched himself out of his chair and threw open his bedroom door. The solid oak door to the haunted bedroom was being pulled slowly from its hinges. George saw no one near it. Marian Wolf arrived at the top of the staircase in time to see the door being tossed into the middle of the hallway. Two large hinges hung limply from the shattered frame.

"My God! What's gone wrong?" George screamed.

His mother didn't answer.

Mother and son knew that nothing human could have pulled that door from its frame.

The next day George moved into a vacant downstairs bedroom.

Despite the terror of that night, no one in the family had ever been physically harmed, or even touched, by the ghost. That changed a few days after the door was torn away and shortly before the family moved away.

George awoke to a soft, almost gentle, stroking of his face. It was the caress of a human hand against his cheek, reassuring in its touch. Then it was gone. In the dim light, he saw one of the cats sitting in an old chair, its back arched rigid. The animal's eyes seemed to be following the progress of someone moving across the room.

George Wolf knew then that Uncle Otto was apologizing for his outlandish behavior. And saying good-bye.

DON'T MESS WITH ELMER

In the hardscrabble Depression years of the 1930s, when a person's economic security was often determined by luck or resourcefulness, tempers sometimes flared over small injustices, whether real or imagined. At least that's how it was in northern Wisconsin between bachelor farmer Roy Nelson* of rural Cumberland and his neighbor Elmer Pederson*. The men had been renting some joint acreage and they shared the hay crop.

One day the men had an argument over the arrangement. No one today remembers what caused the disagreement, only that it led to a perplexing series of events in that pocket of the state.

Soon after the argument, Roy began complaining about a "ghost" on his property—a prankish sprite that left barn doors wide open day and night, filled feed troughs to overflowing with water, and pounded on the walls of Nelson's house all night long.

Roy named Elmer Pederson as the culprit. Neighbors were anxious to preserve harmony in the community so they didn't dare take sides. That and the pair's naturally ornery dispositions, which many feared would result in a lawsuit for slander should either one be publicly criticized. Secretly, they attributed Roy's wild tales to the eccentricities of living alone too long.

But the neutrality didn't last long. When the disturbances at Roy's farm continued, the neighbors got involved. After all, they reasoned, Roy was basically a good man always ready to welcome a visitor with a hot cup of coffee. He kept his Bible open on the kitchen table and paid his help well.

Roy called his unseen tormentor a "Billy goat" for some reason. And he was determined to catch him—or it—in the act.

He persuaded a few nearby farmers to take turns hiding in his woodpile and watch from the windows of his modest farmhouse. Meanwhile, Roy would carry out his own surveillance. He ran a wire from his house to his barn and bought a German shepherd dog whose leash he looped around the wire. The dog was free to run back and forth in hot pursuit of any trespasser, seen or unseen.

Next, Roy borrowed a .38-caliber revolver from his brother-in-law and stood guard on the front porch. Whenever he heard a strange sound, he fired in the air a sound that reportedly echoed three-quarters of a mile away in that quiet neighborhood.

Meanwhile, watchers inside the house usually congregated in the kitchen. If they heard pounding on the walls at the opposite side of the house they ran to that side. Then the thumping would jump back to the kitchen walls. But with men stationed at both ends of the house, the irritating thumps would cease.

Even neighborhood children took their turns on the "ghost watch." A good friend of Roy's volunteered his son's services for a 48-hour shift. Pete was a little boy of 12 years at the time.

"I shook from my belly button both ways," Pete remembers today, "but I didn't dare say no."

He was given a chamber pot and instructed to go upstairs and remain there at all times. Roy carried food and water up to him. A horse blanket with a peephole cut through it had been tacked up over a window. On the first day, while the boy squinted through the hole watching Roy at work in a nearby field, he heard what sounded like someone moving around a jug downstairs. But he knew there was no jug down there.

"That's when I quit growing," he recalls.

Later that evening when Roy returned from the field, he discovered that the mail, which he had picked up at noon, was strewn all over the kitchen. Long after dark and still huddled upstairs, little Pete heard swats from a rolled up newspaper. Roy was yelling at his "Billy goat" to get away.

"After two days of Depression coffee, I went home," Pete says.

A day or so later the boy was helping Roy with the haying on the rental property. As it happened, Elmer was haying at the same time.

Pete says, "At one time we were all within 15 feet of one another. The look they exchanged wasn't one of love, hope, or charity."

The ghostly disturbances ceased a short time later when Elmer died unexpectedly ... of natural causes.

Now that could have been coincidence, or perhaps Elmer himself really was the "spook." Pete isn't sure today if anyone really wanted to catch the culprit. He said chasing after the ghost did cause a good deal of levity in that grim Depression-era year.

Pete doesn't really know who the ghost was.

Perhaps it never really mattered.

A DREAM SO REAL

The Scots may not be the most superstitious people in the world, but some beliefs they hold to tenaciously. One such conviction is that the seventh son of a seventh son has precognitive powers, that is, the ability to foretell future events.

When Robert Laurie was born in Scotland the seventh son of a seventh son, news of his birth spread far and wide. His family learned when he was just a small boy that Robert had the gift as many characterized precognition. In 1854, the Lauries immigrated to Sturgeon Bay, Wisconsin. Here as young Robert grew to manhood, his extraordinary, almost supernatural, powers flourished. His fame spread far and wide.

The problem with precognition is that one can "see" both good and evil. For Robert, his honesty dictated that he disclose whatever the future held.

He told a neighboring family with seven daughters that their eighth child would be a boy. It was and they were joyful.

On another occasion, Robert assured a woman that her fisherman husband would survive the roiling Lake Michigan waters after his boat capsized in a storm. Laurie had "seen" the man clinging to the boat's cabin hatch that had been torn loose from the craft. Some time later, the hatch, bearing its human cargo, was washed up on shore. The sailor was barely conscious, yet he was alive.

Not all of Robert's uncanny predictions were so welcome. Alex Laurie, Robert's older brother, along with another man set forth by boat for Green Bay to buy supplies. Robert said they would never return. The boat must have capsized for neither it nor the two men were ever heard from again.

One night when he was in his sixties, Robert had a dream so vivid that in the morning he recounted it in precise detail to his wife, Catherine. He told her there would soon be a large funeral in Door County. People would attend from great distances, traveling by land and by water to get to the services. He described the glistening horses pulling magnificent carriages, he named the minister, and he named a precise number of mourners.

The only thing he could not name was the deceased. In his dream he could see the person that the casket held.

A month later, a funeral was held, one of the largest in the history of Door County. People did travel from far and near. All of the details were unerringly like those Robert Laurie had told his wife. But among the mourners was one whose heart was heaviest with sorrow—Catherine, the widow of this seventh son of a seventh son.

THE SUMMONING

The second-floor apartment of the private home in Manitowoc met the needs of Randolph and Esther Johnson* back in 1935. Their land-lord lived in separate lodgings downstairs.

The Johnson's bedroom had two doors diagonally across from one another, leaving barely enough room for their double bed. A door near the foot of the bed was never used and kept locked. It led out into a hall-way; an old-fashioned wardrobe cabinet in which the Johnson's kept clothing also blocked the way. A china cabinet in the hallway blocked access from outside the hallway outside the apartment.

A second door near the head of the bed opened into a rear room from which the tenants could reach the stairway leading to the outside door.

On one night after they'd lived there for some time and the couple had gone to bed, Esther had a hard time falling asleep. As she stared off into the inky darkness of the room, the startling apparition of a tall woman wearing a long gray dress and matching sweater floated out of the wardrobe. She moved with folded arms and bowed head around the bed and passed through the door into the rear room.

Esther nudged her husband who slept only a few feet away from the ghost's path. He looked over, grunted, and said, "Can't Mrs. Anderson* walk in her own house if she wants to?" He went back to sleep as did Esther in time.

In the morning Esther and Randolph discovered that their landlord Mason Anderson had died in his sleep some hours before. His wife had come to get him by way of the Johnson's apartment. She'd been dead for 19 years.

HOUSE OF CHIMES

The George Websters moved into an old house in Green Bay in 1968. Everything went well at first. Then, the kitchen screen door, equipped with a tight spring, began opening and slamming shut with no one near it and no wind blowing. George recalls that on one occasion the slamming was preceded by "a loud scraping, swirling noise." He had been standing only 20 feet from the door. He rushed outside to investigate but found nothing that could account for the noise or the movement of the door.

On July 20, 1976, George was home alone doing paperwork for his job as district supervisor for a Chicago-based corporation. He had just started for the back bedroom when he heard the now-familiar slam. Looking toward the door, he saw the apparition of a man approaching — a black clothed specter who seemed to float rather than walk. It came straight toward him and George flattened himself against a wall to let it pass. Then the ghost, as if sensing a head-on collision, veered to the right and passed within two feet of Webster. It turned its head to stare at him, entered a bedroom, and vanished. George estimates that the episode took place in about ten seconds.

Five days later the family left on a vacation trip. The house was locked up and empty, or so they thought. At 9:00 P.M. that night the neighbors, who were taking in Websters' mail, saw the kitchen lights go on and dark apparitions move back and forth in the room.

One day in August, Mrs. Webster watched two white-clad ghosts disappear into the master bedroom just off the kitchen.

Some time later, the family began hearing "scraping and screeching noises in between the walls." Playful mice? Hardly. George says, "These noises would then turn into chimes and bell-like noises." Lights also were being turned on and off by unseen forces both day and night, and neighbors often called the Websters to find out why they had left their basement lights on all night.

On September 3, 1977, the family moved. The old house remained vacant for three months before it sold and, although the electricity was shut off, neighbors reported that the lights continued to go on intermittently during that entire time. George then talked with the former owner of the place, who said he had never witnessed any strange phenomena during his stay in the house.

What does George make of these bizarre manifestations? He has no explanation; he says only that he believed his experiences are "most unusual."

THE GIRL IN WHITE

In the early days of the 20th century, few people in rural Wisconsin traveled by car or even by buggy. Those who owned horses rode them; those less fortunate walked. Young John Groat of Menomonie was among the latter. One hot summer evening, Groat and his neighbor Ed Forness* walked the mile and a half to town. On the way back they decided to visit their girlfriends, Carrie and Anna Chapman*, two sisters who lived with their parents in a farmhouse not far from the road the men traveled and quite near a small stream.

But as the men reached the wooden bridge that carried the roadway over the shallow stream, they stopped to reconsider their visit with the girls. After all it was quite late and they weren't expected.

"Look, John!" Ed Forness suddenly called out, as he pointed off down the gloomy road. "Looks like there's a girl all in white coming down the road."

Forness was right. John saw a girl about the age of Carrie and Anna walking directly toward them, but then she turned abruptly before the bridge, walked down into the stream. And vanished.

The two men dashed to the stream bank where the girl had entered the water. They waded into the knee-deep water, walked back and forth, around and around, but could find no trace of the girl.

John Groat feared that the girl in white must have been either Carrie or Anna and he knew, too, without asking, that Ed shared the same trepidation. But why would either girl be out all alone at night? And how could anyone disappear in such a shallow body of water?

"Ed, we've got to get to the Chapman place right away," Groat said, starting off at a fast pace. "I don't know how it could've been Anna or my Carrie, but we've gotta find out. And if it ain't one of them, well…" his voice trailed off.

At the farmhouse, the girls' parents were still out on the porch. Mrs. Chapman explained that they had had company earlier and that the girls were in the kitchen washing dishes.

"Carrie! Anna!" their father called into the house.

The Girl in White

The girls came out and listened to their boyfriends' story. Both girls were as puzzled as their beaus were. They'd waded the stream many times but there were no deep holes anywhere in it.

A century and more has passed, yet no one has ever offered a satisfactory explanation of who or what those two young men encountered. John Groat always said he would never, ever have told the story if Ed Forness had not been at his side on that remarkable summer night.

THE BURNINGS

In the middle of the 19th century, Norwegians began moving into the sandy jackpine region of northwestern Wisconsin. Here, in the harsh and isolated Indianhead country, the new immigrants broke the land and attempted to wrest a living from the meager soil.

The Einar Larsen* family had just finished building a snug cabin and had moved in. Returning home late one evening, they discovered that a window curtain had burned; an ash pile on the floor was all that remained. Strangely, the floor was not scorched, nor was there any other sign of fire anywhere else in the house. Although perplexed, the Larsens soon put the event out of mind.

About a year later, after another outing to visit neighbors, the family returned and smelled smoke upon entering the house. They soon discovered that a chair cushion was smoldering while the chair itself showed no signs of a burn. Again, they were at a loss as to a cause. Einar Larsen's careful search of the house revealed no clues—everything was in order.

Another full year would pass before the next "burning," only this time it was a far more devastating event. The family again returned home late of an evening to find their house burned to the ground.

Although they rebuilt their home, the Larsens never felt entirely comfortable not knowing who or what caused the mysterious fires. Several months later a fire broke out in the middle of the night and the family barely had time to escape. Feeling lucky to be alive and not wishing to tempt fate further, they abandoned their homestead.

Many years later, a newcomer to the area bought what had been the Larsen land a century before and made plans to build a modern summer cabin. Construction was partway along when the carpenter hired to do the construction arrived one morning to find the charred remains of his apron on the floor exactly where he had left it the previous day. About this time, the newcomer learned the history of the place. He paid off the carpenter and abandoned his plans.

American history is filled with tales of mysterious, spontaneous fires— flames igniting clothing in closets, burning mattresses on unoccupied beds,

The Burnings

and fires erupting in the center of bare floors. There are even accounts of human beings suddenly bursting into flame for no apparent reason.

We do not know how the "burnings" occurred in that cabin in the tangled jackpine forest of northern Wisconsin. If they had been of incendiary origin, it is odd that the house itself didn't burn down the first time or second time the family discovered the remnants of a fire. Some said the fires were all unfortunate coincidences. But others insisted odder, more sinister, and possibly, supernatural forces were at work. Which was the case here? We can only speculate.

THE SPIRITS OF MADELINE ISLAND

Before white men came to Wisconsin there was a land called Moningwunakaunig, "place of the golden-breasted woodpecker." We call it Madeline, largest of the Apostle Islands scattered off Lake Superior's shore near Bayfield.

Madeline Island is a 14,000–acre refuge with white sand beaches hugging impenetrable forests of fir, spruce, pine, and hardwoods, contrasting sharply with wind-sculpted red granite cliffs on the island's lake side. It is an ancient place. For 3,000 years Madeline has known human footsteps. Primitive peoples camped in the forests, taking from the waters and forest their simple diet of fish, meat, and berries when Roman armies were conquering Europe.

Later, the Ojibway (Chippewa) were forced from their ancestral home along the St. Lawrence River and they settled on the Apostle Islands. A great village was built on Madeline with a population, archeologists say, of nearly 12,000. But the area became overpopulated and a terrible famine struck the native people.

Farming was rudimentary, if practiced at all; the men of the tribe could not kill enough fish and game to feed a village the size of a small modern city. In desperation, tribal elders and the medicine men resorted to cannibalism. Young maidens and children were chosen and offered as sacrifices on a primitive altar, their flesh used as food. But, the population rebelled after a time and the old leadership was executed.

Tales began spreading that the island was haunted by the vengeful spirits of the dead women and children. They would rise from the earth near the sacrificial altar and wander over the island.

Legend says a great exodus took place and the entire village was evacuated to the mainland until not a Chippewa remained on Madeline. Various families migrated to locations in northern Wisconsin and Minnesota. Some accounts insist it was several centuries before the Chippewa would again camp on the large island.

Now there are few Indians on the island. Earlier in this century, it is said, some sacrificial tobacco was found scattered at the site of the ancient altar.

70

The Spirits of Madeline Island

Today Madeline Island caters primarily to tourists and several hundred permanent residents. Few traces remain of the island's original inhabitants. A modern yacht harbor and marina occupy the lagoon near which the sacrificial altar was located. Nearby are a lavish resort and a golf course created by the world-famous designer Robert Trent Jones. A few old islanders say the lagoon used to harbor the ghosts of those killed and devoured centuries ago. Although no one has reported any recent apparitions, on a cool dark, foggy night if you sit near the shore of that lagoon at the edge of the old Indian burial ground, and listen intently, you might hear the haunting plaintive cries of the sacrificed.

TWO OJIBWAY GHOSTS

In ancient days, Indians roamed Wisconsin. Game was plentiful in the dense forests, and men, hunting each day, provided well for their families.

One winter evening, a young Ojibway wife, awaiting the return of her husband, became uneasy. He was always home earlier, tired but eager to sit by the fire and spin stories of the day's adventures for her and the child. But now?

Suddenly the silence of the night was broken by the sound of footsteps. The wife hurried to the door of the lodge. Her husband was nowhere in sight. Instead, two strange women stood beyond the doorway, their thin figures wrapped in garments that almost concealed their long, hollow-eyed faces. The hunter's wife did not recognize them. They were not of her tribe and she had no idea where they might have come from. The nearest family lived a distance of several days' travel through the woods. Yet, not wishing to appear inhospitable, she invited them in to warm up by the fire. They accepted her invitation, but instead of going to the fire, huddled in a dark corner of the room.

Suddenly a voice cried out, "Merciful spirit, there are two corpses clothed in garments!" The wife wheeled around. There was no one there, no one except the silent guests. Had she been dreaming? Hearing only the sound of a rising wind?

Then the door burst open and the hunter appeared, dragging behind him the carcass of a large, fat deer. At that instant, the strangers rushed to the animal and began pulling off the choicest bits of white fat. The husband and wife, although astonished by such impropriety, decided that their guests must be famished and so they said nothing.

The next day when the hunter returned from the chase, the same thing occurred.

On the third day, the young man, deciding to cater to the whims of his peculiar visitors, tied a bundle of fat on the top of the carcass he brought home. The women seized it eagerly, then ate the portion of fat that had been set aside for the wife. The hunter, although tempted to rebuke them, remained silent. For some mysterious reason he had had

Two Ojibway Ghosts

unaccountable good luck in bringing down game since the ghostly visitors had come into his home; he thought that perhaps somehow his good fortune had something to do with their presence. Besides, the women didn't cause any trouble; on the contrary, they began to be helpful. Each evening they gathered wood, stacked it by the fire, and returned all implements to the place where they had found them. During the daytime, they huddled unobtrusively in a corner. They never joined a family conversation, nor laughed or joked.

Finally, one evening in early spring, the hunter stayed out later than usual. When he did appear with a carcass, the visitors tore off the fat so rudely that the wife, who had held her anger in check for so many months, was on the verge of lashing out at the usurpers. Although she managed to keep silent, she was certain, this time, that the guests sensed her resentment.

After the family had gone to bed, the husband heard the women weeping. He tried to sleep, but their sobbing seemed incessant. Recalling the looks exchanged between his wife and the guests, he worried that his mate had offended them. Had she spoken sharply to them? Said something that he perhaps hadn't heard? He got up, went over to the women, and asked what was wrong. After assuring him that he had treated them kindly, they spoke further.

"We come from the land of the dead to test the sincerity of the living," they began. They explained that many living people, bereaved by death in a family, say that if only the dead could be restored to life they would devote the rest of their lives to making them happy. The Master of Life had given them "three moons" in which to test the sincerity of those who had lost friends or relatives. "We have been here more than half that time," they said, "but now your wife is so angered by our presence that we have decided we must leave."

The hunter's wife, awakened by now by the voices, arose and stood at her husband's side. The ghosts went on to explain why they had eaten the choicest parts of the hunter's kills. "That was the particular trial selected for you. We know, by your customs, that the white fat is reserved for the wife. In usurping that privilege we have put you both to a severe test of your tempers and feelings. But that is what we were sent to do."

Before the astonished hunter and his wife could respond, the ghosts blessed them and said good-bye.

At that moment, the lodge was plunged into total darkness. But their blessings were made manifest in the years to come. The hunter excelled in the chase, fathered many splendid children, and enjoyed health, wealth, and a long life. Such were the rewards of befriending two lonely ghosts who had come to test him on a winter's night of long ago.

THE COULEE ROAD GHOST

Hudson, Wisconsin, is a small, bustling city clinging to the bluffs of the St. Croix River. The city is a popular suburban home for workers in Minneapolis/St. Paul, Minnesota, only 15 miles to the west. Its scenic river beauty, coupled with pleasant small-town living, makes it a popular locale. Nothing much out of the ordinary happens in Hudson ... except the legendary visits by the ghost of Paschal Aldrich.

The story of the hauntings on what is now called Coulee Road begins nearly 140 years ago with the arrival in Hudson of one of its first residents, Dr. Philip Aldrich.

Aldrich, who was born in Ohio in 1792, could justifiably be called a pioneer entrepreneur. He became over the years a businessman, mail carrier and postmaster, county commissioner, circuit judge, and landowner. No doubt the ease with which he accomplished these tasks was due in some measure to the small population of St. Croix County in 1845 — 1,419 inhabitants. That was according to Dr. Aldrich's own census! In those days, the county included most of northwestern Wisconsin and that part of Minnesota between the Mississippi River and St. Croix River.

Shortly after Aldrich arrived in the county in 1840, the federal government awarded him a contract to carry twice-monthly mail dispatches from Point Douglas to St. Croix Falls. During the summer he piloted a flat-bottomed riverboat, called a bateau, and in the winter he trod the ice-covered river by foot.

Two years later, Dr. Aldrich was elected a county commissioner and continued to be closely associated with the political growth of western Wisconsin for many years. According to newspaper accounts, the first meeting of the St. Croix County Board was held September 9, 1848, at the home of Dr. Aldrich, which stood at the northeast corner of Second Street and Elm in Hudson. The house was a center of many gala social events in early Hudson.

Dr. Aldrich had moved into Hudson during the previous year, 1847. He bought a large tract of land, now called the Aldrich Addition. Aldrich abandoned his mail route via the St. Croix River, and an overland route was begun from Hudson to St. Croix Falls. The mail was delivered on foot once a week, a distance of some eight miles round trip!

In 1849, Aldrich became Hudson's first postmaster, a position he held until 1851. In that same year, he was also granted a license to operate a ferry across the St. Croix River.

A son of Dr. Aldrich, Paschal, owned a home on Buckeye Street that became the first post office. Paschal's wife, Martha, often clerked in the post office and since she could neither read nor write, the patrons picked out their own letters.

Following Dr. Philip Aldrich's death, the large holdings were passed on to Paschal. But the luck of the father was not invested in the son.

Paschal Aldrich and his family moved to a small house at the head of Coulee Road, near present Interstate Highway 94. He farmed a large area for many years, but when a serious illness altered his fortunes, he was forced to sell much of the property. There is some dispute as to the reason for the sale. One newspaper account reports that an unidentified man somehow caused the family to lose its vast holdings during Paschal's illness.

Paschal Aldrich died on October 13, 1860, in that house on Coulee Road. For years afterward, the place was known as the "haunted house." Members of his family and some neighbors said they saw Paschal's ghost wandering the premises at night, reportedly keeping watch over his family. Paschal's solicitude in death was attributed to his near financial ruin during the illness preceding his death.

Mrs. Paschal Aldrich also vowed to come back in the form of a ghost. But her granddaughter, the late Mrs. Wallace Smith, said, "I've never heard if there was ever a second ghost out there or not."

Perhaps one was enough.

THE CHIEFTAIN'S CURSE

The haunted house of legend must be a stately old mansion perched atop a windswept knoll. One enters the grounds through a gate attached by a single hinge to the decrepit fence winding around the property. The building is in a desperate state of disrepair—planks missing from the front veranda, windows boarded up or broken—and, for good measure, a few bats ought to flutter from one of the gable windows. Of course, one visits the mansion at midnight when it is cold and windy, and terror seems to wait just beyond that large, forbidding door.

Well, that's fiction. In fact, one of Wisconsin's more famous haunted houses fits only part of that imaginary picture. In earlier days this house and the land upon which it still stands seemed to be cursed with evil. No fewer than ten people associated with the mansion met unusual deaths. Although there have been no reports of rattling chains or ghostly apparitions, if a house can be haunted with grief and sorrow, it is the Scott mansion in Merrill.

In the early part of the last century an Indian village occupied the west bank of the Wisconsin River in what is now the city of Merrill. French fur traders had often stopped at the village to barter for goods. The peaceful Indians had little fear of the white men. When lumbermen began traveling the river during the big timber drives in northern Wisconsin they were welcomed as brothers by the inhabitants.

The village chief would bring visitors to his wigwam where his only daughter would serve them meals. The men were entranced by the beautiful, shy maiden who soon became known as Jenny to her white guests. But the blissful life of the settlement soon turned to tragedy. A young lumberjack who was particularly fond of Jenny made love to her. The accounts differ as to what happened next. One version asserts that Jenny, ashamed of her act, killed herself. Another tale states that Jenny simply died soon thereafter, probably of the flu, which had been introduced among the Indian peoples by the white men.

Whatever the cause of lovely Jenny's death, her father was grief-stricken. He ordered that she be buried upon a high hill across the river from the settlement. At her burial the old man stood at his daughter's grave, gazed out over the river, and prayed, "Oh, great Father, grant me this place for my child. Let this ground be sacred to her memory." Then he placed a curse upon that earth: "Let it never do any white man any good."

The years passed, the Indians abandoned the settlement, and Jenny and her final resting place were all but forgotten. The village that had grown beside the Indian camp was named to honor S. S. Merrill, the manager of the St. Paul railroad.

But in 1884 there began a series of events so strange that the old chief's grim incantation seemed to echo down through the ages.

T. B. Scott, a wealthy Merrill Mill owner and lumberman, purchased "Jenny's hill" from the government and planned to build a mansion there fit for a timber baron. He knew nothing of Jenny or the curse. Only two years after he bought the land in 1886, Scott died with the house only partially built. He was 57. Scott's widow, Ann, in ill health, tried to complete construction of the mansion. But within a year Ann was dead. It was now left to their son, Walter, to finish his father's work.

Although his mother had urged him to complete the house, Walter apparently abandoned the project. Some years later, however, Walter did visit Chicago to consult an architect. During their meeting, Walter and the architect, a Mr. Sheldon, got into a fight and young Scott was stabbed to death with a letter opener. Sheldon proved self-defense, implying that Walter Scott instigated the struggle.

The Scott estate sold the still-incomplete mansion to a Chicago millionaire, Mr. Kuechle. He wanted the house as a summer retreat and made plans to install lavish additions to the mansion. Kuechle visited the World's Columbian Exposition in Chicago in 1893 and bought a number of decorations for the house, including heavy, hand-carved doors, plate glass windows, embossed mirrors, and a carved mantel. He hired workmen to install the furnishings and complete construction. Kuechle apparently spent little if any time in the mansion. Within a short time, a series of bad investments forced him to mortgage the house to a Chicago tavern owner named Barsanti. Kuechle was able to avoid foreclosure on the mansion when he inherited a large sum of money. Determined to recoup his loses, Kuechle invested the fortune in a contract to build a section of the Northern Pacific Railroad. The man knew nothing of railroads or engineering, soon went bankrupt, and later died in a mental institution.

The Chieftain's Curse

Barsanti took possession, but never lived to see the mansion. He had apparently antagonized a murderous gang known as the Black Hand, and as he waited in Chicago's Union Station to board a train for Merrill, he was stabbed to death by one of the "Hands."

The Barsanti family, in turn, sold the still-vacant and only half-completed mansion to a real estate speculator, George Gibson. His idea was to build a home for elderly lawyers. An office was organized in Merrill to collect donations, and work once again resumed on the mansion.

Late one afternoon Gibson left his office for home to have supper and then he vanished. Search parties were organized to scour the countryside. The Wisconsin River was dragged without success. River banks and booms (sections of the river where freshly cut timber jam up) were carefully watched. There was no apparent motive for Gibson's sudden disappearance. He was a devoted family man, well liked by the townspeople, with no financial problems. Indeed he had looked forward to the day when the mansion would house the aged barristers. But George Gibson was never seen alive or dead after that day.

The mansion reverted to the Barsanti family since all payments on the house had not been made. The family retained possession for several years during which the mansion was never occupied. A reputation for evil was now firmly attached to the old place. Caretakers looked after the house and grounds, mainly to protect it from vandals. One old groundsman was an Englishman called Popcorn Dan, since he also operated a popcorn stand in Merrill. In 1911 he sailed for England and a visit to his childhood home. Returning to America in 1912, however, he made a fatal mistake. Popcorn Dan booked passage on the *S.S. Titanic*.

The Lloydsen family became the mansion's caretakers after Popcorn Dan's death. Mr. Lloydsen died of alcoholism.

Finally, Mrs. Mary Fehlhaber, a Merrill area midwife, bought the mansion for a small sum and took in boarders. One day, while out riding, she became ill, made her way to a nearby farm home, but died before a doctor could reach her side.

In 1919, Herman Fehlhaber, Mary's husband, gave the house and adjoining property to the city of Merrill. Four years later the city gave the property to the Sisters of Mercy of the Holy Cross, an order of Roman Catholic nuns. The Scott mansion is now used as a residence for the sisters, who operate a hospital and small college nearby. Nothing peculiar has happened to the house or its occupants since 1923.

It is only a macabre coincidence that so many people associated with the house met with tragedy during their lives? Or did that curse pronounced so very long ago carry through the decades to torment those who tried to build on "Jenny's hill"? Perhaps now that the mansion and the grounds are being used for humanitarian purposes there is peace on that high knoll.

Should you ever see the Scott mansion at the south end of Merrill, think of Jenny. Is the curse over? Yes, at least for now.

A QUARTET OF WISPS

Will-o'-the-wisp: *n. A phosphorescent light that hovers over swampy ground at night, possibly caused by rotting organic matter.*

That is what the dictionary says, but Wisconsin pioneers often placed the will-o'-the-wisp in the same category as ghosts. Within the vast, dark forests, along river banks and lowlands, the eerie dancing lights would be seen moving and jumping as if they were living, breathing creatures. No theory about "possible rotting organic matter" could dissuade those hardy settlers that anything but the devil could be the culprit.

The Wisp that Roared

Mrs. Adele Cline of Eau Pleine recalls that the lights had the appearance of a man walking along in the dark swinging a lantern, a common method of travel in the early days. Mrs. Cline's father first saw the phenomenon on a homestead near the Big Eau Pleine River in the 1880s. The first encounter took place one night on his way home from a visit to his parents' farm about a mile from his own cabin. The will-o'-the-wisp suddenly appeared beside him and followed him nearly to his doorstep.

Mrs. Cline's parents eventually built a barn on the land and surrounded the yard with a timber fence. The will-o'-the-wisp never entered the yard once the fence was erected.

The family homestead was quite near a small lake formed by the Big Eau Pleine River. Between the barn and lake was a large area covered by rock and slabs of stone. The children used to call it "the acre of stone." All around this section the land was cleared and under cultivation. Mrs. Cline said the light would come up from the river and cross over this stony expanse usually at twilight, although her mother watched as two lights chased each other until the early morning hours.

The light would sometimes travel very fast, "as though it was really in a hurry," while at other times it would hover and slowly fade. A few minutes later it might reappear hundreds of feet away and continue its strange, nocturnal gyrations.

On one occasion Mrs. Cline's young aunt, 12 years old, and an uncle, who was only nine, came to visit the family. The children had been assigned the job of bringing in the livestock. Twilight descended and the youngsters had yet to complete their tasks. As they walked across a pasture the will-o'-the-wisps appeared floating beside them. Their dog took a look at the apparition and bolted for home. He hid for several days under the front porch. The cows also wasted little time in returning to the comforts of the barn.

A few days later Mrs. Cline's grandfather was returning home at dusk when he saw the glowing, bobbing will-o'-the-wisp. At the same instant a thunderous roar bellowed from deep within the earth. The old man had been a soldier in the German Kaiser's East Prussian Army. He was familiar with the roar of cannon fire, yet the sound on that night was more frightening than anything he had ever heard.

Could there have been an underground landslide in an impenetrable cavern? Was there a minor earthquake? The same sound was heard several years later by a neighbor boy returning along the same path. From that night on he carried a gun whenever he was out late.

Mrs. Cline's family eventually moved to an adjoining farm and their original homestead was rented. The new tenants would periodically report seeing a man walking along with a lantern in "the acre of stone."

The last sighting occurred in 1948. A bulldozer operator, who was clearing stone from the farm, visited Mrs. Cline's father and expressed his surprise at having seen the old man out walking all alone the previous evening with only a lantern. "You could have seen the field by riding with me on the bulldozer," he said. Mrs. Cline's father just looked up and smiled. He knew the will-o'-the-wisp had been abroad in the land once again.

The Wisp in the Graveyard

The legendary ghost arises in the dark, brooding silences of cemeteries. But it wasn't exactly the ghost of legend that appeared to Buffalo County pioneers in the autumn of 1889. It was a fireball that hovered above a grave of the old Indian burial grounds on the shores of Oneida Lake. The size of a large orange, it swayed, like an eerie pendulum, 30 feet above the ground. As the whispered word spread among them curious residents of the area gathered nightly on the lakeshore to watch the swinging light. Occasionally, a brave man reached out to catch the light, but it always vanished before his eyes.

A will-o'-the-wisp? Old-timers had a different explanation. They said that a man named Belknap once had recurring dreams in which he saw a crock filled with immense treasures in the old cemetery. He was convinced that if he went there late at night and dug up the crock it would be his.

So vivid were these dreams that finally, one night, Belknap was impelled to action. He set forth with pick and shovel, found the crock, and dug it up. Alas, he had failed to turn around three times as he had been directed in the dream. The minute he bent down to pick up the crock he was stunned by a flash of lighting and the crock vanished.

And since that night the spot has been haunted by the glowing beacon ... the sign of one man's folly.

The Wisp on the Road

The will-o'-the-wisp would often form itself into a bluish-colored fireball. It would then hop and skip across the fields. Some say that if a person is interfered with the wisp he would become lost. Luckily that didn't happen to Alfred Ulrick, Sr., who had several chilling encounters with the will-o'-the-wisp.

Ulrick was a young man 70 years ago when he first encountered the wisp. The mysterious ball of fire was common in rural Wisconsin in those days. It would appear in an open field near his parents' farm in all manner of weather, rainy or dry, and on the darkest of nights as well as when the moon was full. Farm animals, ironically, seemed unafraid of the object. They would continue to graze even when the wisp was close by in the pasture. But, Ulrick says, no one ever tried to interfere with the will-o'-the-wisp.

The closest Ulrick came to a direct encounter with the will-o'-the-wisp was an incident in July of 1909. Ulrick and his father had taken the buggy and a favorite horse named Dick into town for a supply of oats. Their grain hadn't yet been harvested.

Ulrick describes his father, who stood nearly six feet tall and weighed 175 pounds, as a fearless man: "He did not seem to know the meaning of fear, regardless of what the situation was."

On their way home the Ulricks had to travel near an area where the will-o'-the-wisp was known to frolic. Twilight descended on the pair as Dick trotted through the gathering gloom. The night air was cool. A full moon cast a glow across the nightscape. The road stretched out before them "like a white ribbon laid out in the darkness."

Soon, father and son knew they were near the wisp's playground. They began peering into the darkness. A glimpse of the fiery creature would provide ample fuel for a lively tale once they reached home.

And then they saw the will-o'-the-wisp. It was hovering and pulsating not far away. It appeared to be moving toward them. Ulrick's father reined the horse to a walk for a closer look at the mysterious object. Alfred didn't appreciate his father's curiosity. The young boy didn't say anything, but his stomach was churning.

As the object continued to close the distance Ulrick's father brought the horse to a stop. In a few seconds, the will-o'-the-wisp was only a few yards from the wagon. That was young Alfred's limit. "I think my body was covered with more goose-pimples than a chicken has feathers; seconds seemed like hours; and I know I stopped breathing."

His father evidently felt the same dread, for he urged the horse onward. They didn't stop until they reached home. Did the will-o'-the-wisp follow them? Neither father nor son ever looked back.

The Hitchhiking Wisp

Sailors are familiar with a phenomenon called St. Elmo's fire. This round flash of light often appears around ship masts during stormy weather. We know it is an electric charge, which actually does look like a flame. It is named for St. Elmo, the patron saint of sailors. It is also not unusual for St. Elmo's fire to appear on land around church steeples, airplanes, and other objects when weather is unsettled.

In early Wisconsin, St. Elmo's fire was often mistaken for the phantom-like will-o'-the-wisp by those who saw it. Such was the case of K. F. Peabody in Star Prairie.

Automobiles were still a rarity on country roads in the early 1910s, but travelers often ventured out after dark with the aid of strong spotlights. On one particular night Peabody was guiding a horse and rig through a light drizzle. It was late and the road was quite muddy. Suddenly a bright light surrounded the rig. Thinking it was someone coming up from behind, Peabody pulled his rig toward the side of the road and turned to look. Nobody was behind him.

Peabody was startled. Where was the light coming from? Perhaps it was shining on him from somewhere in the dark night sky. He lowered his umbrella. There, on the metal tip, was a bright shimmering flame. Peabody quickly furled the umbrella. The flame jumped to a whip that was held in place next to the wooden buggy seat. As he gazed at the flame he recalled reading about St. Elmo's fire and realized that this must be the explanation. He removed the whip and looked more closely at the flame. It was white, quite brilliant, and similar to the flame of a candle, but it gave off no heat and, in fact, was quite cold.

Peabody returned the whip to its socket and drove on. The flame stayed with him to the top of the ridge. On the downhill side, the flame gradually receded and eventually disappeared when he reached the bottom.

• • •

Whether it danced across a meadow, followed pioneers to their doorsteps, or hitched a ride in a buggy, the will-o'-the-wisp was a unique part of the ghost lore of Wisconsin. To the uneducated pioneer, the wisp's appearance was a source of awe, not fright. We now know that those lights pulsating over that dank swamp in the dead of night were products of swamp gas … don't we?

THE PENDANT

Her name was Jan. A pretty girl. Gold-tinged hair framed a cameo face. Her large, gray-green eyes held the sunlight of today and the dreams of tomorrow. She fell in love; she fell out of love. She knew joy and despair. She studied art in college, and during the summers of her young womanhood she loved to swim, boat, and picnic at her parents' lakeside home near Spooner. Although shy and sensitive, she had the restless, searching mind that longs to know the world, to hold it close. Those who knew her hoped that all good things would come to her.

At 28 she was dead, the loser in a three-year battle against mental illness. Her life had ended at the moment when doctors said that complete recovery was in sight, when bright tomorrows were within her grasp.

For her parents, Marion and Dick Stresau, and the other children, the tomorrows were filled with the special sadness that attends the death of one who has died too soon.

But that sadness was overshadowed by a series of perplexing incidents that began to occur in the Stresau home—incidents that, in time, changed the lives of every member of the family.

It was Marion who had the first experience. She had been sound asleep on that autumn night in 1967, less than two weeks after her daughter's death, when she was suddenly awakened by something. She glanced at the clock. It was just after three in the morning. Then she felt it—the soft touch upon her arm. Had she been dreaming? She was certain that she hadn't been. Someone's touch had awakened her. Her husband, deep in sleep, lay unmoving beside her. Drifting into sleep again, she felt once more the light touch upon her arm. A spider, perhaps? Insects frequently invade homes built in the deep woods. Although now fully awake, Marion was surprisingly unconcerned. "I felt only a strange sense of peace and relaxation," she recalls, "as I drifted toward sleep again."

Her husband, however, had awakened by now and wanted to know what was troubling her. After she muttered something about a spider, Dick got up and turned on the light. Marion got up also, and they threw back the covers and searched the bed, but found nothing.

The Pendant

Many months later, on a trip east, Marion was to learn that her mother had also been awakened at about the same time to see an oval blue mist of cloud float slowly across the end of her bed. The older woman, who had been close to her granddaughter, was convinced that the apparition had been that of Jan. She maintained this belief while, at the same time, rejecting belief in the supernatural.

The morning after Marion's experience, Dick awoke his wife by his restless squirming. "Hey!" he shouted. "There's something moving under my arm!"

He and Marion both leaped out of bed, pulled the bedding, pillows, and mattress off the bed, and examined everything thoroughly. They found no living thing. Dick had been sleeping on his side. Had he had a muscle cramp? Had his arm gone to sleep? No. He was positive that something had been crawling under his arm. Unable to find a logical explanation, they put the matter out of mind and never discussed it again. Marion kept to herself the strange feelings she had that both episodes might have something to do with Jan. Was that possible?

The possibility seemed strengthened a short time later when a friend sent Marion a pamphlet with her sympathy note. Although Marion was not one to be consoled by what she calls "commercialized words of comfort," she admits that she was excited by the author's statement that sometimes the personality of a deceased loved one seems to make contact with the living by the form of a touch. Was Jan really trying to communicate with her parents? Or was Marion merely the victim of "fantasies of a mind recovering from grief," as she wrote in her diary? Neither she nor her husband gave credence to psychic phenomena or superstition of any kind. Yet, there was that persistent feeling. Marion thought it had something to do with the circumstances of Jan's death. There had been the phone call from the mental institution saying that Jan had escaped, that she'd attempted to cross a busy highway and had been hit by a truck. Was it suicide? She'd made previous attempts. Or could it have been an accident? Questions without answers filled Marion's mind.

The week before Christmas, 1967, Marion started to unpack the boxes of tree ornaments. Discovering the tree-top angel that Jan had made many years ago, Marion hesitated. Should she put it on the tree this year or would the memories be too painful? She noticed that the doll's dress was soiled and rumpled and would have to be replaced if the angel were to adorn the tree. Jan would have made a new dress. But now Marion, suddenly overwhelmed by a sense of love and joy, knew that she herself must make the dress. Family Christmas traditions are for tender keeping.

In the morning Marion drove to town and bought the white tulle with silver sparkles that would reflect the tree lights. Back home, she worked all morning, carefully cutting, fitting, and sewing the dress. Just before noon, she stopped to prepare lunch. Suddenly a flash of blinding light filled the room. Although nothing like that had ever before happened, Marion dismissed it as eyestrain. On her way to the kitchen, the light flashed again. Imagination? Or was the phenomenon somehow connected to Jan? Marion couldn't know.

On the Saturday afternoon before Christmas, 13-year-old Steve set out to search the woods for the family's tree. Although he had always gone with his father, Marion decided that this year he was old enough to go by himself. At dusk he returned, dragging a blue spruce with thick clusters of cones. Marion remembers that it was the most beautiful spruce she had ever seen. Steve told his mother an uncanny story. He said he had hiked a long way and couldn't find any suitable tree. Then, when he was ready to give up, the spruce suddenly appeared before him. "Almost like in a dream," he said.

He took the tree into the kitchen to cut off the lower branches. Marion was working at the sink, her back to her son. Suddenly, Steve shouted, "What was that flash of light?"

Marion wheeled around. She had said nothing to anyone about the flashes she had seen, but after Steve described a "very bright, white light," she knew that they both witnessed the same phenomenon.

That night at dinner Steve told his father about the light and tried to pinpoint its source. Where could it have come from? The drapes were all closed, which eliminated the possibility of an outside source of light reflecting upon something inside the house. No one could explain it.

On Christmas Eve, Steve's sister, Pat, arrived home from college for the holidays. After a long, cold drive, she welcomed the cheerful warmth of the blazing fire on the hearth. She settled into the orange leather swivel chair that her mother usually occupied, and Marion sat on a hassock in front of Pat. The family was engaged in animated conversation, catching up on Pat's news, laughing and talking, when all of a sudden Pat's chair tipped

The Pendant

over backward, coming to rest against a window ledge. Pat, with her legs higher than her head, was unable to right herself. Her parents set the chair up, but the chair tipped backward again almost immediately. Pat, bewildered, stammered, "I … I didn't do a thing!"

Marion, who had been facing her daughter, knew she had made no movement that could have upset the chair. The two women exchanged places and the chair did not move again. If other family members forgot about the incident, Marion did not. There was something inexplicable about the whole thing. The chair had been used for years by boisterous teenagers and never before had it tipped over.

The next morning, Marion tried an experiment. She found that the only way she could tip the chair back was by bracing her feet against the hassock and pushing. Yet Pat hadn't had her feet on the hassock because her mother had been sitting on it. Again, Marion thought of Jan. Could she somehow have resented the fact that her sister had occupied the chair usually reserved for her mother? And could she have indicated her displeasure in a physical way?

Future events were more puzzling. Several nights after the chair incident, Steve went to spend the night with a friend, leaving his parents and Pat the only ones home. Marion and Dick were sound asleep when Marion was awakened by loud banging on the wall. There was a pause, then the blows began again. The family's dog began barking, but the blows continued intermittently for 15 or 20 minutes. Marion reasoned that Pat was doing exercises in her room, and she was annoyed by her daughter's lack of consideration. Why didn't Pat quit? Surely she could hear the dog barking. Dick, a sound sleeper, was not awakened by the disturbance.

In the morning Marion spoke to Pat about her exercising at unorthodox hours. A startled Pat replied, "It wasn't me—I haven't done exercises for years. I was sitting up in bed scared to death! I didn't move out of the bed the whole time the banging was going on."

The family searched outside the house. Their home did not have shutters or loose siding or doors that might have banged in the wind, nor could they recall any neighboring homes with appurtenances that might have created the sounds. Besides, Marion says, "It had been a deeply cold, still night." There were no footprints or animal tracks in the fresh snow. Could the two women have imagined the noises? Perhaps. And the dog also? Not likely.

Haunted Wisconsin

The strange events of a Christmas season. Marion pondered them often, and then one day she confided in Steve that she too had seen flashes of light. In turn, he told his mother that for some strange reason he had felt a warmth and goodness during the holiday season that he didn't think had anything to do with the gift aspect. Both shared the tenuous thought that the mysterious happenings were somehow related to Jan, that she was trying to reach them, to share once again in the happiness of a special time. The closeness of Jan seemed a reality, and Marion wished she could be sure.

According to Marion's diary, the next strange occurrence is dated February 18, 1968. Pat was at home on her mid-semester vacation. She, Steve, and Dick were outdoors on that Sunday afternoon when Marion decided to tidy up the living room. As she reached for the clutter of newspapers on the coffee table, she noticed a clipping—a picture of three young women skating at an indoor rink in Duluth. It had been so carefully torn from the paper that the sides were nearly scissors-straight. She read the girls' names in the caption below the picture but knew none of them. Nor did she know why anyone in her family would be interested in such a picture. Puzzled, she put the clipping aside.

When the three came into the house, Marion asked them about the picture. Pat and her father recalled having seen it when flipping through the paper that morning, but that was all. Had it been torn from their paper? Since the rest of the sheet had already been burned in the fireplace, there was no way to check. Could it have come from someone else's paper? The possibility was remote because the Stresaus had bought their newspaper at the drugstore. Had the clipping been left by someone? No. There had been no guests in the house that day.

The next morning, Marion threw the clipping away but later, on impulse, retrieved it. A few days later, she showed it to a friend who claimed to have some talent in the extrasensory perception field. The friend thought that the meaning of the picture was quite clear. She explained that the three smiling women holding hands were symbolic figures representing Marion, Pat, and Jan. The joining of hands symbolized the closeness and happiness they had always shared. Marion thought the symbolism made sense, but it didn't explain how the picture had been removed from the newspaper.

On the following Sunday, just before noon, Marion and Dick

90

The Pendant

arrived home from a trip to find Steve studying boat-building catalogs, excited about the plans for a particular boat that he hoped to build that summer. Marion was immediately aware of the odor of glycerin and rosewater. As she moved closer to Steve the scent became stronger. The only thing in the house with that scent was a bottle of hand lotion that Jan had left. But what would Steve have been doing with it? Then, as if reading his mother's mind, the boy looked up and said, "What is that awful perfume smell? It's been driving me nuts all morning. Must be some of Pat's stuff."

Steve went off to check and about that time Pat, still in pajamas, came into the room. She said she hadn't seen the bottle of lotion since her mother had given it to her several days previously, and that no one had been in the room. Steve opened a number of bottles on Pat's bureau, and when he found the lotion bottle that had belonged to Jan, he identified the smell immediately. But how could the odor have filled the room when no one had opened the bottle? No one knew, but again Marion wondered if Jan was trying to make her presence known. Jan was the only one in the family who had ever used that particular lotion.

In the summer of 1969, the last unexplained manifestation took place. Marion, Dick, and Steve had been talking about a book they had all read and enjoyed and Jan's name came into the conversation. Marion recalls that "there was a happy feeling of closeness among the three of us that evening." When darkness closed in, Steve and his father went into Steve's room and Marion sat reading. The cat was curled on the hassock. Soon Marion noticed the cat seemed to be staring at something across the room in the partly closed door of the studio/writing room. The cat's pupils were large and black but it didn't act frightened. "I followed her gaze," Marion wrote in her diary, "but could see nothing unusual, not even shadows, as the room was well illuminated."

Suddenly the dog, which had been asleep at Marion's feet, bounded up and, facing the opposite direction, stared at the glass-paneled door that opened onto the porch. The terrier's tail began wagging and she trotted to the door ready to greet a family member. Marion was startled by the dog's behavior because Tuffy, like many small dogs, was an excellent watchdog, accepting only the family and barking furiously at the approach of any strange human or animal. Yet the two other family members were still in Steve's room; Marion could hear their voices.

Haunted Wisconsin

Perplexed, she got up, opened the sliding door, and let Tuffy out. The dog circled the area beyond the porch and, finding no one and evidently picking up no scent, bounded back inside. Several minutes later, Marion realized that the studio door was directly in line with the glass door. Whatever the cat had seen in the studio door must have been reflected in the glass door across the room. Could that be? According to ghost lore, animals often have the ability to see discarnate entities that are invisible to humans. Marion concluded that Jan's presence must be in the room and that the animals, recognizing it, were not afraid.

The dog and cat then wandered off and Marion resumed her reading. Suddenly, a clattering noise shattered the silence. It was as if something metallic had crashed to the floor, and the noise seemed to have come from the studio doorway. Marion got up and checked the room and both sides of the door. The cat, alarmed by the noise, ran into the studio also and sniffed and pawed around. Marion found nothing that could have explained the commotion.

The touch in the night ... the brilliant lights ... the tipping chair ... the banging on the wall ... the newspaper clipping ... the aroma of glycerin and rosemary ... the presence felt only by the animals.

Were these only a series of unconnected events? The imaginings of a sensitive, bereaved family? Or had the ghost of Jan returned to brighten the tomorrows of those she had loved? One classic theory is that the ghost of a person who has died an unexpected death often returns to familiar places. Another theory holds that ghosts of those who do not know how to go on to further spiritual development after death come back to stay with loved ones. Speculation, of course.

But the Stresaus were not content to speculate. They wanted proof of Jan's continuing existence and they found it. The search was long-encouraging at times, disheartening at other times. It began with the reading and study of books in the psychic field and culminated in the family's participation in a prayer group near Chicago. It was from this prayer circle that the Stresaus believe they received irrefutable evidence of Jan's survival after death.

One of the psychics, in a state of semitrance, described a pendant – teardrop shaped and edged with small seed pearls and filigree work. The pendant's stone was described as being mottled in color. This information was not significant at first. Marion was certain that there was no pendant of that type in the family.

Then, one day about three weeks after the family had returned home, Marion decided that she could no longer postpone sorting through the boxes of Jan's personal effects that had been sent on from the girl's city apartment after she had become ill. Although she had gone through everything earlier in order to send to the hospital the things Jan had wanted, Marion dreaded facing the sad task again—making the difficult decisions as to the final disposition of clothing, letters, jewelry, and other things that Jan had accumulated over the years. But the job had to be done and on Friday morning Marion started.

In the bottom of a large packing box, she found her daughter's green leather jewel case. The top tray with compartments held an undistinguished jumble of jewelry—pins, loose beads including a collection of baby pearls, and a couple filigreed gold earrings. Marion picked up a round glass bead and was about to toss it into her giveaway pile when she saw something moving inside the bead. She held it up for a closer look and, in doing so, nearly dropped it. The bead was not round at all; it was a teardrop-shaped globe. And something inside was moving indeed. Tiny, iridescent white chips floated in a liquid and, as Marion moved it, the particles changed position, flashing darts of red, aquamarine, and purple-blue. The pointed end of the globe was inserted into a four-pronged silver shaft to which was attached a ring for a chain. A pendant! Yet it wasn't the one the psychic had described; it had no mottled stone.

Marion then laid aside the pendant and resumed her sorting. But, drawn irresistibly to the pendant, she kept glancing over at it. Then she realized that, in looking at it from that particular angle of vision, it did appear to be a mottled stone, the chips motionless in the liquid. But there were no small seed pearls or filigree work that the psychic had "seen." Or? Of course. The pendant, lying in the compartment of the case, had been surrounded by pearls and the filigree must have referred to the gold earrings close by! Deeply moved, Marion sat staring at the jewel in her palm.

The next day at the jeweler's, where she bought a silver chain for the pendant, she learned that the iridescent chips inside the globe were cuttings from a flame opal suspended in glycerin. The jeweler added that she had never seen a floating opal so large and so beautiful.

It was not until a couple days later that Marion realized the full implications of her discovery. No one in the prayer group, not even the family members, had had any knowledge of the existence of the pendant. Where had this knowledge come from? Only from Jan! Then Marion recalled her entreaty at the close of the prayer circle in which she had said softly, as though her daughter were actually present, "If there could be something that only you know about..."

The pendant on the silver chain is the family's most cherished possession.

THE LADY IN BROWN

Can some people survive physical death and somehow remain behind, in an altered state, to watch over a home for which they had a strong emotional attachment in life? That question has perplexed ghost hunters for decades. Scores of tales detail nightly visitations to houses by the ghosts of former tenants.

Brenda Weidner knows all about such appearances. She lived for five years in a haunted house southwest of Durand. Brenda, her husband, Robert, and the couple's two-year-old son moved into a rented, rural, two-story frame home in 1970. There was no indication the house was anything but what it appeared to be—a rather old structure in a grove of elm and oak trees on a country road. It was not unlike thousands of other homes throughout Wisconsin.

Everything seemed normal the first year. Robert Weidner drove each day to a factory where he worked the night shift. Mrs. Weidner stayed home with young Derek. But the idyllic country life was shattered late one evening in the spring as Brenda waited for her husband to return home. It was that night when she first heard the pounding in the walls, gently at first, almost too faint to detect. Then the sound grew in intensity. What was it like? "The walls would vibrate and the curtains would shake," Brenda remembers. "I thought at first it was someone outside with a baseball bat. It happened first on one living room wall and then on another wall, and then back and forth. It would go on for five or ten minutes. Just like someone was inside the wall trying to get out." When the hammering ceased, Brenda sat frozen on the couch, afraid to move and reluctant to search outside in the cold, starless, black of night.

The sounds continued periodically over the next several years. The rapping would usually begin after 10:00 P.M. and continue for several minutes. Were squirrels chasing across the roof? Small animals trapped in the walls frantically searching for an escape route? Brenda doesn't think so. The sounds were absent during the day and at other times of the night. Robert searched the house and grounds when he returned home that first night but found nothing that could have produced the thumping. Robert never heard the sounds on that night or any night thereafter.

Were the noises merely the product of an overly active imagination? Was there an entirely plausible answer? A few months after the pounding in the walls began, Brenda learned she was not the only person to have heard the strange noises.

A local teenage girl had been employed by the Weidners to watch over Derek when the couple went out of an evening, but the young woman became "unavailable" after only a short while. Brenda and her husband were perplexed.

"We couldn't figure out what happened and I was quite upset by it," Brenda recalls. "I asked her what we had done. And she said nothing ... it's the house that upset her. She said she couldn't stand the pounding inside the walls; it happened in the living room wall behind the stove and then would move across to the other wall. That's where I heard it, too." Neither Brenda nor her husband had ever mentioned the pounding noises to the girl.

Brenda also discovered that the pounding in the walls was not the only frightening experience the young girl had in the home. "Every time she shut off the basement lights they would go on again and the basement door would open. She could shut off the lights and close the door and go back in there in five minutes and the lights would be on again and the door open. She just couldn't take it any more. She didn't want to tell me, but every time I called she would have excuses. I finally found out why. It was the house."

The babysitter's chilling encounters and Brenda's earlier experiences proved to be just the first in a series of strange encounters with the unknown.

Young Derek provided the first hint as to an identity for the unseen tenant. The boy's bedroom was adjacent to the living room and only a few feet from the small kitchen. Brenda was preparing lunch one afternoon when she heard her son's voice coming from behind the closed door of his room. The young mother stopped her activity, crossed the living room, and stood outside the bedroom. She heard only her son's muffled voice. The boy would speak a few words, stop, and then continue. Brenda thought at the time the child was carrying on a conversation with someone. But only his voice was audible. For several minutes Brenda listened. At length the boy emerged from the room with a confused expres-

The Lady in Brown

sion. "Mommy," he said, "I just talked to an old, old lady in my room." Brenda glanced into the small bedroom and saw no one. She asked him if he were positive it was an old woman. Yes, the child replied, vigorously nodding his head.

He wasn't scared, Brenda says, just bewildered by the experience. She would have dismissed the child's report but for the earlier experience and her knowledge that Derek had never before made up imaginary people, as do many children. Brenda began to wonder if there was a connection between this mysterious "old woman" and the knockings.

Other events began to take place that reinforced Brenda's belief that some unseen entity was at work in the house. On some occasions she would hear moaning, or groans, whenever she worked in the kitchen area. It would come from behind, but no one was in the house. "It was like someone was in pain," she said.

What was causing the turmoil? Could there be a natural explanation? Or did young Derek actually see someone—or something—in his bedroom? Brenda had never taken seriously the stories of haunted houses or ghosts. But she began to wonder if there wasn't some truth to those tales. Was she experiencing supernatural phenomena?

Determined to learn more about the house and its history, Brenda began questioning neighbors and the present owner of the house, the elderly son of the original owners. Gradually she pieced together the story of Mrs. Gerda Biermann, the late wife of the house's builder. Her entire life had been spent in the house, and she died there in the early 1950s. But what startled Brenda were two peculiar facts relating to the woman's last days on earth: Gerda Biermann had died in the room now occupied by young Derek Weidner, and she reportedly had told a housekeeper that she would never leave that house! Was it possible that this woman had been Derek's mysterious visitor? And was she responsible for the other mischief in the house?

A few months later, something happened that seemed to indicate that perhaps Gerda's vow was more than the idle ramblings of a dying woman.

Brenda was sitting on the couch in the comfortably furnished living room, watching a television program and waiting for her husband to arrive home. It was now shortly after midnight. She expected him within a few minutes. Suddenly Brenda heard the kitchen door swing open and then close moments later. "Robert, is that you?" she called out.

There was no answer. Surprised, she rose quickly and walked into the kitchen. It wasn't Robert ... the nearly transparent image of a woman wearing a brown dress hovered near the outside door! The specter hung motionless in the air, its vacant eyes staring past the frightened young woman. Brenda gazed at the vision, noting that although the body was perfectly outlined, a vaporous mist seemed to form an aura around the figure. Several inches of space separated the specter's feet from the kitchen floor.

Suddenly the ghost began to move, floating slowly across the room. Within seconds it disappeared into the pantry. Brenda walked cautiously over and peered in. The tiny storage room was vacant. A basement door at the far end of the pantry was locked shut. An overhead light was off. The room was silent and dark.

Brenda was dazed. It was the first time a "physical" presence had presented itself to her. As she turned to walk into the living room, her thoughts raced back to all she had learned of the late Gerda Biermann. Yes, she realized, the specter in the kitchen did fit the description of Mrs. Biermann. The dress was plain and old-fashioned, the face looked haggard and old. Yet Brenda couldn't grasp the possibilities of having just seen a ghost.

She hadn't dreamed the entire episode, she decided, and returned to the kitchen for a glass of water to calm her frayed nerves. But what she beheld didn't help assuage her: the pantry light was now on, the basement door stood wide open, and the basement lights were ablaze! How? Why? She had just checked the pantry minutes before. And yet her eyes didn't lie. She gazed down the rough, wooded basement steps but saw and heard nothing. She switched off the lights and closed the basement door. Now she understood the babysitter's take about the basement and its self-propelled lights. What hand had turned them on? What fingers had encircled the basement doorknob and pulled it softly open?

Until the Weidner family moved out of the house, Brenda often found the basement door open and the downstairs lights switched on without reason. Was there a significance in this bizarre routine? Did Gerda Biermann lead Brenda to the basement door for some purpose? Brenda searched the ancient, earthen cellar several times without success. It was old and musty and rather forbidding, but it contained nothing out of the ordinary as far as Brenda could tell.

The Lady in Brown

Other puzzling events occurred. As Brenda recalls, "I had a vase of flowers on the kitchen counter that would move all the time. I'd put it back, but it would move from in front of the radio to beside it. It happened one time when Bob and my son were there. I asked Bob to please quit moving the vase but he said he hadn't touched it. Now, I never saw it move … but it was moved!" Perhaps Gerda preferred the vase beside the radio!

The Weidner's dog, a German shepherd, also sensed a ghostly presence in the house. Brenda said that on numerous occasions "the dog would crouch down on her stomach. She was petrified. I knew that she [Gerda] was around. That dog was absolutely frightened of something."

One particular episode involving the animal stands out in Brenda's mind. One day while she was working in another part of the house, a crash resounded from the kitchen. The dog sprang to its feet and followed Brenda to the source of the disturbance, but Brenda could find nothing broken or out of place. "I never could explain it. I checked everything but there was nothing wrong. Just that loud crash. My dog heard it…" And so did Brenda.

Shortly before the Weidners moved from the house. Brenda had her final, and in many ways most chilling, encounter with the ghost of Gerda Biermann.

The late woman's son had recently built a new porch onto the rear of the house. Brenda recalls what happened a few days after the porch was completed:

"This was in the winter, about February. I was in the kitchen fixing a meal. My dog was with me and Derek was taking a nap. There was a door that led to the porch from the kitchen, which we always kept closed. And then I heard a woman's voice on the porch. But I knew it was empty. I heard her say, "Look what my son has done to the house. He build this porch." My dog's ears went up and its fur stood on end and she started to growl. Then the voice outside started talking in what sounded like German. She started rambling and mumbling. I opened the door but the voice stopped. My dog ran out and sniffed at the corners, on the steps, everyplace. Her fur was up. She knew someone had been out there. And I checked the doors and windows and they were all locked fro the inside. Snow was on the ground and there were no footprints or tire tracks. But there had been that voice. I heard it with my own ears. That's when I knew for sure it was Gerda Biermann. She was German and I understand she often spoke the language. And the voice had been talking about what her son had done to the house. And that was the last I ever heard from her."

The Biermann holds any wandering ghosts within its weathered walls. No one else seems to have had the same experiences Brenda witnessed during her five years in the house, and she was the sole target for most of the events. Her husband found the basement lights on and its door open on one occasion, but dismissed that episode as coincidence. Derek was too young to remember now his puzzling conversation that afternoon in his bedroom. The babysitter felt there was something terrifying enough in that house to refuse work there. And the large family dog whimpered and grew frightened on the occasions when Brenda saw or felt Gerda Biermann's ghost in the house.

Was it all imagination? There are far more questions than answers to this puzzle. Brenda Weidner is visibly shaken to this day when she recounts the events of her life in the Biermann house. One thing is certain—she will never forget that old farmhouse on a country road southwest of Durand. It isn't unlike thousand of other houses with one, macabre exception: it has a ghost!

THE PSYCHIC SISTERS

Rachel Harper* and Diane Bonner* are sisters who share a curious talent: the ability to act as a magnet for ghosts!

The first time a ghost visited Rachel Harper was on a Monday night in March of 1976. Rachel lay next to her slumbering husband in the bedroom of their small frame home near Neillsville. Her two young children and husband had been asleep for hours. Rachel was still alert, gazing at the darkened ceiling, somewhere between wakefulness and sleep.

Suddenly she felt a presence in the room. A third person was watching her. Rachel looked across the room and saw a male human form pulsating in a foglike haze.

Rachel recognized the figure. His name was Billy-Billy Fulham*— and he had been dead for nearly ten years! She'd been his high school sweetheart. But, as with many teenage romances, love withered and the couple went their separate ways—Rachel to marriage and homemaking and Billy to the army shortly after graduation.

No one knew precisely what happened, but Billy left his army camp one night without permission and was killed in an automobile accident. The young man who had died too soon was buried in the cemetery in the small town where he'd grown to manhood.

Rachel couldn't attend the funeral, but she often thought of Billy during the ensuing years. He had an intense love for the outdoors, and whenever Rachel gazed at a particularly spectacular sunset, or walked across a low hill after a gentle rain, or trod softly in a misty morning fog she remembered Billy and how he would have reveled in these simple pleasures.

All these memories flooded back to her as he floated toward her in that night-shrouded room. Rachel could sense a deep sorrow, almost as if he wanted to be consoled over a great loss. And then Billy vanished as suddenly as he had materialized.

The next morning Rachel told her husband about the strange visit during the night. "It wasn't a dream," Rachel told her disbelieving husband. "Billy was in that room."

Rachel had remembered her dreams before, as many of us do. But

Billy was most definitely not the product of fragmented experiences released in the eerie world of dreams.

Her husband scoffed at the incident. Rachel, too, was outwardly jocular over the "ghost." Yet, she was secretly distressed and puzzled by the visit. Rachel wanted to dismiss it as a hallucination or imagination ... or something.

On the next night, however, Billy came again. Just as on the previous evening, he was trying to communicate with Rachel. But there was still some barrier between him and Rachel.

"It was as if he couldn't totally communicate," Rachel remembers. "There was this sadness, though, this deep depression. I couldn't understand what he was saying." Rachel also felt that Billy was trying to draw her away; he wanted her to come with him.

For three consecutive nights Billy appeared and tried to make Rachel understand his sense of sorrow.

On the fourth night, Billy came as before. But this time Rachel left with him! There was no conscious movement, Rachel says, no action. She felt herself being lifted by the shoulders and suddenly accelerated to "a different dimension."

Rachel found herself in a place of whiteness and such brilliant light that it seemed as if all the camera lights in the world had been turned on at once.

Where was this place? What was this place? Rachel doesn't know. "It was cold. The beings I saw weren't human and they weren't three-dimensional. But, they had faces, and you recognized them as people but could only see faces."

Rachel again sensed a suffering, an emptiness in the beings around her; they needed to be released from some indefinable shackles.

The couple passed through this world of silence and moved into a void occupied by a single stone bench with intricate, etched scrollwork on the backrest. There was no talk. No sound at all. Just a pounding silence.

As suddenly as she had entered this realm, Rachel was back in her home, lying next to her husband. Was it a dream? She still wasn't sure.

By the following day Rachel was afraid for darkness to fall. What was Billy trying to say? Why was he coming to her?

On Friday night, Rachel lay awake wondering if the pattern of the previous evenings would be repeated. She was not to be disappointed. Rachel saw him in the doorway, shimmering and beckoning toward her.

The Psychic Sisters

He wore the same sorrowful countenance about him. But something was wrong. Rachel knew then that he was saying good-bye. Billy had been unable to reach her. He seemed to want to make her understand that something was wrong.

When Rachel awoke the next morning the episode was imprinted on her mind. She was frightened.

Rachel decided to telephone Billy's mother. It has been years since they'd last spoken to each other, and perhaps Mrs. Fulham* could understand the reason for Billy's visits.

Mrs. Fulham answered after several rings and seemed delighted to hear from Rachel. Casual conversation followed. Rachel asked the woman how she had been.

"Well, all right, under the circumstances." Mrs. Fulham replied.

"What do you mean?"

"Rachel, my husband died last Sunday night."

She froze at the words. So, that was it.

Billy first appeared the night after his father died. That was the sorrow he felt. Somehow, Billy knew that Rachel could tell his mother how sad he was and how much he wanted to be there to comfort his mother … but could not.

Rachel tried to tell Mrs. Fulham about Billy but the woman refused to listen. "I don't want to hear about it or talk about such things," Mrs. Fulham said.

But the puzzle had been solved. The final missing piece had been put into place. The visits of the ghost had not been a product of Rachel's imagination.

As the months passed, Rachel gradually eased Billy Fulham from her mind. But she was not able to escape the ghost of Billy Fulham.

It was just past 9:30 in the evening nearly a year later. Rachel was propped up in bed reading a novel. Suddenly she felt Billy coming down the hallway. Rachel doesn't know how she knew, only that she looked up and fully expected to see him standing in her doorway once again.

But he was not there.

"You could just feel him though," Rachel said. "It was like electricity charging through the air."

She spoke out loud and told him that she couldn't go through the same experience again. The ghost never reappeared.

Why had he seemed to return? Or did he? Rachel remembered the stunning revelation by Mrs. Fulham after Billy's first visit.

Rachel reached over to a bedside telephone and dialed Mrs. Fulham. The old woman was in clear distress. "What has happened?" Rachel asked. Earlier in the day, Mrs. Fulham said, her bank mortgage had been canceled. She had been unable to make the monthly payments and would have to move within 30 days!

Two visits from a dead soldier. And two tragic events in the life of his mother. Coincidence? Or a hand reaching out from the grave trying to console a grief-stricken mother?

Rachel Harper is not the only member of her family to have experienced hauntings. Diane Bonner, Rachel's younger sister by several years, has encountered three ghosts and seen a vivid dream turn inexplicably into reality.

Diane moved with Rachel and her mother to Chippewa Falls in the summer of 1968. She was a junior in high school and on that particular Sunday night in August looked forward to a new school the next morning. She and her sister were staying with their grandmother until a house could be found to rent.

At 10:00 that night Diane went to bed. How long she had been asleep she doesn't know. But she was suddenly awake and alert, sitting up in bed. Through an open window stars shone in the distant heavens.

Then she saw the old man.

He was at the foot of the bed surrounded by a vaporous mist. Diane could only see his upper torso, but it seemed solid, almost three-dimensional. He wore work trousers and a blue short-sleeved shirt. A full white beard reached to his chest. Diane saw that his white hair was receded to nearly the middle of his head. A bushy moustache curled over his upper lip.

Extraordinary blue eyes gazed at Diane as she sat immobile on the bed. A kind of light seemed to emanate from them.

Nothing was said and the old man did not move. As quickly as he had come, the ghost vanished.

Diane managed to fall back asleep, but the next day after school she tried to find her mysterious intruder's identity. Diane saw her grandmother conversing with a neighbor. The young girl told the woman about her visitor. Her grandmother scoffed at the tale, but the neighbor woman stared at the girl.

"Why, that sounds like old Mr. Banks,*" the neighbor said. "He died in that house 20 years ago!"

Mr. Banks never visited Diane again.

A few years later Diane had an encounter with a ghost strikingly similar to her sister Rachel's. It was early in 1971, shortly after Diane had graduated from high school. A good friend of hers, Tom Kearsley,* had just been told by a physician that his headaches were a result of an inoperable brain tumor. He apparently had been born with it.

Keasley was one the most popular boys in Diane's high school class. He was the type of boy nearly everyone respected and liked, always ready to help his friends without the thought of himself. Selfless was the word used often to describe his outlook on life.

As the youngest child in his family, Tom was particularly close to his parents and especially his father, whom he idolized.

Diane and her boyfriend, whom she would later marry, were the only close friends to whom Tom confided the tragic news. Six months after the tumor was first diagnosed Tom, Diane, and a group of friends attended a party on Friday night. The next morning Diane learned that Tom had been rushed to a hospital and doctors were preparing to perform brain surgery. Before the operation could begin, Tom Kearsley died.

"I didn't find out about his death until later in the afternoon," Diane said. "But about 11:00 in the morning I suddenly felt my skin tingle and I immediately thought of Tom. A friend called later and said Tom had died about 10:30 that morning."

He was buried the following Tuesday. The next night Diane awoke with a start at 11:30 P.M. She looked across the room and Tom was standing only a few feet away from her bed. He looked as he did in life, as if he had never died.

Diane relates what happened next. "There was no verbal communication between us, but it was almost as if I could read his thoughts. And he said, 'Diane, I know everyone feels bad about my death, but please tell them not to worry. I'm happy here.' And then he left."

It was very difficult for his friends to accept Tom's death. Whenever they would gather the conversation inevitably turned to Tom and how he was missed so very much. Diane accepted his death better than most of his grieving friends and relatives. "He was only nineteen but he had a very good life. People adored him. What more could anyone want?" she would remind them.

Perhaps that is why the ghost of Tom Kearsley came once again to Diane. It was about a week after his burial. Just as before she awoke in the middle of the night to see a vague form of a man standing before her.

"Please tell everyone to leave me alone," the ghost told Diane. "I know everyone is still upset. But, please, have them remember the good times and leave me alone."

Even after life Tom was concerned and moved by friends in distress. Diane carried out his commands, and the ghost was released from his earthly wanderings.

Two years later Diane had her third session with a ghost. By then married, she and her husband were in a hundred-year-old frame house on Elm Street in Chippewa Falls.

Shortly after the couple moved in, Diane was busying herself with makeup in front of a large mirror in the upstairs bathroom. She reached down for a brush, and when she glanced back into the mirror she saw two reflections! A disembodied head of an old woman was staring at her from somewhere over Diane's shoulder.

The head of the ancient crone was weathered and deeply etched with wrinkles. Her cheeks were sunken and the face had such a total look of emaciation that Diane could barely distinguish the woman's lips and mouth. Long gray hair was pulled tightly back into a bun and parted straight down the middle. The woman seemed to have no eyes, only a leathery face that didn't move or speak.

Diane turned to look behind her but saw only the empty room. When she looked back into the mirror the face had vanished.

She never again encountered the old woman in the mirror, and she never discovered who the ghost might have been.

Diane Bonner's last encounter with the unknown happened upon her father's death in October of 1977. Her parents were divorced in 1960. Diane and Rachel had always lived with their mother and rarely saw their father.

Diane clearly remembers the "dream" she had the night before she learned of her father's death.

"The dream wasn't about my father, but he kept appearing in it," Diane recalls. "I don't believe I'd dreamed about him since he left us."

The Psychic Sisters

At the end of the dream, Diane saw herself at a table with a stack of large-denomination bills in front of her. A stranger was beside her. The money was hers, he said. But its source or purpose was not clear.

The next evening Diane's mother called. She had somber news. "Well," Diane replied, "if it has anything to do with money it has to be good news."

Her mother was strangely silent. Then she told her daughter that Diane's father had died the night before. The most unsettling news came next. Diane would receive an inheritance from her father's estate. Depending upon the settlement, she could receive as much as $10,000.

How had her mother known about the inheritance so shortly after her former husband's death? Diane learned that her father had discussed his will with his former wife only a few weeks before, but he had made Diane's mother promise to keep the terms of the estate confidential.

In this instance, a dream turned out to be incredibly accurate.

Ordinary Wisconsin sisters with extraordinary experiences. Why have these events happened to Rachel Harper and Diane Bonner? Do they have a peculiar ability to see beyond our world and somehow attract restless spirits from another dimension? There are some who may have that ability. Rachel and Diane are two of them.

Southern Specters

SOMEONE TO WATCH OVER ME

The historic Chances Restaurant in Rochester had just gone through some extensive remodeling, including the installing of a new roof, when co-owner Debbie Schuerman got one of those telephone calls every business owner dreads—an alert from her security firm that the electronic alarm had gone off and a motion detector had identified movement in the dining room. Even worse, the call came in the middle of a rainy night and the last thing she wanted to do was to go along with sheriff's deputies as they checked the premises.

"We went in knowing which section of the alarm system had been set off," Debbie says. "We started looking room by room, looking for someone inside."

The deputies were concerned about a burglar or vandals; Debbie didn't really know what to expect. This wasn't the first time the alarm had interrupted her night's sleep. A systematic search failed to turn up any plausible reason for the motion detector to have activated, especially since it is configured to have what is termed "pet sensors," that is moving objects must weigh over 40 pounds to set it off. Spiders, mice, squirrels, or even most household pets, would not affect the alarm.

Debbie and the sheriff's deputies made sure everything was secure inside before they reset the alarm and started through the back hallway to the rear door. At that point she discovered the real reason she thinks she had been "summoned" to the restaurant.

"I got water in my face as were walking down the hallway," Debbie says. "That section is an add-on. The water was coming down through the doorway there."

She didn't think it looked serious. Apparently the roofers hadn't completely covered the seam between the old section of the restaurant and the newer portion. She'd call the roof company in the morning and have them fix the problem. But as she was locking up she saw the real danger—the leak was only a few inches from a light fixture. She got some rags to plug the small crack through which the water was dripping and then she shut off the power to the light fixture.

No doubt the deputies were startled when Debbie turned toward the empty restaurant and called out,

"THANK YOU! I'll catch you in the morning. Keep an eye on the place!"

With that she also thanked the puzzled deputies, turned the key in the lock for the last time and went home.

And to whom was she speaking?

It might have been Sadie, the African American cook, or the Civil War Soldier or perhaps his love, the lady in green. They are just three of the seven ghosts that Debbie and her family believe stand watch at their century and a half old establishment.

Debbie Schuerman has learned to be sensitive to what is not obvious.

"When we get an alarm that is motion activated, I come in and look for electrical problems or other hazards. Can I smell gas? Do I see smoke? The sheriff's department looks for someone to be here."

But in 14 years, none of the alarms has meant a living intruder. The Schuermans have never had a break-in or a burglary while other businesses in the small, western Racine County community have been burglarized.

The owners think they know why.

Chances may be the oldest continually operating wayside tavern and restaurant in the state. Early settlers Levi Godfrey and John Wade staked a claim on the Fox River near the present site of Chances in the early 1830s and soon built a double log house that was opened as the first tavern in western Racine County. Although the quarters were primitive, that didn't impede travelers between Racine and southwest Wisconsin from stopping there to share meals and spend the night sleeping on the packed dirt floor.

According to legend, disgruntled Indians burned the log cabin in the early 1840s. Peter Campbell bought the property and built the existing brick building in 1843. The Union House, as he named it, continued to serve travelers on the old Plank Road from Racine to Janesville. Rochester was the third largest city in Wisconsin at the time and Campbell's hostelry was one of the most popular stops along what could be considered the interstate highway of its day.

A large stone addition with 18-inch thick walls was added to the Union House in 1856. An expanded dining room was situated downstairs while a 2,000 square foot dance hall took up most of the second floor. The original springboard dance floor is still intact and is thought to be among the last of its type in the state.

Unfortunately, the 1850s also brought the decline of business along the Plank Road when railroads bypassed Rochester in favor of nearby Burlington. The Union House closed as a hotel, but it has continued in business as a tavern and restaurant almost uninterrupted to this day.

Perhaps the Union House's most fascinating period came during the years just prior to the Civil War when it and the Willard House, across the Fox River, were purportedly used to hide slaves as part of the Underground Railroad. Local legend has it that escaping African Americans were clandestinely taken up the Fox River to tunnels on the riverbank which led either to the basement of the Union House or the Willard House. The slaves hid in the cellars until they could be sent on their way to their next stop and eventual freedom in Canada. An odd, circular hole in the Chances basement wall is routinely pointed out as a possible entrance to the old passageway, the Schuermans believe.

Over the past 150 years, the inn has gone through countless owners and several name changes. Until Tom and Debbie Schuerman bought the business, it had been known in the modern era as Big John's and the Rochester Inn.

"We fell in love with the place because of its history," remembers Debbie about their 1987 decision to buy the then-closed restaurant. Neither Debbie nor her husband had owned or managed a business, but both had familiarity with the food and liquor trade.

"We jumped in with both feet, thus the name. We took 'chances.' We're still taking lots of them, but whatever we did has been working," Debbie says.

The couple set about cleaning the well-maintained building, adding a few room dividers and shortening the bar, which once extended into the dining room. Today, the front portion of the inn holds an entrance hallway, the cozy bar, and restrooms, while the rear portion accommodates two separate dining rooms. In one dining area, Debbie displays her collection of antique dishes and teapots. She wants to make it look like "her grandmother's dining room," she says. The second floor is no longer used, but it was used as a dance hall until shortly before the Schuermans bought the business. A small apartment was even built at one end. Today, the area is closed to the public and used only for storage.

The two-story, brick building on County Highway D occupies a prominent place in the little downtown Rochester business district. Since the building was in "pretty decent shape," Debbie says, it didn't take long to get Chances open for public business on May 13, 1987. From the original pressed tin ceiling in the dining room, to the brick and stone walls and period furnishings, the old wayside looks today much as it did a century ago, as is clear when a visitor studies old photographs of the building which adorn the walls.

What the Schuermans didn't reckon with was that along with the period furnishings and landmark building would be added a few other-worldly residents almost as old as Chances itself.

"We didn't have any idea that the place had any so-called spirits or ghosts," Debbie says matter-of-factly. "There was no indication of that when we bought it. But as we were hiring employees, one of the people we hired started telling me the stories about the spirits that were here. Her husband's family was one of the past owners. I didn't think much of it."

Perhaps she should have.

Shortly after the restaurant opened, Debbie began to notice small annoyances. Chairs at the dining room were pulled away from the tables each morning when she came in to clean before opening for the day. "You had to push the chairs in just to walk through the room," she recalls.

Then it was her shoes that went missing. "It drove me nuts," Debbie says. "I wore high heels to work. I'd bring in a pair of flats so that through the night as my feet got tired I'd slip into my flats and put my heels back in the liquor room. The next day I'd come in and they'd be gone. I think I lost half a dozen pairs of heels before I finally decided I wasn't going to wear high heels any more."

At first, Debbie thought someone was trying to tell her something by playing these peculiar practical jokes. But they continued to vanish even when she started hiding the high heels after she had changed into flats.

"I decided I couldn't afford it anymore so I just kept wearing my flats. My feet were more comfortable and I didn't have shoes disappearing."

It took a long time and a lot of convincing before she thought perhaps something, well, odd was going on. Apparently Chances had a ghostly reputation not spelled out in the Schuermans' purchase agreement.

"I thought there was always some logical explanation to it. That's how I felt about it. But within the first year, we would get small groups of people who claimed to be psychics coming to dinner. Some of them would say, 'they like you.' The spirits were going to watch over us, protect us and make sure we're happy," Debbie says. She usually nodded politely and smiled when visitors told her that, not quite knowing how else to react.

She wasn't won over until a night a couple of years after Chances opened. A night on which the Schuermans came perilously close to losing all that they were working so hard to build. Debbie was bartending on a Wednesday around 8:00 P.M. when she discovered that she had run out of CO_2 gas pressure for the tavern's soft drink and beer hoses. The problem was that the CO_2 tanks that fed the bar's spigots were located in the basement, a room in which Debbie is decidedly uncomfortable. "I don't know what it is, but it's only at night. Not that it's an uneasy feeling, not that I'm afraid. It's just one place where I've never been comfortable. And I don't go down there alone."

So with the help of a knowledgeable customer who volunteered to help her, Debbie went to the basement room where the gas tanks are located and supervised while he exchanged the empty tank for a full one.

"Then I heard this hissing sound above my head," Debbie says, shivering at the memory. "I have a phobia about snakes and I thought that's what it was."

She stayed crouched and backed away but couldn't resist trying to see the source of the sound.

"And as I was looking up I saw that there was a water leak from the ice drain sinks in the kitchen. The water was coming down on top of a light fixture and had even blown the glass off the light bulb. The filaments were still connected and glowing."

The hissing was coming from the water hitting the live electrical wires.

Once they had quickly changed the CO_2 tank, Debbie and the customer, also a volunteer firefighter, disconnected the power to the light fixture and capped the wires on what they both knew had been a very real and potentially catastrophic fire hazard.

"The porcelain on the fixture was black and the floorboards were the same. The heat was very intense. If we hadn't noticed it that night our business would have gone up in flames," Debbie says.

Early the next day, the company that replaced and maintained the CO_2 tanks came out to replace the one Debbie said was empty. But after checking the tank, the service man came back upstairs looking perplexed.

"He asked me why we'd taken the tank offline the night before," she remembers. "I told him. He said the tank was half-full, had pressure, and that there was nothing wrong. It shouldn't have had to be changed."

Then she remembered the visiting psychics who had told her the spirits of Chances liked her and her husband and that they would be around to see that no harm befell them.

"I was being protected," Debbie says, shaking her head at the memory. "Because I had no CO_2 and I had to go downstairs, we found that hazard." She doesn't know how the ghosts made it all happen, but because she had been drawn to the basement she was able to discover the faulty light socket and prevent the building from being damaged or destroyed.

"The gentleman who went down to help me knew it was something waiting to combust. The light was on. It would have heated up until it combusted and started the floorboards on fire. We would have had a fire."

A few years later, the episode with the leaky roof offered more corroboration that the Chances ghosts have been able to warn the owners when something is amiss or there is danger. Often this has come in the form of the burglar alarm being activated, such as the night of the roof leak.

"I call them attention-getters," Debbie says of the times she's been called after hours when the alarm goes off. "Most every time I've found something (wrong). It does make me nervous when I can't find anything. We had three squad cars show up for one. I looked for everything, I made sure the garbage in the bar had been taken out" in case a burning cigarette had been accidentally thrown away. When the alarm company tested the system everything checked out just fine.

"After awhile, I figure that if I missed something, the ghosts will set the alarm off again. That's the confidence I have. But I want them to make it more obvious the next time," she adds emphatically.

A peculiar incident with cut phone lines may indicate that the ghosts do more than patrol for building defects. They may scare off would-be intruders.

"I was working late and had left the bartender here and went home," Debbie recalls. "I remembered something and I tried to call back but I couldn't get through. The line rang and rang. I knew the bartender was here and I almost drove back."

When Debbie came in the next morning she called the night bartender and asked her why she had closed up so soon. She said she hadn't.

"I called her from home because our phones here were dead. The phone company came out and found that the line had been cut on the outside of the building. Whoever it was never got in."

The severed phone lines also deactivated the dialer on the alarm system, so if someone had broken in the automatic dialer would not have functioned and authorities would not have been notified.

Debbie suspects potential burglars were frightened away by…something. "The opportunity was there, but they never made it in. It was the perfect time because the bartender was alone or they could have set something up for later. My thought is that somebody did cut the phone lines so that sometime during the night they could get in undetected. And nothing ever happened."

The identity of the seven ghosts who may haunt Chances is as shrouded in legend as is the history of the tavern itself. A fire destroyed the Rochester town hall years ago taking with it city records dealing with the history of many Rochester businesses and residents.

Only one ghost has a name, Sadie, a black woman and runaway slave who cooked at the Union House. The others are known by their physical descriptions, including two women, one wearing a green gown the other attired in a blue dress.

Sadie was the first ghost Debbie became aware of.

"This is where she ended up settling and for some reason she lived in the basement. She would only come up to cook," Debbie Schuerman says, adding that what she has learned of the resident spirits has come from previous owners. "I didn't like the fact that she had no name, so I named her Sadie."

She is the "kitchen spirit" because she usually doesn't go beyond that area. If there are odd things going on back there, it's Sadie who is thought to be responsible.

"Our chefs change their clothes in a bathroom back there," Debbie uses as an example. "I've been here when they've come running out white as can be and with their clothes in hand because as they're bending over they were touched. They're just terrified."

Other problems associated with Sadie involve stove burners being shut off while food is cooking, a basement door off the kitchen that will not stay closed (it leads to the basement), and food that vanishes.

"She doesn't seem to like them very much," Debbie says of Sadie's attitude toward chefs in "her" former kitchen.

Although no one has actually seen Sadie, the same cannot be said for the mysterious entity known as the Civil War Soldier, whose haunt is confined to the first floor of Chances.

Stacy Kopchinski is Debbie and Tom Schuerman's 24-year-old married daughter. She works at Chances and helps manage the facility and is one of only a few people who say they've seen the soldier.

For Stacy, the sighting came on a bright, early weekday morning as she vacuumed the carpet under tables in the dining room. "I don't know why but I turned around, and I saw him sitting there at the bar as if he were waiting for someone to come and serve him a cocktail. He had on a hat with a brim and a long coat. He was dark and looked very much like a real person."

So real in fact, that Stacy grabbed a fork off the table, fearful that an intruder had somehow gotten in. Then he was gone.

"I thought, What the heck? I looked in the men's and women's bathroom and then I called my dad and asked him to come right down. It was scarier thinking a real person had gotten in," Stacy remembers. The front door was still locked and, of course, no one could have walked past her undetected through the dining room.

A cleaning woman is also said to have seen him and promptly quit.

The soldier displays another irksome bit of behavior—he pinches female customers and wait staff.

"He's a ladies man," Debbie Schuerman says. "We've always thought he's the one who pinches ladies' butts, or pats your butt all the time. Then you'll get this cold feeling like something is there and you're swiping it away all the time."

At other times it feels as if you've sat in something wet and cold, she says. The sense of being touched is annoying, but Debbie maintains she hardly pays attention to it anymore. "He's doing it all the time."

Stacy Kopchinski recalls the time she was seating a couple at a table when the woman quickly turned around and glared at her." She thought I'd pinched her!" Stacy laughs.

The old soldier may long for female companionship because, by legend, his girlfriend in life is the lady in the green dress who has only been seen haunting the second floor. She was said to have been a prostitute plying her trade at the Union House.

"The tale we've been told is that the Civil War soldier and the prostitute were a couple. She fell in love with him but decided she was unworthy of his love because of what she did and killed herself upstairs," Debbie recounts. "But the soldier was so distraught over what she did that he committed suicide downstairs. The two can never get together because they're on different (spectral) planes."

Although Debbie has not seen the spectral woman on the second floor, her daughter Stacy has driven by the restaurant late at night and has seen, at least twice, the face of a blonde-haired woman staring out the upstairs windows. Christmas-type candles in the windows and several lights on the front of the building have illuminated her face. On some other occasions, customers have asked if someone lives upstairs because they've seen someone looking out one of the windows.

Debbie also recounts the story of a former bartender who actually lived in a small apartment built on one end of the second floor. He is said to have heard faint harp music. When he looked around for its source, he saw the woman in the green dress standing in a far corner of the old dance floor. He scurried away downstairs each time he heard the music, but eventually decided to stand his ground to see what she would do. Apparently, she floated right to him and passed through his body leaving him with a cold, clammy sensation. A decidedly unpleasant odor lingered in the air.

However, there are enough other odd goings-on up on the second floor that any more sightings of an actual ghost might be somewhat anticlimactic. There are the footsteps, the boxes that move self-propelled across the springwood floor and … the music.

"Ah, the music, that's the biggest thing that's happened to me," Debbie concedes about the first time it happened. "I had been working a lot of hours and very late. I'd gone upstairs to do inventory on a Sunday morning. All of a sudden I hear this music, beautiful music that sounds like it's from an old piano. I wondered where it was coming from, but no matter where I walked around the ballroom, it was always the same volume. I thought someone was playing a joke, so I quickly opened the door thinking someone was there. I went downstairs where a cook and his assistant were getting ready for Sunday brunch and a bartender setting up. Everybody's doing their job, there's no music, no nothing."

Debbie didn't bother to ask anyone about the music. She went back upstairs to continue with the inventory and after a few minutes the music started up again. It was calming, she says, but unnerving at the same time because she couldn't figure out the source. Debbie was tired from working long hours and taking care of the myriad details necessary to operate a successful business.

"I kicked a box across the room and just as it hit the floor the music stopped," Debbie remembers. "Then I thought (the ghosts) were only trying to be good, to be nice. I apologized. I said I was sorry and that they could play music for me any time they wanted. But I've never heard it again. It's like I really insulted them."

In the quiet early morning hours or late at night there's additional activity in the old ballroom. "You have the feeling someone else is here," Debbie says. "Either you hear movement or some muffled talking. Footsteps, too, a click, click, click across the floor. Like someone walking in heels. Very well defined. It makes you wonder if someone is up there. You do get used to it ... because you hear it all the time."

Another female ghost, this one wearing a dark, blue dress made with what Debbie terms dotted Swiss material lingers, along with the soldier, only on the first floor. Several people have seen her, including a former waitress and Stacy Kopchinski.

The waitress watched as the woman walked calmly through the dining room and into the kitchen. The figure looked so real that the waitress followed her back to the kitchen trying to find her.

"I have no clue as to who she is," Debbie says. "She's just always here. When you're sitting at the bar late at night and the lights are off in the dining room, all of a sudden the doors to the kitchen will open up. We've run back to see if somebody had walked into the kitchen but nobody would be there. The doors swing open so the lights in the kitchen filter in and draw our attention to them. There was a period of time when she was around a lot. It was always after the dining room closed and she was always going into the kitchen."

A fourth presence dwells with the lady in green on the shuttered second floor. He is a bearded man glimpsed once by Tom Schuerman.

According to his wife, Tom had turned off several spotlights that had been used to illuminate some carved gargoyles on the exterior facade of the restaurant.

"Tom had gone up to shut them off that night. He was going through the old kitchen upstairs and passed a mirror hanging above the kitchen

118

sink. He always sees his belt buckle reflected in it. Except this night as he went through and looked there was an older, bearded, dark-haired man's face looking back at him from the mirror. Tom came downstairs and called me. He told me about it and said we're not turning those lights off again. Ever since then they've always remained on."

A week later, the mirror fell off the wall and shattered on the floor. The Schuermans believe the spectral face appeared as a not-so-subtle suggestion to keep the lights on the gargoyles.

The last two ghosts at Chances have only been seen in a painting of the restaurant that hangs on a dining room wall. They are twin children, a boy and a girl, portrayed playing around a kid's wagon in the foreground of the picture.

"I had a waitress who used to work for us commission a painting of the building," Debbie says. "The artist is a psychic. When she gave me the painting, I asked her where she got the idea for the kids in the painting and she said that they're playing here, this is their play area. Someone had told me about the kids before but I didn't want to believe it."

Debbie thinks the children are the ones who pull the chairs out from the tables and cause other little nuisances, "doing their playful things."

In fact, all the ghosts at Chances are illustrated in the picture. "She painted everyone she felt was here," Debbie says of the painter/psychic, who claimed she didn't know much about the identities of the spirits. Oddly, Debbie notes that the artist dropped off the finished painting and walked back out. "She said, 'I'm sorry, I can't go in there. I don't feel comfortable,'" Debbie recalls. She didn't give a reason for her uneasiness, a sensation that Debbie most definitely does not share.

"What I've come to terms with over the years is that the ghosts are souls that are lost, that they're in this in-between stage with unfinished business. I don't know what that unfinished business is, but I've always thought that if the Civil War soldier could be reunited with his love upstairs then their business would be finished and they'd move on," Debbie explains.

Does she ever want to help them "move on?" Absolutely not.

"This is their home and we're the guests more or less. I get very protective of them. We have a comfortable coexistence. We're comfortable with them. They help us and we entertain them, I guess. I do have this sense when it comes to them of calm and peace."

That does not mean, however, that she would want to live with their steady presence. "I don't know if I'd feel this way if they were in my house. I can walk away from it here every day."

She does have the habit, however, of locking the doors, turning around and calling "good night" to the lingerers, just as she did years ago after she discovered the water leakage.

Stacy Kopchinski seems almost as comfortable with her unseen helpmates as does her mother. "It's just nice to know they're here, especially when I'm alone closing up the bar. Sometimes you can feel them everywhere, then you know they're all out, but then there are other long periods when they're not around," Stacy says.

Except for a short paragraph on their menu, the Schuermans have not exploited or commercialized their unique guests. That would be taking advantage of them, Debbie says. And besides, if changes have been made in the building that the ghosts haven't liked, or if there are visitors to whom they've taken a disliking, "we'll know," Debbie says.

But mother and daughter—and many others associated with Chances—keep a wary eye open around the place. Debbie does not go alone into the basement and Stacy avoids the second floor whenever possible. It's not that they are scared in any traditional sense of the word, but they remain more or less always on guard.

"Sometimes it's the fear of actually confronting something face to face. You know they're here, but what would you do if one of them was actually standing there?" Debbie asks.

What would you do indeed?

MRS. COURTNEY'S RETURN

Mr. and Mrs. William Courtney had never gotten along. Mrs. Courtney had left her moody Irish-Canadian husband at least once, but she eventually returned to him and their small farm in Brooks' Corners, a section of Vinland about seven miles north of Oshkosh.

The uneasy truce between the bickering pair ended on November 4, 1873, when Mrs. Courtney died of natural causes. Not long after William Courtney discovered his wife's body in her bedroom, he moved out of the house and into the home of his mother-in-law about a mile away. He returned to the farm only to do chores.

Courtney kept on the hired girl, but not for long.

Several days after Mrs. Courtney's funeral, the girl heard sharp raps on the windowpanes in a room adjoining the bedroom where she had died. The girl lifted a corner of the window curtain and peered out. Although she could see no one, the girl was badly frightened and fled to a neighbor's house. She quit that day.

Hiram Mericle and his family lived on an adjoining farm only a few hundred feet from the Courtney place. Shortly after the hired girl quit, Hiram noticed a light burning in the Courtney house. He knew the place was empty so with two of his older children he went to the house. From the front yard, they could see that the light was coming from Mrs. Courtney's old bedroom. As they approached closer, the light dimmed and finally went out. Mericle and his children went home quite puzzled. But then early the next morning as Mericle prepared for chores he saw the light again shining as brightly as before.

Other neighbors soon noticed lights in the Courtney house. When several of the neighbors went to investigate, they claimed to have seen a shadowy form pass in front of the light. "Look, it's Mrs. Courtney!" one of them screamed.

From then on everyone in Brooks' Corners said Mrs. Courtney haunted her old house. Lights of varying shapes and forms continued to appear regularly. Sometimes they were circles about six or seven inches in diameter, with smaller lights circling the larger ones. At other times, the lights took oval shapes. The most startling observation was that the light was most frequently seen was a flame with clearly defined edges; all around was inky darkness.

The light came from all parts of the main house and also in the one-story rear addition that housed the kitchen.

By November 20, 1873, the *Oshkosh Weekly Times* had heard of the phenomena and dispatched a reporter to check out the story.

The reporter reached the house of Jacob Whitacre by nightfall. He lived about a half mile from Courtney's. The newspaperman ate supper with the Whitacres and listened to the stories told by the family; each had seen the lights at one time or another. The Whitacres appeared to be intelligent, straightforward people who had obviously seen something for which they had no logical explanation.

After supper, Jacob Whitacre led his guest to the mystery house. There a group of about a hundred men and boys had already gathered in the deep, late-fall snow, stamping their feet to keep warm and comparing notes on what each had seen. A bright light suddenly appeared in one of the windows and just as quickly vanished, again plunging the house into darkness. Gusts of wind churned the loose snow and finally the reporter grew cold and disappointed at not witnessing further manifestations. He and Whitacre walked to the Mericle's farm to warm up. They made a second trip back in a few hours and arrived in time to see a series of bright lights in the house exploding like flashes of lightning.

On November 21st and 22nd, large crowds continued to converge on the haunted house but no lights appeared. The Oshkosh newsman speculated that since a family was planning to move into the house no more lights of a ghostly nature would be seen. He didn't explain how he had arrived at this conclusion.

The reporter continued to try and solve the mystery lights. He interviewed William Courtney who claimed the lights were the work of a prankster who had gained access to the house through an unlocked cellar door. Courtney also said he had found the kitchen door kicked in. He thought the culprit was someone who wanted to rent the place and was trying to scare off the man to whom Courtney had promised it.

The hundreds of nightly witnesses did not agree. Many told the reporter that no one in their right mind would brave the wild winds and deep snows to break into a vacant house night after night. Observers

Mrs. Courtney's Return

noted that the light they saw did not reflect on anything around it, often flashed like lightning, and sometimes changed shape or created haloes. It seemed unlikely that the Courtneys' kerosene and oil lamps could have produced such characteristics.

The puzzle was never really solved. The Oshkosh newsman did not think the witnesses were fantasizing, although the possibility of pranksters at work was never completely dismissed.

Of course, many reasoned, the lights could have been of supernatural origin signaling the return of Mrs. Courtney. Perhaps, they said, she was trying to gain a few hours of peace and quiet in a house of such unhappiness.

VOICE ON THE BRIDGE

The village of Omro, Wisconsin was a center of Spiritualist activity in the 1870s. In this little settlement near Oshkosh, the First Spiritualist Society hosted eminent Spiritualists and mediums from all over the United States—the Davenport brothers, Moses Hull of Boston, Benjamin Todd of Michigan, Susan Johnson of California, and many others. Séances multiplied, spirits materialized, but, with peculiar irony, the combined efforts of local and visiting mediums failed to solve the murder of a local man.

Sometime between 9:00 and 10:00 P.M., farmer John Sullivan left Omro, where he had spent the day trading. His thoughts must have been on home and a good night's sleep after the long day in town.

His movements were later reconstructed, as there were no eyewitnesses. Several people who lived near the Fox River said they heard a cry followed by a gunshot. A short time later, Sullivan's body with a single, fatal gunshot wound was found at the side of a footbridge spanning the river. No one saw the assault. Law enforcement officials were baffled. Sullivan had no known enemies nor was he carrying a large amount of money after having spent most of what he had on supplies.

Séances buzzed with questions directed toward the nether world asking for the identity of the killer; there was never an answer.

Then some weeks later, a Mr. Wilson happened to be crossing the same bridge at the same time of night when out of the darkness he noticed what appeared to be a man just ahead of him shouldering a rifle. A voice from out of nowhere whispered, "That is the gun that killed John Sullivan!" Wilson heard a terrified scream, a loud gunshot, and then the man and rifle vanished.

Wilson ran back to the village to relate his experience. He swore that he would recognize the murder weapon—and the murderer—if he ever saw them again. He later claimed that he had indeed seen both but would not identify the culprit nor the weapon. The spirits weren't talking either. Sullivan's murder remained unsolved.

HE CAME BY NIGHT

The winter nights were long and lonely for the families of 19th century Wisconsin lumberjacks. While their men lived in lumber camps as they cleared the great northern pine forests, families were left behind in scores of small settlements, sometimes hardly more than clusters of log shanties, scattered across the state. From Brule in the northwest through Minocqua, Hazelhurst, Conover, and Split Rock toward the east, the villages were as remote as any place on earth for months at a time.

One such village was West Algoma, near Lake Winnebago and since incorporated into the city of Oshkosh.

The legend has persisted that in one particular year a century and more ago, West Algoma's isolation was disrupted each winter night by the terrifying appearance of a towering figure swathed in a black cape.

The stranger's routine never varied. At the stroke of midnight he would emerge from the shadows at the edge of town, walk slowly with the aid of a crooked cane down the wooden sidewalk and then vanish into the night. He never spoke aloud to anyone nor did he alter his gait. His arrival time varied by less than a minute.

Townsfolk hid behind barred doors and curtained windows, afraid to interfere with or question the walker. Few slept until he was gone.

On one particular night, however, a teenage boy accosted the stranger. He claimed that beneath the figure's dark cap he had seen a pallid, expressionless face devoid of life. The boy fled terrified.

Night after night, week after week, and month after month of that long winter the stranger walked the streets of West Algoma. But on that day in spring when the men returned from the piney woods the visitor vanished, never to return.

THE PHANTOM RIDER OF PUMPKIN HOLLOW

As dusk settles on quiet autumn nights over the south line road in the village of Oak Hill, near Sullivan, old-timers say a ghostly Indian brave still gallops through the gathering darkness. His pony is fast, and wears a garland of sliced pumpkin around its neck. A whole pumpkin encircles the barrel of the Indian's musket, which he carries high above his head. The legend of the phantom rider begins in early pioneer days and bears more than a casual resemblance to Washington Irving's "Legend of Sleepy Hollow."

Harry Osgood operated a tavern on the south line road frequented by ox drivers and travelers on their way to Milwaukee. The structure was little more than a log shelter along the rutted trail. Nevertheless, it was a favorite stop.

Early one fall evening, an Indian arrived at the tavern astride a lively pinto pony. The man was tipsy but somehow managed his way into the establishment and demanded more whiskey. Osgood refused the request, fearing the consequences of such an act. Instead, he gave the brave a number of ripe, bright orange pumpkins. The Indian was delighted and proceeded to impale the largest pumpkin on the barrel of his rifle. He cut the others into chunks and with some string draped them around his pony's neck. Pleased with his work, he set off down the road.

A short way off, Doc Powers, a pioneer physician in the region, was riding toward the tavern after making calls at several homesteads. As he gazed down the trail, he saw the pumpkin-becked Indian galloping toward him. The trail was narrow near the spot where the two met. Powers demanded to pass first but the Indian refused. Instead, he bashed the physician over the head with the rifle and Powers fell from his horse.

What happened next is unclear. Some say the physician recovered his senses and grabbed the rifle from the Indian, smashing the weapon on a tree trunk until it was bent. With the remnants, Powers pummeled the youth until the Indian fled across the marsh. Both horses bolted into the forest. Powers knew that men from the tavern would help in finding

126

his horse.

Another version of the story claims the doctor lay unconscious for some time. When he awoke, pieces of the pumpkin littered the road, but the Indian was nowhere to be seen. The doctor's horse was found a short way off.

Whichever version is correct, Doc Powers swore vengeance on the Indian who attacked him. Powers made his way to the tavern, where proprietor Osgood agreed to help him search for his horse. When the pair reached the spot where the attack had occurred, Powers shook his head over the chunks of pumpkin scattered about. He said the name of the area really ought to be changed from Pleasant Valley to Pumpkin Hollow. And so it was.

The Indian was never seen again at the tavern or anywhere in the region. Wayfarers, however, frequently reported the ghost of an Indian bedecked with pumpkins galloping up and down the south line road for many years. And, some say, when the chill autumn wind scatters brittle leaves down Pumpkin Hollow, the Indian brave can still be seen in his garish costume.

THE POSSESSION OF CARL SEIGE

Can an evil spirit take over a person's mind, body, and soul? Man has always thought so. In every culture, in every period of history, demonic possession has been recognized. Loud, obscene curses issue from the mouth of the victim, his body contorts, and his eyes gleam with hatred. Often, his environment is beset by paranormal manifestations — poundings in the walls, levitation of furniture, and the presence of fireballs.

The causes of demonic possession are little understood, but the condition seems to occur in individuals with weak egos, unmet psychological needs, or some obscure, if undetected, character flaw. Since possession closely resembles some forms of mental illness, medical treatment is usually tried first. For intractable cases that do not respond to medication, the religious rite of exorcism may be performed to cast out the "demons." No one knows how many exorcisms are performed in this country in a given year because the possessed usually insist upon anonymity. But Carl Seige, of Watertown, was not so fortunate. He was harassed by demons for 20 years and the whole town knew it. His exorcism, along with more lurid details of his sensational case, was reported by Milwaukee newspapers and reprinted by papers in other parts of the state.

The diabolical manifestations first appeared in 1848. Carl was then five years old and living with his family in their native Germany. One day one of Carl's sisters found a duck's egg under a tree beside the door of their small hut. With typical childlike curiosity, she picked up the egg and took it to her mother. Mrs. Seige noticed that the egg had a small pinhole in one end. She cautioned her daughter to put the egg back where she had found it. The girl did. At that moment, the family dog appeared, seized the egg, and ate it. Immediately, he was stricken blind and, raging with fright, ran in wide circles through the yard. The child fled, screaming. The dog was promptly shot.

A short time later, the little girl was seized with blindness and spasms and soon was bedridden. She lingered in agony for a year. After her death, Carl was attacked with blindness and severe pains that continued for a number of months, leaving him lame and with a withered hand

The Possession of Carl Seige

twisted into a grotesque shape. But he would manage. His sight was partially restored. And his life had been spared.

But when Carl turned 12 years old, uncontrollable seizures set in. His head was jerked like a puppet by unseen forces, his shoulders twisted, and he was often thrown violently to the ground where he struck out at all who tried to approach him. He frothed at the mouth and his eyes filled with malevolence. If a "fit" overtook him while eating, his hands struck his dinner plate, upsetting it and scattering food all over the floor. Sometimes a spell would last an entire day. Between attacks, he prayed for deliverance and made the sign of the cross. But his prayers went unanswered. So did those of his pious Lutheran family. German doctors, using roots and herbs and all the medicines available at that time, were unable to cure, or even alleviate, the dreadful symptoms of Carl's strange malady.

Finally, in the spring of 1867, when Carl was 24 years old, the despairing family—father, mother, three sons, and five daughters—immigrated to the German community of Watertown, Wisconsin. But troubles followed them. The 16-year-old daughter, a beautiful young woman, was sent to live in the home of the local Lutheran minister to help with the housework and the care of the family's several children. Before long, she became pregnant by the minister and bore a son. In sorrow and shame, she returned to her own family.

But her return precipitated a series of terrifying events. Her brother's demonic symptoms greatly increased. Now the violence was focused upon the baby. Screaming that he intended to kill the infant, Carl would spring toward the child with eyes wild in his pale face and froth glistening on his lips. His sister, terror-stricken, clutched the baby and ran from the room. She slept only fitfully at night, keeping the infant close, and during the day she never let it out of her sight. As fears and tensions built, the whole family suffered strange, recurring illnesses marked by dizziness and severe headaches.

In the evenings, unearthly noise shook the house. Open doors would slam shut with no one near them, the window panes rattled loudly, even on windless nights, and weird, hollow noises emanated from one of the rooms. Seige inspected the house thoroughly and found nothing that could account for the phenomena. Late one evening, to the family's horror, an enormous ball of fire appeared on the top of the cooking stove. As they watched, frozen with fear, Carl dashed forward and struck the fireball with his fist. It broke apart, scattering small glowing spheres into all the corners of the room. Yet, nothing burned, and the fire gradually disappeared.

Shortly after this incident, the family cow, tied in the back yard, started behaving strangely. She began to rear on her hind legs, smite her tail, and shake her horns with savage fury. Carl, watching her from the kitchen window, gave great shouts of joy. Seige could not get near the beast to milk her, and he and his wife were convinced that somehow the demons had gotten into the cow.

The peasant family, who had sought sanctuary in the New World from the evil, supernatural forces that beleaguered them, was engulfed by fear and despair. At first they had tried to keep Carl's illness a secret. But as his attacks increased with awesome intensity, Seige knew that he must seek outside help. In the winter of 1868, he called in a Dr. Quinney, son of a prominent Stockbridge Indian chief.

Quinney listened to the young man's history, then administered an herb physic. He also applied poultices to Carl's shoulders in an attempt to draw out evil spirits. When the compresses were removed the next day, they were covered with bristles! Those bristles were of different colors and ranged in size from half an inch to three inches in length. The Indian doctor could not account for them. But an explanation was offered later by the spirit of a long-deceased Mohawk Indian speaking through a Milwaukee medium. This spirit claimed that the bristles were actually "long hairy worms generated by microscopic animals" found in a spring in Germany, whose waters Carl had drunk as a child. The spirit said that these worms were feeding upon Carl's muscles and would eventually kill him.

The parents were not so sure. Some time after the bristles appeared Carl had a violent seizure during which he gave the names of the devils possessing him. One was named Wilhelm Buhrer. Seige recalled that Buhrer was a desperate man who had murdered a hog drover in Germany many years ago for his money. Was the soul of the entity tormenting Carl? Perhaps this accounted for the presence of the bristles. Some people thought so.

When Dr. Quinney could offer no further help, the family turned to a spiritualist medium. He arrived at the house to find Carl black in the face and gasping for breath. It seems that a snake was inside the young man, pushing its head up into his throat. The lashings of its tail were

The Possession of Carl Seige

believed to be felt under Carl's ribs! The medium pushed a goose quill down Carl's throat then waved the quill over his head. Finally, Carl became quiet and was helped into bed. Relief, however, was short lived.

When the demons returned, the Seiges decided to appeal to the local priest. He declined to intervene, however, because Carl was not Catholic. When the Catholic bishop visited Watertown and heard the story, however, he agreed to arrange for an exorcism.

In early November of 1869, Carl was brought to the Catholic church in Watertown for the rites. The church was filled. Catholics, Protestants, and those of no particular religious persuasion crammed the pews. An awesome hush spread over the congregation as Carl Seige was laid upon the altar. His face was wan and drawn, his slender, wasted body almost corpselike in appearance. Seven priests, in cassocks, white surplices, and purple stoles, took their places beside the stricken man. Their faces held no fear, yet each, in his heart, recognized the dangers inherent in the ritual—of engaging in conversation with the demons, of being attacked psychologically in such ways that they themselves might be possessed by the evil spirits they sought to cast out.

"Almighty Father, Everlasting God ..."

They recited in unison, each priest tracing the sign of the cross over the young man's head.

"We beseech thee, this day, to help us cast out from thy beloved servant, Carl Seige ..."

Each priest sprinkled holy water upon the victim.

" ... Those demons that torment and seek to destroy... and by thy infinite mercy..."

Each priest laid hands upon the prostrate form before them.

"In the name of the Father, and of the Son, and of the Holy Ghost ..."

Then came the Latin words of ancient prayers, powerful incantations used for centuries to drive evil from the earth. The holy men knelt in a circle around Carl. At the back of the altar a picture of the Holy Virgin glowed in the candlelight, and flanking her were orbs of burning incense giving off a heavy, pungent fragrance.

The prayers, the sprinklings of holy water, the sign of the cross were repeated—over and over with soft, yet urgent insistence.

Suddenly Carl's head jerked, and from his gaping mouth the evil spirit spewed invectives. It shouted obscenities in German, threatening to surround the church with its own water, which it would purify. The forces of God and Satan had met. The priests' faces, shadowed by the flickering candlelight, were set like stone in mortar. The demon laughed raucously at the prayers, telling the priests they had not found the right one. Then it began speaking in tongues—snatches of Irish and Latin mingled with strange utterings that resembled no spoken language. Undeterred, the priests continued their prayers, beads of sweat sparkling their brows. They spoke with confidence, with a discipline born of long training. And the congregation watched, moved, unmoving.

When the last cold rays of the setting sun vanished below the windowsills of the church, the exorcism was halted. The exhausted priests were cautiously optimistic—four demons had been cast out. But there were more.

On the next day, Carl was again placed upon the altar before the picture of the Holy Virgin, and the priests began once more the long ritual. Three more demons were cast out.

And on the third, and final, day, the last demon agreed to leave if all the persons assembled would leave with him. All but three acquiesced and, to great joy and relief of Carl, the churchmen, and the congregation, the devil departed. The miracle had been made manifest.

A subdued and grateful Carl, along with his family, joined the Catholic Church. They hung a crucifix on the wall and bought prayer books and rosaries. And Carl attended mass each morning.

One month later, however, another devil appeared. This one was successfully cast out, but not before shouting, with glee, that four more demons remained.

Here, the story of the possessed man fades from the newspapers. In 1870, the press had more important stories to write. Wisconsin communities were astir with the issuance of railway bonds, and overseas Napoleon III was marching troops across the face of Europe to touch off the Franco-Prussian War. No matter. The sensationalism created by Carl Seige had already peaked.

No one now living witnessed Carl's exorcism. Nor can anyone ever know the nature or the dimensions of his illness. Was he mentally ill? Or was he really possessed by supernatural, earthbound entities that invaded his mind, body, and soul to torment him with their evil thoughts and fears? Today's physician may have diagnosed Carl as an epileptic.

The Possession of Carl Seige

There is one postscript to the story of the Seige family. The minister who had fathered Carl's nephew was arrested on a charge of seduction and committed to the county jail. After being confined for a month, he tore his blankets into strips and hanged himself in his cell. It is said that the boy and his mother lived happily in her parent's home.

MURDER ON THE BOARDWALK

Back in the 1890s, Oshkosh was a bustling frontier city that spilled across the plain. Sawmills on both banks of the Fox River hummed incessantly, turning out pine lumber and shingles, while factories produced finished wood products. Lumberjacks roared into town on payday and their heavy drinking in Main Street saloons often ended in brawls.

One night a rural man who had been shopping in the city started homeward carrying a rocking chair. His young son accompanied him. The sidewalks at that time were high boardwalks, and as the pair passed a large grove of gnarled oak trees, the father decided to rest for a moment. He put down the chair and, elated over the splendid bargain he had struck with the shopkeeper, sat down to rock.

Suddenly from out of the darkness beyond the trees two drunks appeared. Resentful of the man's obvious delight in his new chair, and spoiling for a fight, they taunted the stranger. The quarrel soon go out of hand and the drunks killed the man and ran off.

The boy, meanwhile, had dived under the boardwalk. When the assailants left, the child raced across the street for help. By the time the neighbors arrived, the father was dead in his chair.

For years afterward, travelers claimed that they heard the creaks of the rocker and the groans of the dying man in the grove where he had been slain. And those who are keen of ear say that the eerie sounds can still be heard, carried by the wild wind of a stormy night.

FOOTSTEPS IN THE DARK

The house at the crest of High Street in Pewaukee projects the solidity of a medieval fort. Built in the 19th century when the octagon craze swept the Midwest, the three-story, eight-sided cement structure, with walls 18 inches thick, has a permanence about it that contemporary houses lack. Yet the severity of its lines is softened by the dark wood framing, long windows, the carpenter's lace that embellishes a second-floor porch, and the towering ash and maple trees that surround it. To the casual observer, the house appears to be only an intriguing architectural folly; to those familiar with its history, it is remembered as the house of haunting footsteps—the abode of some unseen, unknown, ghostly night walker

The site originally held a log house. But after this structure burned to the ground, Deacon West, a blacksmith, bought the property and had a house erected on it in the late 1850s. Several years later, West too lost his home in a devastating fire. Only the massive walls remained.

The next owner, Ira Rowe, sold the place to N.P. Iglehart, a colonel from Kentucky. Iglehart, who spent his summers in Pewaukee, rebuilt the house into its present form in about 1873. He also discovered springs on the property and soon established a small home business, bottling the water and selling under the label Oakton Springs Water.

In the early 1900s, Audrey D. Hyle, a Milwaukee attorney, owned the house. And it was during his ownership that the unearthly footsteps were first heard. Someone or something wandered through the vast rooms and corridors each night at exactly 10:45 P.M. It was never seen and it never bothered anyone. Sleeping residents were sometimes half awakened, but drifted back into sleep as the footsteps faded.

In the 1930s, Mr. and Mrs. Joseph Zupet lived in the haunted house, and by this time the nocturnal visitor had varied its wanderings slightly. It now ascended the staircase from the front hall to the second floor at precisely 10:50 P.M. and descended by another staircase into the garden at precisely 1:20 A.M. Sometimes it paused outside a closed bedroom door, then moved on down the wide hallway. Whatever it was searching for was never known. Nothing was ever disturbed and nothing was ever taken.

Nevertheless, the Zupets became apprehensive about their resident ghost and invited a mystic by the name of Koran to visit their home. He was performing at the Milwaukee Theater at the time and welcomed the opportunity to make the 20-mile trip to Pewaukee. Koran made a thorough investigation and, although he did not identify the unseen guest, he did assure the homeowners that it was a friendly one. But after three years of residence, the Zupets put the house up for sale.

Tales of the haunted house spread, however, and no one wanted to live there. For a number of years the octagon house remained vacant. The housing shortage of World War II brought a succession of renters. Finally, in 1948, Mr. and Mrs. John T. Oswald of Milwaukee bought the house and lived in it until 1966, when they sold it to the present owners.

Insofar as is known, neither family was ever visited by the mysterious, if friendly, phantom.

THE HILLE CURSE

Mrs. Dorothy Ransome had a very clear idea of who the phantom was who approached her farmhouse near Waukesha, Wisconsin, and then vanished at the kitchen door. The ghost was named John Hille, and he built the house over a century ago. What the ghost of John Hille may not have known is that those appearances were just another chapter in a saga of bizarre, and often tragic, events that led many to believe the farm known as Ravensholme was cursed. Over a dozen people associated with the farm, including seven members of the Hille family and two of Mrs. Ransome's grandchildren, met with strange and untimely deaths.

Mrs. Ransome and her husband, Ralph, have lived on the farm since 1971, although they purchased the property in 1948. The ghost of John Hille has been making regular trips to their back door since the early 1970s. It was after the ghost's first appearance that Mrs. Ransome began delving into the history of the farm. She discovered a chilling legacy.

The history of the farmstead began in 1848, the year Wisconsin was admitted to the Union. John Hille, 37 years old at the time, brought his young wife, Magdelena, and several children to settle the 146 acres of virgin wilderness bordering the Fox River, six miles southwest of Waukesha. Hille had been born in Hanover, Germany, and immigrated to America in 1837 following the deaths of both parents. He apprenticed to a cabinetmaker in his native city and brought that skill to New York where he worked until his move to the Wisconsin frontier. Magdelena Jaquiltard Hille was also an immigrant. She met and subsequently married John in 1837, five years after her own family reached the East Coast from France.

The Hilles began their new life near Waukesha in a log cabin. Gradually they built their holdings into a prosperous 215-acre farm with several granaries, barns, sheds, and a spacious stone farmhouse constructed with granite boulders Hille cleared from nearby fields.

By 1880 the Hille family numbered eight. Two children had died: Michael, in childhood, and John, Jr., when he was 30 years old. The curse claimed its first victim in 1898. Magdelena Hille had been ill and a doctor was called. No one knows precisely what happened, but somehow the family physician mistakenly gave Mrs. Hille a fatal dose of poison. A short time later John Hille, the immigrant who had turned a Wisconsin forest into thriving farmland, died at nearly 90 years of age. His death was attributed to natural causes. Shortly thereafter a son, who had been an invalid for some time, followed his parents and two brothers in death.

The family which had been eight was now five.

Two sons, Oscar and William, and a sister, Hulda, inherited the large estate. Several other children had moved away and showed no interest in farming. By all accounts, the trio that remained on the farm was well respected by their neighbors and thrifty in their financial affairs, making the farm one of the most profitable in the county.

Nearly a decade passed before tragedy again struck the Hille family.

Oscar Hille died in 1916. He had taken a bull to a water trough early one morning. The animal had been led back to its stall and tethered to a post when it suddenly bolted and crushed Oscar against a wall. He died two days later of internal injuries.

The strangest of all deaths attributed to the curse was the macabre scenario played out at the Hille farm two years after Oscar's death.

The war in Europe had reached into America's midlands as young men marched off to battle the Kaiser. At home, sewing circles formed to make warm woolen clothing for the forces overseas, the Red Cross and YMCA asked for donations, and the purchase of Liberty Bonds and War Stamps was a strong measure of patriotism.

William and Hulda were particularly touched by the war. Both their parents had been born in the land now being torn asunder by battle. They had many Old World customs, and their hearts must have ached at the suffering and loss on both sides. William didn't like to discuss the war. "It's useless to argue," he often said. His reticence to talk about the war and his Germanic background, may have led some of his neighbors to suspect him of disloyalty, although members of his family later convincingly rebutted such speculation. The suspicions stalked William and Hulda with tragic consequences.

The morning of July 11, 1918, broke gently over the lazily moving Fox River a hundred yards behind the Hille house. The couple went about their chores as they did each day, but there was tenseness about them, almost as if their world would soon crumble. Several weeks earlier, a man named Elder Krause had ingratiated himself with the Hilles and persuaded them to take

The Hille Curse

him on as a hired man. Krause told his new employers that he was from South Milwaukee. But after several days his behavior changed abruptly. Krause said he was actually an "agent" of the U.S. Secret Service and was there because of reports that the couple was disloyal. It soon became apparent that the story was false and Krause's actual purpose was to extort money from William and Hulda. He enlisted the aid of a neighbor boy, Ernest Fentz, who performed odd jobs for William. Newspaper accounts of the day say Krause and Fentz threatened the Hilles with "exposure" as disloyal Americans unless they acquiesced to their demands.

There is little, if any, evidence that either William or Hulda were disloyal; on the contrary, they gave generously to the war effort. But a packet of letters found later in the Hille farmhouse indicated something mysterious and sinister in Krause's ways. One note from Hulda alluded to some past misdeed that was so bad that she had torn up the letter Krause sent threatening her with its exposure.

Fentz's role in the blackmail is unclear. William Hille had always liked the boy, buying him gifts and often allowing him to ride in a car Hille had recently purchased. Hille turned against the boy when he teamed up with Krause in the blackmail scheme. Fentz was fired from his job at the Hille farm in late June and told never to return.

The climax to this peculiar chain of events took place shortly before noon on July 11. Elder Krause stopped by the home of young Fentz, saying he wanted him to come along to the Hille farm because he "had a good position for him." The lad's father tried to persuade his stepson not to go, but Fentz wouldn't listen and left with Krause.

At the farm, William apparently relented and gave Krause and Fentz $30 for "protection against exposure." Fentz handed Hille a crudely drawn receipt for the money. It is not known what information would be "exposed" or from whom the Hilles would be safe. Krause, Fentz, and William then fell to arguing. Hulda Hille, who was deeply fearful that the pair was "after them," telephoned a neighbor, Mrs. William Dingeldine, and asked her to hurry over. The woman had just arrived at the kitchen door when a sharp explosion reverberated from the direction of the living room. Seconds later William walked into the kitchen holding a shotgun. When he saw Mrs. Dingeldine he offered to shake hands, but instead she tried to grab the gun. Hulda stopped her neighbor. "Let him go," she said. "It is for the best. They're after us anyway, and you cannot prevent this. We will be dead before anyone can get here."

Ernest Fentz was already dead. His body lay slumped in a rocking chair in the living room, the left side of his face blown away by William's shotgun.

Hille pushed past Mrs. Dingeldine and started for the barn. She tried to reason with him, but he brushed her aside, echoing his sister's grim prediction: "They are after me," he said.

Hulda then handed a small wooden box to her neighbor and told her to leave. Hulda said there were valuable papers in the container and feared that Krause, who was still somewhere on the farm, might find them if he searched the house. Mrs. Dingeldine ran toward the road and home to telephone neighbors for help. When she reached the gate, shotgun blasts came from the direction of a barn. At about the same time she also heard Hulda yelling at Krause to "stay away from here." Krause had apparently heard the sound of gunfire and came to investigate. After the woman's warning he fled across a nearby field.

At the Hille farm a slaughter had begun. William had methodically killed five horses with shots fired into their heads. Back in the kitchen, he then shot and killed a pet dog. Hulda, too, heard the shooting as she lay in bed upstairs, an empty bottle of arsenic and a razor blade next to her on a table. The poison would act swiftly enough, she decided, as life drained from her body. The last sound she heard was her brother climbing the stairs and entering his bedroom. He sat in a favorite chair and balanced the shotgun against his legs, its barrel pointing directly at his midsection. Against the trigger was the tip of a long, thin strip of wood. That would be his remote triggering device when the time came. He looked for one last time out the window to his beloved farm and remembered that it was the land his father and mother had wrestled from a savage wilderness and made thrive. Now he was an old man, and "they" were after him. The crashing roar of the gun shattered the stillness. William's upper torso was ripped away. Down the hall, his sister also lay dead.

One man murdered, two people dead by their own hands, and six farm animals slaughtered. Why? What motivated this orgy of violence? A coroner's inquest and the recollections of the three surviving Hille sisters tried to shed some light on the tragedy.

The sisters argued that their brother and sister were "loyal American citizens." They said Elder Krause's only object in coming to work for William and Hulda had been to get money from them on one pretext or another, and when he could not persuade them in any way he made threats by posing as a "secret service man." William gave Krause the $30, hoping to be rid of him. When Krause and Fentz didn't seem satisfied and William threatened to call the authorities, an argument took place that led to the deaths.

The coroner's inquest left many questions unanswered. Krause was finally located in St. Paul, Minnesota, trying to enlist in the army. Waukesha authorities were said to have gone after Krause to bring him back, but his testimony was not included in the coroner's report.

The most mysterious aspect of the inquest dealt with a letter found in the box given to Mrs. Dingeldine by Hulda Hille. In the note, Hulda predicted her own death!

It read: "Say girls, the other night there was a slapping noise on the wall. I knew what that meant, so good-bye. All be good with Eliza. There are only these three left. We will try our best to get our rights. Don't take it hard because Bill would have to be in prison for life; he [Krause] was telling Bill about the Japs [sic] coming over and how they will come. And then Bill—we would go in the house and shoot them. Give the machine to H. and A. That is W's wish."

On the opposite side of the sheet of paper Hulda listed the pallbearers she wanted at her funeral.

What crime had William committed that would be punishable by life imprisonment? How did Hulda know in advance that their deaths were imminent? Was the slapping noise an omen? The questions cannot be satisfactorily answered. We can only surmise that the harassment of the elderly couple by Krause and Fentz had caused an initial consternation that became fear and paranoia. William and Hulda were convinced that some unspoken past deed or utterance would cause their arrest and imprisonment. Sadly, there is little evidence to support their fears. They were trapped by the diabolical pretenses of Elder Krause and Ernest Fentz…and the Hille curse.

The farm reverted to Mrs. Jacob Hahn of Delafield, Wisconsin, one of the three surviving sisters. Over the next decades a cloud of disaster has hung over all those who live in the great old stone farmhouse.

Mrs. Hahn sold the farm in late 1918 to H.S. Kuhtz. The Kuhtz family built a milkhouse and enlarged the barn. But Kuhtz went bankrupt in 1927 and Mrs. Hahn took the farm back.

From 1927 until 1929, a young couple whose names have been lost to history rented the house. They too suffered the Hille curse. Two of their children died of the baffling crib death.

After 1929 no one lived on the farm for nearly 20 years, but that didn't prevent the curse from working its evil. In 1932 a man named Pratt was killed while dynamiting stone in a farm pasture.

On a clear, bright, beautiful morning in September of 1948, Mr. and Mrs. Ralph Ransome first saw the stone house standing abandoned amid weeds and bittersweet as the couple drove slowly down River Road. The Ransomes owned several health spas in Chicago and were looking for property to which they might retire someday. As Dorothy Ransome gazed at the house sitting way back in a grove of 13 massive oak trees, she knew it was the house for her. They proceeded to walk around the yard and peer into the dimly lit rooms through dust-encrusted windows. Mrs. Ransome was determined to find the owner. Incredibly, the house was still in the possession of Mrs. Jacob Hahn, the last surviving Hille sister. The octogenarian agreed to sell the house only after the Ransomes promised to restore the home to its original splendor.

Various architects said it would be extraordinarily expensive to restore the house, but Dorothy Ransome insisted that it be saved since she had made that promise to Mrs. Hahn.

Work on the restoration began in 1948 and was completed four years later. The roof was removed and the interior of the house was torn out and rebuilt. The only part of the house to remain intact was the 18-inch-thick fieldstone walls. The Ransomes lavished vast sums on the house's rebirth. Stained glass from an old funeral home was fitted into several windows; a marble fireplace, which has been the centerpiece of a New Orleans mansion, went into the living room. Crystal chandeliers from the old McCormick mansion in Chicago were wired into the dining room and parlor. Finally, the house stood proud and beautiful, surrounded by spacious lawns and clipped hedges.

In 1953, Anita Ransome, their only daughter, met and married young Andrew Kennedy while they were both students at Northwestern University. The couple moved to the farm that same year, while the Ransomes continued their business obligations in Chicago.

Meanwhile, they began to hear about the tragedies connected with the old farm. Neighbors warned them that terrible things happened to

The Hille Curse

anyone who lived at the old Hille house. Tear it down, the neighbors told them, or dynamite it, but don't live on that farm! The Ransomes were to learn they were not immune to the legacy.

The first calamity in the Ransome family was not, however, directly connected with the farm. Their grandson, seven-year old Philip Kennedy, drowned in 1963 while swimming in Lake Mendota, in Madison, during a family outing. Nine years later the farm would claim its most recent victim. Ralph and Dorothy Ransome had retired in 1971 and moved to the farm they called Ravensholme, adapted from the original English spelling of Ralph Ransome's last name. Their daughter and son-in-law had separated. Five-year-old Ransome Kennedy was living with his grandparents on the farm, enjoying the delights and distractions a young boy can find in the country. But, on March 17, 1972, while young Ransome was playing in the barn he fell into an auger and was crushed to death. The curse had struck again.

Dorothy Ransome first saw the ghost during the summer of 1972. On several occasions she would be sitting at the kitchen table stringing beans or reading, when a furtive, fleeting shadow, the figure of man, would slip across the backyard and come toward the kitchen door. When she reached the door no one was ever there.

"At first I thought it was a shadow," Mrs. Ransome says. "But this has persisted. He comes across the back, although I have seen him out on the driveway. It's old John Hille. He's got an old black coat on, a crouched hat, and walks fast but he's old. And his coat is way up in back and hangs in the front. Each time I see him he comes to the kitchen door." That was the door John Hille always used.

Dorothy Ransome isn't afraid of the ghost at all. She thinks he is happy and pleased that his farm has been well cared for. He appears at different times of the day and never at night. He is always moving very quickly with his arms swinging at his sides as if he is in a hurry.

When Mrs. Ransome sees the ghost and goes to the back door, her cat will often sit up and stare at the door at the same instant the specter appears.

Why would John Hille haunt his old farm? Because, Dorothy Ransome reasons, he put his whole being into the farm. "He built this house with his own hands. Cleared all the land, too. His family was raised here. I think he loved it so deeply and it meant so much to him that his spirit is still around. The neighbors are scared to death of this place. But I have nothing but love for it."

Mrs. Ransome cannot, however, understand the tragedies that have afflicted her home. "The neighbors still say there is a curse on this farm. We laughed at it at first, but there has been a constant stream of tragedies right straight through. It's always been the same."

Perhaps it always will be.

MARIE

The old two-story, brick house in the sixteen-hundred block of Milwaukee's National Avenue looks out of place in a neighborhood of undistinguished apartment buildings, light industrial firms, and small businesses. The place is easy to miss—lofty buildings on either side seem to cast it in perpetual shadow. Sitting rather forlornly as it does atop a raised yard, the house looks every bit its nearly century and a half of existence. But even so there are a few indications of its once grand appearance—little touches of filigreed wood trim and some decorative patterns in the brick facade around the narrow windows.

Thousands of Milwaukeeans pass along that block every day, ignoring this house just as they would most any other inner city dwelling long past its prime. Certainly Gerald Cummings was in that category. A retired trucking company executive, he lives only a few blocks away.

But for Gerry, as he likes to be called, all of that changed late on a night in September. As he drove down that block of National Avenue, his attention was suddenly drawn to a young woman standing in the street frantically gesturing to passing traffic. She appeared to be in some sort of trouble. Gerry stopped to see if he could help. The young woman jumped in the van without a word and silently pointed down the street.

What occurred next will stay with Gerry for as long as he lives.

"The color was drained out of my face," Gerry says his wife told him as she met him at the door when he got home. "She wanted to know what the matter was."

Gerry hesitated, looked at her, and quietly said: "Audrey, I think I picked up a ghost."

Not just any ghost, mind you, but a revenant known as Marie who was known to haunt that house on National Avenue. Although Gerry Cummings isn't entirely certain it was the ghostly Marie he encountered on that late summer night, his bizarre experience raises intriguing questions not easily answered.

The case becomes even more interesting since the retired Cummings had never heard of Marie, nor did he know anything about that house until several years later. If he had known about the ghost, perhaps he would not have been so willing to stop for a strange young woman in distress!

The story that Cummings would eventually learn began during an early summer in the late 1970s when two men—Paul Ranieri and Jeff Hicks—found the perfect house to which they could apply their considerable restoration abilities. They'd looked for nearly a year before discovering what was reportedly the oldest brick home in Milwaukee still on its original foundation. Built between 1836 and 1840, eight years before Wisconsin statehood, the house had at various times been a private home, an inn, a restaurant and, until Ranieri and Hicks bought it, a rooming house. But during the 1970s summer the men found it, the house was unoccupied, neglected, and in desperate need of repair. Although it had been scheduled for demolition, the pair could see its architectural and historical uniqueness. After negotiations with the owners, Ranieri and Hicks bought it in August 1977.

Within just a few weeks, it became apparent that along with the house came a ghost who called herself Marie. Marie was a young, attractive lady that the men eventually suspected may have lived in the house decades before and, according to some records, had either committed suicide or inexplicably disappeared without a trace.

Marie was not shy about making it clear she loved the house, even carrying on a conversation about renovation plans. More often than not, however, Marie was an unseen presence, a hovering custodian whose arrival was signaled by a sudden, sweeping coldness in a room, as if all the windows had been thrown open on a January day.

Over the ensuing months and years, Ranieri and Hicks became, if not entirely comfortable with Marie, at least tolerant of her infrequent forays into the corporeal world.

The condition of the house was such that Ranieri and Hicks knew they could not move in for some time. However, a separate, attached apartment at the rear of the house was in good condition and could be leased out.

Donald Erbs was the renter. He was the first person to "meet" Marie.

"I didn't see her come in," Erbs recalled of his first, startling experience of seeing an attractive young woman unexpectedly sitting in a chair across from him. "I don't know if she appeared...but all at once she was there."

He wasn't frightened. At first, he thought she had some business

Marie

being in the house—an outside door was not far away—and had simply wandered onto the second floor living room of his apartment. This room was separated from the rest of the house by a long hallway with separate doors to his living quarters, the main house, and the outside. He assumed she had somehow slipped quietly up the steps to his room.

He tried to ask her questions but she didn't answer, although she stared directly at him with what he described as a kind of dreamlike expression on her face. It was also that face, however, that seemed out of sync with the rest of the room. There was a glow about her, Erbs said, "like she was giving off a light. As if somebody had a spotlight on her ... almost overexposed and much brighter than her surroundings."

Her clothing, too, was peculiar. She was barefoot beneath a sort of ankle-length nightgown with lace at the sleeves and neck. Her long brown hair fell around her shoulders.

Then she surprised him by beginning to talk about the house!

"She told me a little about who built the house, which section had been built when, and why certain remodeling had been done," Erbs said. Just exactly how she came to know all of this she didn't explain.

The mysterious visitor then got up and walked out of the room. Erbs followed, but she was gone as abruptly as she had appeared. He reckons that she was out of his sight for no more than a few seconds. Although she appeared to be quite real, Erbs said there is no earthly way she could have gotten away so quickly.

"A ghost, or spirit. Of that I am sure. For some reason she picked me to talk to. I don't know why," he said. Although she appeared as a solid form, Erbs didn't think for a moment she could be a living person.

Erbs told Paul Ranieri about his nocturnal visitor who confirmed that no one had given permission to anyone to be in the house nor did he know of anyone who matched this woman's description. He was as puzzled about the visit as Erbs.

On the following Saturday the new owners spent the day stripping yellowed wallpaper from the plaster walls and preparing the hardwood floors for refinishing. Erbs also put up a small shelving unit he'd brought from another apartment. After he was done with the job, he walked over to the main part of the house to work with Hicks and Ranieri. A crash came from the room he'd just left. The shelf had fallen to the floor, but a plant that Erbs had placed on the shelf was sitting intact on the floor a few feet away, as if it had been removed from the shelf before it fell.

It had been. Erbs discovered that later in the evening as he watched television. Without warning, the same woman appeared in a chair next to him.

Less startled than the first time, Erbs asked her if she had anything to do with the falling shelf. Yes, she allowed, but it was an accident. She had been looking around his apartment and had bumped into it. The plant she'd managed to catch as it slid off the shelf.

Erbs was satisfied with her explanation. By the way, who was she, he wanted to know.

"Marie," the woman replied. She assured him she meant no harm. In fact, she was very happy that the house was being fixed up. She even told him her father was a carpenter and might be of some assistance!

Just as before, the conversation ended abruptly when the woman he now knew as Marie got up and walked out into the quiet of the night. Again Erbs looked and listened but detected no retreating footsteps or slamming doors.

Paul Ranieri himself was the next one to see Marie. It was a day in the following month of September, after tiring hours of renovation and house repair. He sat in the still-unfinished front room. As he mulled over the day's work, Ranieri had the impression of being watched, of knowing in some way that he was not the only one in the room. Glancing toward the staircase in the front hallway, he drew back as the lucent form of a woman suddenly materialized, brushed past within inches of where he sat, glided through an archway and then seemingly melted into a wall. She said nothing, nor did she look toward him.

He realized the woman was remarkably similar in appearance to the person Donald Erbs had encountered, right down to the dark hair and long gown.

"I wasn't really afraid," Ranieri said, adding that for a few seconds, almost echoing Erbs' first impression, he thought she was an unexpected visitor. But there was one significant difference—Erbs said Marie was a solid figure whereas Ranieri quickly realized the person he watched was a ghost—walls and the few pieces of furniture were visible through her torso.

However, Erbs' next encounter with Marie about ten days later seemed to confirm that both men had seen the same woman.

It was about 10:30 in the evening when Erbs climbed the steps to his bedroom. When he reached the top landing, he glanced into the small living room where he had first encountered Marie. He jumped when he saw a transparent Marie standing near the door. He quickly backed away and she vanished. He thought she had been frightened by his startled behavior.

A few weeks later, Erbs was again visited by Marie in his apartment shortly after Ranieri and Hicks had started probing around the earthen-floored basement which was, as with many old houses, damp, small, and cramped by today's standards. It was sectioned off into several rooms with rough-hewn doors between the various cubicles. Broken dishware, musty jars and old furniture lay scattered about. The men wondered if it might be useful to conduct a more formal survey of the basement debris considering the history of the house. They contacted an urban archeologist at a local university who agreed to take a look. Work down there was suspended until he could schedule the visit.

That's when Marie paid her next call on Erbs. She was concerned about why the men weren't working in the basement anymore. He explained, but it didn't seem to satisfy her. She asked him to follow her and guided him down to the basement. Once there she pointed to a wall. Puzzled, Erbs walked over to take a look. He couldn't see anything interesting, but when he turned to ask her a question she had again departed.

Erbs along with Ranieri and Hicks took a more careful look at the wall the next day and discovered that a section was newer than the rest. They knocked out those bricks and started digging in a tight crawl space beyond. They found pottery shards, pieces of jewelry, and bones, later determined to be from a dog that had apparently been buried there.

Those aged dog bones may explain two other odd events during the house's early renovation. Late one night as Ranieri lay in bed reading he noticed his pet cat cowering under a chair on the far side of the room. As he leaned over the edge of his bed to calm the cat, Ranieri came eyeball to eyeball with an aged bull terrier looking decidedly unfriendly. The problem was the only dog in the house was a Siberian Husky, and it was downstairs.

Jeff Hicks also had an encounter with a ghost dog. It was late October as he worked late one evening again in the basement. He heard what he thought were metal tags on a dog's collar coming up from behind him. Thinking it was their Husky, he turned around but saw nothing. The door leading to the upstairs was shut.

Although Hicks was the only one of the three who did not see Marie, he thought he felt her presence in another way. He had discovered a door in the basement wedged open. He tried unsuccessfully to close the door but could move it only a few inches. It stuck fast on the uneven floor. About a week later, he discovered the door completely closed. From that point on he was able to open and close the door at least halfway before it became stuck again.

Marie had told Donald Erbs that her father could help with the restoration.

There was also the matter of the basement lights. They seemed to have minds of their own. As often as eight to ten times a week, Ranieri or Hicks found the lights down there ablaze. The pair was doubly puzzled: Not only had no one been downstairs, but three separate light switches had to be flipped on and that can only be done from the basement itself.

Gerry Cummings knew nothing of these events of a decade before on that late September night when he stopped to help what he thought was a young woman in distress. And even if he had known the house's haunted history, it's doubtful that would have fully prepared him for his experience.

A lifelong Milwaukee resident, who once had a tryout with the Green Bay Packers in the mid-1950s, Gerry is an unassuming retiree who lives quietly with his wife Audrey near 38th and Greenfield, less than two miles from the house on National Avenue. He graduated from a Catholic boy's high school in 1949 and went directly to work for his father's appliance delivery trucking business on South Ruthton Avenue. He worked there all his life, eventually taking over the ownership of the business after his dad died. He sold the business to his son-in-law a decade ago and retired.

"I had a good career," Gerry says. "We had a very nice situation. I miss my friends there and the people I worked with."

His life revolved around his work, his family, and that moment of glory in 1955 when he came this close to playing with the vaunted Packers. It's a part of his life he discloses early on in a conversation. But ironically it was his lack of a college education that was his downfall in professional football.

"That was a big deal. The Packers wanted college boys. A sports announcer in Milwaukee by the name of Earl Gillespie helped me get my tryout. I was very lucky. Actually, my dad was kind of against me trying out. He was afraid I was going to get hurt. At that time, football was very different that it is now. I played two positions on offense and defense.

Marie

Guard or tackle. That's not like it is now."

He did go on to play semiprofessional football for a few years until turning his full attention to the trucking company. But he still savors another connection to the home of the green and gold.

"My mother's relatives came from Green Bay. She just happened to be up there visiting at the time I was born. So I always say I'm from Green Bay because that's where I was born," he says smiling.

Gerry's encounter with the woman on National Avenue occurred a few years before his retirement.

"The date was September 20. I was watching a bowling team my wife and I backed then called Cummings Trucking. They bowled a 9:00 P.M. shift, at what was called LinMor Lanes, over at the corner of 18th and Greenfield. So after they got done bowling I left, probably around midnight. I went to an all-night restaurant between National and Mineral on 16th Street," Gerry remembers of that Friday night.

He said he left the restaurant sometime between 1:00 and 2:00 A.M. to head home. He climbed into his van, which was parked across the street from the restaurant, drove down to National Avenue and made a left turn. The traffic was still considerable even at that time of the night.

"That's where everything started," he says. "The girl was standing out in front waving her hands. She looked like she was in trouble, but nobody would stop for her. She was motioning like she wanted help. A lot of people wouldn't pull over but I did."

The woman was directly in front of the house Paul Ranieri and Jeff Hicks had remodeled. She appeared to be in her early twenties with dark, reddish hair falling to her shoulders. She wore a light jacket, slacks, and a blouse. She did not carry a purse or handbag of any sort, which, Gerry said "was another strange thing. What was she doing out so late without any kind of identification?"

Gerry stopped and asked her if she was all right. She nodded.

"I asked her if she wanted a ride someplace. She got in the van and I asked her where she wanted to go," Gerry remembers. What was particularly odd is that the woman appeared to be mute because she grunted and pointed down National Avenue in a westerly direction, the same way he was headed. Gerry gave her a pencil and paper and asked her to write down what her name was and where she wanted to be taken.

"All she wrote was that her name was 'Mary,'" Gerry said. She seemed confused at other questions and somewhat agitated. "I felt sorry for her because I had no idea what was wrong."

He drove down National Avenue toward 26th Street. She frenetically waved for him to turn at that corner. A block later she again motioned for him to turn and then indicated she wanted him to stop in the middle of the block, on Mineral Street. There was no sign of life on the street. It's primarily a residential area, but there are two churches at either end of the block. A large, older three-story house and garage were opposite where he stopped his van. No lights were on in that house, or in any other building on the block. A few cars were parked along the street. Street lamps from Mineral Street and National Avenue intersections provided scant illumination.

She murmured something, he thinks she said "You nice man," opened the door and climbed out of the van.

"She pushed the door but it didn't close all the way," Gerry says. He waited for her to push it closed. The dome light stayed on. He peered through the passenger side window but he couldn't see her. He was concerned that she may have fallen down. He got out of the van and walked around to the passenger side.

"She was nowhere around. No place. No sign of her whatsoever. I don't know how she could have gotten away… It was only a matter of ten or fifteen seconds between the time she got out and the time I got out," he says, shaking his head.

Gerry says there is no place she could have gone in such a brief moment. He looked up and down the street and listened for footsteps, but there was absolutely no other sign of life on that entire block. The few dark houses were not close enough for her to run into and it didn't make any sense to him that she would have been hiding.

He drove around the block still looking for her. When he gave up, he headed on home to tell his wife about his peculiar experience. "The color was drained out of my face. I told her the story. I said I think I picked up a ghost," he said. His wife thought then it might have been a ghostly hitchhiker and assured him she had heard of it happening to others.

Gerry Cummings allowed the incident to recede in his mind until the following year when his wife gave him a copy of the first edition of this book for Father's Day. She inscribed it, "For My Own Ghost Hunter."

"I read (the book) and pointed out the story (of Marie) to my wife and I showed her the picture of the window of the house. She said for goodness sakes that says the house is on National Avenue. I thought that had to be it," he said. Coincidentally, Audrey Cummings worked at an insurance company in the same block of National Avenue.

An old photograph of a young woman that Paul Ranieri and Jeff Hicks found in the house was included with the original story of Marie. The men thought it might have been Marie. It shows a young woman in her twenties with bare shoulders above a low-cut gown and bobbed hair fashionable in the 1920s and 1930s.

Gerry Cummings considers the similarity between the girl he saw who called herself Mary and the photograph in the book. "The girl I picked up had longer hair, darker, to her shoulders, kind of red from what I could make out when the light went on in the van. I looked at the picture (in the book) a few times to see if it could have been her. I really can't say for sure."

So what really happened to Gerry Cummings on that late Friday night in September?

The simple truth is, he doesn't know to this day if the woman was a real woman in some sort of crisis, or Marie of National Avenue asking a nice man for a ride ... where? The destination the hitchhiker directed him to seemed pointless: no late night businesses to work at, no homes with welcoming porch lights, no parked automobile to start up and drive away.

"The strange thing was that she disappeared so fast. I wasn't frightened, but I couldn't imagine what had happened to her," he says, still perplexed.

As one can imagine, too, Gerry takes some good-natured ribbing when he tells people the story. "They think I'm weird. For a while everyone thought it was a joke."

But it was never a joke to Gerry Cummings. He knows what happened. And though it remains an insoluble mystery, the possibility he gave a lift to a ghost ranks right up there with a Packers' tryout as an exciting milestone for this Milwaukee retiree.

TERROR IN THE NIGHT

Darkness wrapped the old clapboard farmhouse near Cedarburg on that early March night. Barb Yashinsky lay sleeping. The late winter day had been long and exhausting from her family's move into the rural home they'd just purchased. At 2:00 A.M.. in the morning Barb was jerked awake.

"I thought it was a cat fight," she said of the noise, noting the time on the bedside alarm clock. "And you know what they sound like."

Barb was now listening intently. She decided the sounds were more like those of a weeping child. She wondered if her Kate had awakened and become frightened by the strange surroundings. Barb got up, crossed the darkened hallway, and opened the door to her daughter's bedroom. Little two-year-old Kate was sound asleep.

Then Barb thought she heard a woman's voice blending with the crying. More curious than frightened, she walked downstairs and looked through the house. Everything seemed in order. She even found a flashlight and went outdoors to look around the yard.

Satisfied that there was nothing else to be seen, she returned to the house. The muffled crying and indistinct voice persisted. At times they seemed to be coming from a closet in the bedroom she shared with her husband Michael, who slept soundly. No more than 20 minutes later, the upsetting sounds subsided and Barb drifted off to sleep. She decided not to tell her husband about the episode.

Within less than two years, Barb and Michael would finally come to grips with what their brains told them was not possible—that they had moved into a haunted house.

The house was well over a century old when Barb and Michael Yashinsky moved in. There was still much work to be done to convert it into a comfortable and cheerful home. Barb was eager to get the remodeling underway. They had bought the house from a man who restored rundown homes for resale, yet he had made only minimal cosmetic changes to the place. Barb and Michael had bought it "for a song," they said, after it stood empty for nearly a year. New wiring and central heat-

Terror in the Night

ing had been put in before their arrival, but there was still a great deal of painting to be done outside and in. It would be a busy spring and summer. Barb was a schoolteacher and planned to return to work that next fall so she was most anxious to complete work on the house.

But the long, hard days of painting and cleaning did not bring the anticipated rewards. She said she was nervous and restless all during those first months after they had moved in.

"I was never satisfied with anything, which isn't like me," Barb said. "I couldn't find enough to keep me occupied. (I thought) what I was doing was boring. I found lots of reasons to yell at the baby for no reason at all, but I thought I just needed to get back to work."

The couple was able to finish most of the necessary work on the house by late summer. Barb returned to her classroom job on schedule. Michael Yashinsky was a chef who worked nights and cared for their daughter during the day. Barb's mother, Margaret, filled in for an hour or two on those days when her daughter wasn't able to get home before Michael left for work. Margaret also babysat those evenings when Barb had a school function to attend. A return to the classroom did little to alleviate Barb's self-described "nervousness."

One night in November of 1975 Kate awoke crying with what her mother thought was only a nightmare. It was odd, as the child had always been a sound sleeper. Barb went into her room.

"I felt the closing in of fear and apprehension which I was to experience many times," Barb said. She took her daughter into her arms. Kate asked if 'the man' would come again. Barb didn't know what she was talking about and wrote it off as a small child with a large imagination.

The next night Barb was again awakened by Kate ... only this time the girl was screaming in what seemed like utter terror. She told her mother that 'the man' had come again, although this time he had brought frightening animals, circus animals," she said.

Kate was a bright and verbal child, Barb said, yet she could not provide any sort of description of the man or the animals. Barb held her tightly until she quieted down and fell back asleep.

"This left me with a lot of questions and a lot of fears," Barb said.

On the next night, a weekend, Michael had decided to stay downstairs watching television when his wife went to bed. She had not been asleep long when she felt a stinging slap across her face.

"Barbara!" a deep male voice cried out.

She flung an arm out to defend herself. It fell across the other side of the bed, where Michael slept. He was not there.

"I was frozen to the bed," she recalls. "I do remember praying and then getting enough courage to move. But I (felt) real heavy. I couldn't get myself up. I always scoffed when you see heroines in movies who can't move. I thought it's silly—you can always do anything you want. Your own will is stronger."

Barb finally found her way downstairs where she confronted Michael. She still thought he was responsible, but he was stunned. He had never left his seat in front of the television.

Michael remembers that night as if it were yesterday. "Barbara isn't the type to dream. That's why I couldn't figure it out. I'm a very logical individual. I couldn't figure out the logic for something like that. Knowing her as I do, she never lies. It just wasn't Barb."

Meanwhile, Michael began noticing other oddities in the house for which his logical mind could find no explanation. Intense cold often filled the kitchen, the upstairs hallway, and Kate's bedroom, which was situated directly over the kitchen. At first Michael and Barb reasoned that the poorly caulked windows were the cause. But new windows and extensive caulking did not lessen the chill, especially in Kate's room. With hot air pouring from the register in Kate's room, Michael could still see his breath. "I'm so cold," the little girl complained to her parents in the middle of the night.

In the upstairs hallway, newly applied wallpaper kept peeling. No amount of glue or pressure could keep it sealed to the plaster.

On a morning of the following spring of 1976, Michael had an especially disturbing experience.

"Something like a vapor was coming up from under our bedroom door," he said, noting that the hazy substance didn't look or smell like smoke. "Something like steam. A heavy, damp kind of thing, whitish like a fog. And it was transparent, yet you could see the lines of where it started and where it stopped. It was subsiding as I looked at it, going back under the door."

Michael nudged Barb and asked her if she smelled anything. But she was still asleep. When he looked back toward the bedroom door, the vapor was gone. Michael finally roused Barb and she got up to check on

Terror in the Night

Kate who was sleeping peacefully.

A few days later, Michael awoke to find a similar blanket of vapor, but this time it surrounded the bed.

"It reminded me of a screen completely encompassing the bed," he said. "You could look through it. But this time it had no odor."

Michael's personal experiences upset Barb even more.

"The next months left me fighting a battle to remain calm in the evening," she said. "We didn't seem to notice anything during the day. I rarely went to bed without Mike. I'd sleep on the sofa until he'd come home. I'd check on Kate a great many times."

Barb and Michael had kept their peculiar experiences to themselves, yet continued to probe for answers. The events were usually spaced far enough apart that they came unexpectedly, which only led to the couple's distress. Neither one subscribed to a belief in psychic phenomena; they had no interest in the subject. But all that changed in the fall of 1976 when Barb was ready to go back to teaching again.

Barb's mother, Margaret, was a straightforward woman in both her speech and manner. One day she asked Barb straight out if she thought something was "wrong" with the house. Margaret said the kitchen was often so bitterly cold that she had to put on a sweater while she cooked or did her crossword puzzles. Yet at the same time the adjoining living room and dining room were very warm, Margaret said.

Barb took some relief in knowing that Margaret, too, thought something odd was going on. "She's the most stable person I have ever met; a very calm, quiet, sedate lady full of common sense and very much in control of her surroundings," Barb said of her mother.

Her mother suggested that the house be blessed, but Barb was hesitant. "This person or whatever it is isn't aggressive or violent," she reasoned. "Who knows why it's here?"

The house was never blessed. And that may have been a mistake if an event the following January was any indication.

Michael had been playing with Kate before her bedtime. When she got tired he scooped her into his arms and carried her up the stairs, her head snuggled against his shoulder. Michael didn't bother to turn on the lights since he knew the way by heart. But when he opened the door to his daughter's room, he stopped short. A short, squat vaporous form shimmered in the middle of the room. Clearly it was a man.

"The lines of it were moving, vibrating. I've never seen anything like it. You could see somewhat through it but nowhere near like the (vapor) around the bed. I reached over, turned on the light, and it was gone."

The room was intensely cold.

Nevertheless Michael put Kate to bed. He did not tell his wife of the experience at that time.

The sensitivity of animals to reported supernatural events is well documented. Household pets such as dogs, cats, and even birds seem to be more sensitive to the unseen world than their human companions.

Such was the case with Benji, a massive Great Pyrenees owned by the Yashinskys. He slept on the floor in the master bedroom. His behavior one night was another signal to Barb and Michael that all was not well. The couple was sitting on the edge of the bed talking. Benji was curled up on the floor. Suddenly the dog leaped to his feet, looked toward Barb and growled. She was momentarily frightened thinking it "had gone nuts or something" and was about to attack her.

However, in one great leap, he bounded past her and into the corner of the room, facing the closet where Barb had first heard the crying voice. Benji stood growling for a moment, then, looking as if he had made a fool of himself, returned to the couple with his head down and a rather woeful look on his great face.

Interestingly, that was the only time their dog had ever acted oddly in the house. Neither Barb or Michael had heard or seen anything out of the ordinary, yet they could make little sense of the way their dog had acted. All they could figure out is that the room had been in near total darkness so perhaps it had been a passing ... shadow.

On the 13th of January, less than two years after they moved in with great expectations, the Yashinskys packed up the furniture and moved out.

"We wanted to get out of there," Michael said. "Whatever it was seemed more and more disturbed."

Barb thought their lives would continue to change for the worse.

"It might start throwing pots and pans, rumpling bedding, or become hostile in some way. It's silly to talk about it like this, but you wonder. If Katie saw a man bringing animals maybe he was just interested in her as a child."

Or maybe not. That was her greatest fear. The unknown and unknowable future. She didn't know whether the presence in their home was aggra-

Terror in the Night

vated with them and thus might harm any one of them, or whether the entities were merely curious.

The Yashinskys had tried to discover something of the history of the house. The original homestead stayed in the builder's family for nearly a century except for one, brief period of time. The last member of the family had been a reclusive bachelor who died in the place. He reportedly never saw any outsiders save for his widowed sister-in-law. He heated only a few rooms downstairs and had closed off the second floor.

A descendant of the original family provided another intriguing bit of information: a miserly ancestor was thought to have secreted a sizable quantity of old coins somewhere in the house. At least one search by family members years before included knocking out some walls.

A neighbor family in whom the Yashinskys confided their troubling experiences said they'd never seen or heard anything odd in or around the house. Yet, their daughter often babysat for the Yashinskys and habitually turned on every light in the house when she was there.

The short, squat figure Michael had seen in the bedroom might have been a member of that builder's family—when Barb was able to track down living descendants, they were strikingly similar in physical stature.

The couple could find no evidence with which to identify the crying woman or child Barb had heard.

"It's changed my ideas about people who I previously thought were crackpots for seeing ghosts or trying to film ghosts," Barb said, finally coming to terms with what she determined was the supernatural basis for the problems in her home. "Although our experiences weren't particularly frightening, you kind of want to forget. We'll probably wrestle with this the rest of our lives."

Her husband agreed.

"I've gone over and over it in my mind, many times," Michael said. "I'm not an extremely well-read person, but I know what I know and I know what I saw. Nothing will ever change that. This happened to me."

In the years following their adventure in the old farmhouse, the Yashinskys found their new home blissfully terror-free. Even little Kate noticed the change. "Oh, mama," she often said, "it's so nice and warm in my room."

MUFFLED SCREAMS

There is something about an old house that invites rumors of ghosts. For instance, take that old unpainted frame house in Milwaukee's Sixth Ward back in 1875. The neighbors knew it was haunted. The square, two-story home was one of the oldest in the city. It stood high on the west bluff of the river, southeast of the old reservoir. Its windows offered a splendid view of the city—for anyone brave enough to live there—and the house itself, if not elegant, was spacious enough with a full basement, four rooms on the first floor, two large rooms and two closets on the second, and a garret.

Yet for all the house's amenities, no one ever lived there for very long. Year after year, tenants moved in and just as promptly moved out.

In final desperation after a Polish family moved out, Herman Hegner, who lived next door and had been put in charge of renting out the place, decided to conduct his own investigation. He watched the house closely on the first night that it was vacant. Sure enough, shortly after midnight he saw the room in the southwest corner of the first floor fill with light. Fearing the house had caught on fire, Hegner raced next door. The light blinked out just before he got up to the window where it shone through. He groped in his pocket for the door key as the light sprang on again with blinding brilliance then off just as suddenly.

Hegner put the key in the lock. The old door groaned on its hinges as he pushed it open. He moved stealthily from room to room, peering into dark corners and musty closets. Nothing. He found nothing at all. Although Hegner was perplexed, he was certain of the light and equally as certain that no living being was in the house to produce it.

In July of 1875, a newly arrived Bohemian family of five moved into the house. On their first night they settled down on the first floor. The parents were jolted awake by heavy footsteps from the floor above. A muffled scream trembled in the air, then came the resounding crash of a heavy body falling to the floor. Though the very walls seemed to vibrate, the children did not awaken.

On the second night, the sequence of events was repeated but with

160

increased violence. At 1:00 A.M. the terror-stricken family fled to Hegner's house to spend the rest of the night. At first light they gathered their meager possessions and left the city.

As word of the haunted house spread, two recently arrived Englishmen asked Hegner for permission to spend the night in the house to either expose the delusion or to "capture" the ghost. George Heath and Henry Jordan picked up the house key on Sunday evening, August 8, 1875. Armed with nothing more than their own courage and a few warm blankets, Heath and Jordan said they'd report back in the morning. Both men worked at the Milwaukee and St. Paul Railroad car shops and were considered responsible and trustworthy men.

But early the next morning when Hegner went next door to check on the men, he found the front door standing open. Inside, piles of crumbled plaster lay on the floor; the bare walls were streaked with water stains from a leaky roof. Worse still, the kitchen floor was worn through in several places exposing the square-cut log floor beams. Even the ladder leading to the garret was laced with cobwebs.

Hegner found the pile of blankets but no Heath and Jordan.

What happened the night before was pieced together by a newspaper reporter who tracked down George Heath and got the story.

Heath said that he and Jordan had checked all through the house just after sunset to make certain no one was hiding inside. Satisfied the place was empty, the men went back to work at the railroad shops until after 10:00 P.M. They walked back up the hill to the house and sat around smoking until they got tired and went to sleep.

"I was awakened by Jordan," Heath told the newsman. "He had heard some noise upstairs. We sat up for a moment and then heard someone walking across the floor."

Heath said they heard a scuffle, a smothered cry, and then a body falling to the floor.

"I proposed to go upstairs," Heath recalled. He was just about to light their candle when a blinding white light surrounded them.

"For a moment my eyes were dazzled so that I could distinguish nothing. Then Jordan pointed toward the stairway ... through the open door. I looked but saw nothing."

Heath said the light lasted for no more than a minute before going out. He managed to light the candle and glanced at his pocket watch. It was 25 minutes past midnight.

"I was not frightened in the least and insisted upon going upstairs," Heath bragged to the newsman. "At first Jordan hesitated but when I moved he followed. We searched rooms and closets, but found no trace of anything living or dead."

The men decided to stay awake. They blew out their candle and sat silently, waiting. Their patience was rewarded. In about 15 minutes the stealthy footsteps again came from above. Then a brief pause, a muffled cry, a struggle, a fall. Then silence. Within what seemed like only seconds, the blinding light again filled the downstairs room in which the men huddled.

Heath wanted to make another search, but Jordan refused to spend another minute in the house. Heath reluctantly agreed and both men left.

The newsman asked Heath for an explanation. He could give none, but he insisted ghosts had nothing to do with it. But if not ghosts, what?

GIDDINGS' HAUNTED BOARDINGHOUSE

Nobody ran a boardinghouse with the aplomb of Mrs. William Giddings. She filled her south side Milwaukee home with employees of the local tannery and catered to her men with calm efficiency. The two-story frame house, at the corner of Allis and Whitcomb streets in Allen's Addition, soon earned a reputation as a haven of solitude where nothing more disturbing that the death of a kitten ever occurred.

But that was before August 8, 1874. At 9:00 A.M. on that Saturday, Mr. Giddings was at work at the rolling bill; his wife and Mary Spiegel, the hired girl, were alone in the house working in the kitchen. Mary, the daughter of a neighboring Polish family, was a slow-witted child whose father brutalized her so severely that she welcomed the opportunity to "hire out." Although living in a constant state of nervous apprehension, she was treated with compassion and charity by her employer.

The women were making pies for dinner when suddenly spoons leaped from their holder and flew in all directions around the room. Only momentarily startled, the older woman continued to work — until a trap door in the kitchen floor began to rise and fall. Mrs. Giddings asked 14-year old Mary to stand on it. When the youngster was unable to hold down the heaving door, the woman knew some prankster had gotten into the cellar. She lifted the door, descended, but saw no one.

Climbing back into the kitchen, she found everything in motion. Dishes flew from the china closet and smashed on the floor. An oil lamp soared from its shelf and shattered. Chairs rose to the ceiling and one broke upon hitting the floor. The stove danced. One of the pies fell from the table, a dish of beans spilled, and eggs whirled out of the pantry that was open to the kitchen. One egg, following a trajectory, cut across a corner to hit Mrs. Giddings where she sat.

Mary, greatly frightened, was sent to get the neighbors, Mrs. Mead and Mrs. Rowland, to come sit with them. As the women approached Giddings' house, a pail of flowers at the door leaped over the 5 1/2-foot wooden fence into the next yard. It was brought back but again flew over the same fence.

Haunted Wisconsin

Once inside, the four women sat in a circle. Mary began peeling potatoes for dinner. As she talked, the knife flew out of her hand, along with the potato from the pan in her lap; both hit Mrs. Rowland. In the next moment, a dish on the table cracked in two. None of the group was near enough to the table to have reached the dish. One piece fell to the floor; the other remained on the table. Corn, boiling on the stove, leaped out of its pot.

The resolute Mrs. Giddings tried to keep her composure. The next door neighbor, Mrs. Mead, lost hers. Visibly upset, she announced that she was going home. No sooner had she reached her own yard than a heavy stick of wood was hurled over the fence at her. Mary was at the far end of Giddings' yard and reportedly couldn't have lifted the stick anyway.

Pails of water also traveled over the fence and back again, and no more than one pail in four was spilled.

Curiosity soon brought throngs of neighbor women to the house and terror kept them there. Finally, the bewildered Mrs. Giddings sent Mary to get George W. Allen and his brother, Rufus, owners of the Wisconsin Leather Company. The men were at their tannery near Giddings' home and they came promptly to the house, bringing with them a Dr. Meacham and Dr. Nathaniel A. Gray, an eminent Milwaukee obstetrician.

While George Allen tried to calm the women, a stove-lid lifter flew off the wood stove, hurtled 10 feet through the air, and struck Allen on the leg. No one was closer to the stove than he. Then, a pie rose from the table, flew past him, and smashed against the stove. To avoid further bombardments, Allen left the room.

By this time the floor was littered with debris of broken dishes, splintered wood, shards of glass, and spilled food. Mrs. Giddings asked Mary to sweep, and as she did so, Dr. Meacham kept a close, scrutinizing eye on her. From where he stood, he had a full view of the pantry and of the servant. As he watched, a small china dish sailed horizontally out of the pantry. He dodged it and it slid to the floor, spilling the cards it contained, but not breaking.

Mary then began to wash the floor, but the pail of soapy water skated to the outer edges of the room into the crowd of frightened onlookers. As Mary got off her knees to chase the pail, she was hit hard on the head by a bowl flying out of the pantry. The men searched the pantry, the kitchen, and the dining room but found no devices that might have propelled objects into space.

164

Giddings' Haunted Roadhouse

The manifestations continued until late afternoon. By that time, reporters from the local press had arrived to interview the men and all the women still present. They questioned each eyewitness independently and were completely satisfied that there had been no collusion. Since the phenomena occurred only in Mary's presence, there was some speculation that she might have thrown some of the objects. But the scrupulous observations made by the witnesses and the unnatural ballistics of the moving objects exonerated the girl. That the phenomena had indeed occurred without human agency was vouched for by literally scores of eyewitnesses who were highly regarded and generally considered to be beyond impeachment.

One reporter also had a talk with Mary. He found her to be a pitiable creature fearful of staying in the house or of doing anything. She could not explain how the manifestations had occurred, and she denied all responsibility for them. The reporter also learned that the child would sometimes get up in the night to fight imaginary enemies. Mrs. Spiegel, who was present during the interview and who spoke no English, thought that the note-taking newsman was a law enforcement officer gathering evidence to support a charge of witchcraft against her daughter. She scolded Mary repeatedly and the girl huddled deep in her chair and trembled and cried.

Saturday evening, the Giddingses decided that they could not keep the girl and they told her to go home. She begged to stay and when her pleadings were of no avail she hid herself in the woodshed. Her father found her there and, in order to make amends, beat the child severely.

The next that was heard of Mary was her attempted suicide in the river. An unnamed gentleman rescued her, soaked and shivering, and took her to Giddings' house. When asked why she had tried to kill herself, she said she was so hounded by everybody that she could no longer endure her life.

Again her former employers sent her back to her parents, and the charitable Mrs. Giddings sent along a dish of food. The next day Mary returned the empty dish. No sooner had she put it on the kitchen table than the tea kettle leaped off the stove, hit the floor, and was damaged beyond repair. Giddings, hearing the commotion and fearing further destruction of his property, drove Mary out of the house.

Two days later she was taken back to the house by Dr. Chauncey C.

Robinson, a prominent physician of the city who had taken an interest in the girl and wanted to question Mrs. Giddings about the strange phenomena. The family and the boarders were eating dinner; the moment Mary and the doctor entered the room, knives and forks flew off the table.

According to new accounts, Mary was finally taken into the home of a well-known physician in the Seventh Ward.

Was Mary the focus of the upheaval? Parapsychologists believe that neurotic conditions are among factors that conduce to poltergeist activity, and it was the consensus of the time that Mary was neurotic. Did her neurosis and somnambulism facilitate the unconscious release of paranormal powers? Or were the levitations the result of some natural phenomenon—the movement of underground water? A localized earthquake? Natural settling of the house? Mass hallucination?

Because all normal explanations seemed preposterous, the little servant girl attracted international attention. In *Ghosts and Poltergeists*, author Herbert Thurston, a Jesuit investigator of psychic phenomena, includes the story of Mary Spiegel. He calls it a "remarkable American case."

HOUSE OF EVIL

Violent death is often the catalyst for the appearance of a ghost. Those who die at the hands of a murderer or take their own lives are said to frequently leave behind strong energy impressions that may manifest in the activity of a ghost or poltergeist.

Present-day Milwaukee residents passing the corner of 12th Street and State are unaware that they are within a few feet of the location of one of that city's most famous haunted houses. The brick house is gone now, but its sinister reputation persisted for many years. It belonged to Major Hobart. He left earth too soon and his house was never the same.

Hobart, a former army officer, calmly hanged himself for unexplained reasons one afternoon. He was found swinging from a chandelier in the large two-story home. After Hobart's demise, many families lived in the house, but few remained for more than several months. The terrified residents reported doors opening and closing without human assistance, footfalls clattering up the staircase when all were in bed, groans echoing from various rooms, and chains being dragged across the floors.

When the house was vacant, and that was frequently, neighbors would notice lights through the dusty windows, solidifying the house's reputation for evil.

After several years, no realtor could sell the brick mansion, so infamous had its reputation become. At last it was razed, and with it was lost the last, unearthly traces of Major Hobart, late of the United States Army.

THE FACE ON THE BEDROOM CURTAIN

Early on Saturday morning, September 21, 1878, Milwaukee resident Mary Tubey died. Although the circumstances of her death were not unusual, her youth made her passing especially poignant to her relatives.

A block away, on Hill Street between 7th and 8th, her stepbrother, Dan Connell, had finished his noon dinner and was sitting in the front room, silent and alone with his grief. The door to the bedroom was open, and from where he sat he had a clear view of the window in that room. Suddenly he saw Mary's face on the curtain. Was it just a shadow? A pattern created by the folds of the material? No, the longer he looked, the clearer the face became.

Connell called his wife, and she too saw the strange likeness. They tried to divert their uneasiness by keeping busy in the house, but their curiosity impelled them to check the curtain several times during the afternoon. The face was always there ... shimmering, smiling ... in exactly the same place. Had Mary returned to say good-bye, or were the Connells, in their sorrow, imagining her presence?

Later that day the story got out, and neighbors by the dozens swarmed through the front and back doors of the small brown cottage. Some glanced at the curtain and, seeing nothing, held their laughter until they got outdoors; others were profoundly moved by what they believed they saw. A policeman, who visited the house at 3:00 P.M., said later that he had never seen anything plainer in his life.

When the size of the crowds became unmanageable and the Connells were chilled to the bone from the cold air blowing through the open doorways, they barricaded the entrances and refused to admit more visitors.

The next day, Sunday, the crowds swelled into the hundreds. The doors were opened again and the curious callers filed past the window curtain. At dusk the phantom vanished but the visitors did not. From all parts of the city they came, and many were deeply disappointed upon learning that there was no longer anything to be seen.

The following week, a local reporter called on Mrs. Connell and also interviewed a number of neighbors who claimed to have seen the face on

168

the curtain. Some said emphatically that they could not be deceived, and all cross-questioning failed to shake them. They were so solemn about the affair that the reporter decided it was folly to hint that they were victims of imagination.

THE RESTLESS SERVANT GIRL

In 1908, Dr. Gerhard Bading and his wife were living in a house they had rented on Milwaukee's west side, on Upper Wells Street between 25th and 26th streets. It was a large clapboard house with double stairways typical of the era. One staircase connected the front of the house to the upstairs hall and the other connected the rear portion of the upstairs hall to the kitchen. The hallway and both stairways were carpeted. That year, the Badings decided to take a short trip, and, not wishing to leave the house unattended, they asked their friend, Dr. E.J.W. Notz, to occupy the place in their absence.

Notz moved in on the appointed day and that night went upstairs to bed and fell promptly asleep. Shortly after midnight he was awakened by a thundering crash followed by footsteps padding in the hallway. He sat up in bed, then thought he heard the footsteps going down the rear stairway. They were definitely footsteps. He was certain he was not alone in the house. He got up quickly, turned on lights, and searched the attic, second floor, first floor, and basement. There was no one anywhere, nor could Notz find evidence of anything that might have caused the disturbance. Satisfied and much relieved, he went back to bed and fell asleep, until ...

A sudden crash, then hurried footsteps across the hall and down the stairway awoke him again. He got up and searched the house for the invisible prowler. He found no one. Nothing has been disturbed.

The commotion erupted a third time before morning, and the same sequence occurred during Notz's second night in the house. Uneasy and thoroughly baffled by this time, he mentioned the matter to some relative living in the city; they had no explanation either.

When the Badings returned, Notz told them of his experiences, but they showed no surprise. They said they had heard those noises so often that they weren't greatly disturbed by them.

Later, Notz learned that people in the neighborhood believed the house was haunted by the ghost of a servant girl who had committed suicide on the premises. She had been sent to the house early one fall day to open it up and get it ready for its owner, the proprietor of a resort hotel

170

The Restless Servant Girl

in the Waukesha Lakes area. The girl was apparently suffering from depression and, once in the house, was unable to complete her work. After her death, her restless ghost roamed the hall and stairways, frightening every family who ever lived there.

THE LEGACY OF MARY BUTH FARM

The weather was warm for December 31. Wispy strands of fog clung to the gently rolling fields of southeastern Wisconsin as the thermometer hovered near 30 degrees. At the end of a long paved road near Germantown, the Tom Walton family prepared to celebrate New Year's Day in their 140-year old farmhouse. Somewhere a clock struck midnight. Family members and several guests toasted each other for success and happiness in the coming 12 months.

But, according to what Walton later told a news reporter, the evening had not been cheerful. There was a tinge of something sinister, something almost evil intruding upon celebration. Walton, a professor of education at the University of Wisconsin–Milwaukee, remembered that night. The whole evening had been very strange. Small things happened at first. The house suddenly cooled for no apparent reason. A candle burned much faster than its twin sitting nearby. The television set lost power—again without explanation. And then, outside the wide living room window, she appeared. An old woman, dressed in a rough black dress, stared in at the assembled family and guests. Before Walton could act, she was gone.

Who was she ... that vague, dark phantom staring in at the startled assemblage? Walton had a hunch—a hunch that led back in time to 1838.

In that year, John and Mary Buth built the farm as one of Wisconsin's pioneer homesteads. In its early days, the Buth cabin and land were used as a trading post for early settlers and traders. Near the farm, Indians camped by a small stream. The decades have brought innumerable changes to the original house, but a section of the original log cabin forms a part of the present two-story frame house. Sturdy log ceiling beams now support part of the second floor. The place is still known as Mary Buth Farm.

John and Mary Buth had three children: Herman, who died at age 70 in 1917; Carl, who died at age 74 in 1923; and Mary, the only daughter and the farm's namesake, 76 at her death in 1926. None of the children married. A weed-shrouded cemetery near the farm holds their remains.

How does this explain the Waltons' eerie New Year's night? The Buth

The Legacy of Mary Buth Farm

farm has a history of being haunted. The ghosts of Mary Buth and her mother were said to roam the farm by day and inhabit the house at night. Tom Walton had heard neighbors tell stories of peculiar events occurring in or near the Buth farm. Walton and his family moved to the farm in 1961 and didn't place much faith in the tales until that night in 1965.

On that evening Walton changed his mind. The fleeting apparition outside the window left him perplexed. The next morning he discovered that a pepper plant near the window had wilted leaves on one side while the other half remained green and healthy. The other small incidents that night added to the mystery.

Over the next months and years, until 1976 when the family moved away, the Waltons were to have other baffling experiences. An overnight visitor told Walton that he had seen in the yard a young girl who vanished into the early morning mist. The Buth farm is quite isolated from nearby houses.

One afternoon, Walton was alone in the house when the clear, distinct notes of a violin floated through the house. No radio was playing. The stereo was turned off. The violin music alone echoed through the silent rooms. Later, Walton learned that Herman Buth had played violin as a hobby.

On another occasion, when the kitchen was being remodeled, the Waltons' plumber said he had heard footsteps walking across the upstairs floor. The plumber had been alone in the house at the time.

What caused these victims? To find out, Walton asked a psychic and writer, Mary Leader, to visit the home. After a session with an Ouija board, Mrs. Leader said at least two ghosts haunted the Buth farm. She identified them as Mary Buth (the mother) and her daughter, Mary. Mrs. Leader said the daughter was an evil ghost lurking outside the home and searching for her missing lover. According to local lore, Mary had been left standing at the altar on her wedding day. The mother was the "inside" ghost protecting the house from her daughter. Mrs. Leader could not explain the violin music Walton had heard.

Some neighbors scoff at the idea of either Mary coming back to haunt the house. One resident said several years ago, "She [Mary, the younger] just wasn't the type who would come around and haunt [the farm]. Sure she was an old maid and probably a little eccentric, but she had a good heart." Mary reportedly cared for the mentally retarded people in the vicinity during an era when they were shunned by most of society.

Few contemporary accounts remain of the elder Mary. She was 93 at her death in 1899, outliving her husband by 46 years.

Nearly everyone agrees that young Mary and her brothers were hardworking farmers who cut wood with a handsaw and offered the use of their farm as a resting place for peddlers traveling from Milwaukee. Is it possible that one of these itinerant salesmen proposed to Mary and then jilted her when a new territory beckoned? It has been known to happen.

A former resident of the farm, whose family lived in the house from 1945 to 1954, says he never saw a ghost there. But, he says, a coven of witches did want to buy the farm at one time.

The John Ewens family moved to the Buth Farm in 1976. They, too, have been told the ghost stories. Ewens said neighborhood children believe the house is haunted and are reluctant to visit.

Do the spirits of Mary Buth, mother and daughter, haunt the ancient structure? Is Herman Buth still fiddling at the house he lived in all his life? Tom Walton still can't explain the strange things that happened on that New Year's Eve in 1965. As far as he is concerned, the ghosts were very much a part of his family's life at Mary Buth Farm.

THE STRANGE CASE OF HENRY JAMES BROPHY

At noon on Tuesday, March 9, 1909, schoolboy Henry James Brophy, 11 years old, arrived home for lunch. He opened the side door of his home in Mt. Horeb and was immediately struck in the back by a snowball that broke and splattered across the kitchen floor. The boy spun around, but there was no one in sight.

At the same time the next day, the same thing happened.

Early on Thursday evening of that week, cups suddenly flew from the dinner table and crashed to the floor. Lamp chimneys disintegrated. Spools of thread unwound. Bars of soap soared through the air.

And so it went for one of the strangest cases of alleged poltergeist activity ever recorded in the state of Wisconsin.

Little Henry Brophy lived with his grandparents, Mr. and Mrs. Knut K. Lunde in Mt. Horeb following his mother's second marriage to Patrick Trainor. It is not known what happened to Henry's natural father or why he was not able to live with his mother and stepfather.

The boy attended the village grade school. A shy, delicate child with few close friends, Henry was the possessor of no extraordinary talents…or so everyone thought. But he was soon the center of attention in a state of affairs that led those in the community to believe that Henry was either psychically gifted or was a superb manipulator and clever fraud. Which conclusion was correct has never been satisfactorily determined.

Friday, March 12, brought a visit from Henry's mother from Madison to attend a family funeral and spend the night with her parents and her sister, who also lived in the Lunde home. Early that evening, Mrs. Trainor is said to have sat down to play the organ. In that instant, household utensils allegedly took to the air, banging against the walls and crashing to the floor. Knut Lunde became so agitated that he sent for a local minister, a Reverend Mostrom. When the minister arrived with a friend, Sam Thompson, a hymnal on a windowsill near the door fell to the floor at their feet.

"There, you see it!" Knut Lunde said.

Reverend Mostrom listened attentively as the Lundes explained

175

what had been going on. Since most of the unexplained events occurred near Henry, Sam Thompson kept the child by his side.

"Look out!" Henry cried as a butcher knife flew from the kitchen table, arced through the air, and fell at Thompson's feet. Thompson said later that the boy could not have touched it. Later, a hatpin mimicked the knife's arc. Neither Thompson nor Mostrom could explain what happened.

Nightly thereafter, the family and a steady number of curiosity seekers reported objects flying around the house. Doors crashed to the floor after screws in the hinges were mysteriously loosened. Kerosene lamp chimneys shattered. A wood stovetop toppled to the floor. A drawer under a sewing machine came free and soared high into the air, knocked plaster from a wall, and scattered bobbins, thread, and needles in every direction. Mrs. Lunde had to duck when a table knife leapt through the air at her before it clattered to the floor!

News of the Lunde house phenomena spread rapidly beyond the confines of the little town, attracting the attention of newsmen and self-described clairvoyants from across the Midwest. On a single night in March, 200 people left muddy footprints as they tramped through the house. No one in that group saw any manifestations, only damage the Lundes said had been caused by flying household objects.

If the Lundes and their visitors could not explain what was happening, some of Mt. Horeb's residents believed they could—even if their reasoning was bizarre to say the least.

Two prominent citizens came to the Lunde house to claim it had become "electrified" since both a telephone and electricity had been installed. The electrification caused the disturbances, the pair insisted, so cutting the electric wires would put an end to what they termed the "spell" that had descended upon the house. The distraught family feared darkness more than the chaos and tossed out the intruders.

The family had concluded early on that Henry was somehow responsible for the turmoil—either by design or by supernatural means. The phenomena always occurred in Henry's presence and the flying objects always seemed to travel toward the child. His family reasoned that if the child was removed from the house and the strange manifestations continued, then perhaps "electricity" was the cause.

So it was that Henry was sent to visit the homes of his uncles Hans and Andrew Lunde in the settlement of Springdale. Henry spent one day

The Strange Case of Henry James Brophy

at Hans' house during which only a few small items took flight. But it was a far different story later at Andrew's home. No sooner had Henry arrived than a pail of water began spinning, then spilled across the kitchen floor. After that had been mopped up, Henry spied a mirror on the wall. "You'd better take that down," he warned. Andrew laughed. A moment later, the mirror crashed to the floor.

Meanwhile, all was peaceful at the Lunde home in Mt. Horeb. Rather than take this as a sign that little Henry instigated the mischief, Mrs. Lunde insisted that there must be a supernatural origin. A Mt. Horeb cheesemaker told her that in the Old Country a bag of salt was the time-honored "remedy" to exorcise evil spirits. Accordingly, she sent word to Springdale and Andrew Lunde put a bag of salt in Henry's pocket.

That didn't seem to work. A neighbor boy who came over to play was hit in the face by the salt bag when it supposedly flew out of Henry's pocket! Later a set of marbles the boys were playing with disappeared. Only Henry could find them secreted around the house, even a few tucked deeply into bed quilts.

Andrew tried an experiment after the neighbor boy left. He put Henry in a chair and then held a cigar box full of marbles in front of him. The marbles leaped from the box, though the uncle swore Henry could not have touched them.

That night Henry complained about noises coming from the wall next to his bed. His uncle took a look around but could find nothing to explain what Henry said he was hearing. But the next morning, Andrew found a large hole in the plaster wall next to Henry's bed. By this time, the boy's uncle was tired of the problems his nephew was causing and talked his brother Hans into taking Henry back to Mt. Horeb.

"I took a basket of eggs along and set them on a chair in the house," Hans later said. "While we were standing there one egg flew out of the basket and struck Henry in the face. I saw it leave the basket with my own eyes. There was no one anywhere near the basket. Two more eggs jumped out...on the floor and one jumped off the table."

Henry was also examined by physician and Spiritualist Dr. George Kingsley of Madison. The Spiritualist Movement in Wisconsin was still quite renowned at that time with a major center in Whitewater. During the short time Henry was in Dr. Kingsley's office, the doctor pronounced the boy a "splendid medium" for his age, destined to become one of the world's greatest spiritualists! He said that although the boy did not yet have the "spirits" under control, he would gain power over them later on.

Other clairvoyants were more specific in their assessment of the child. Some claimed they saw three spirits — two women and one man — hovering near him. They did not explain who the spirits were. Henry's mother recalled that when her son was quite small, he had been cared for by two women Spiritualists, one of whom later died. Some people thought she had passed her supernatural powers onto Henry.

The seers also said that the three spirits were "oppressed" by crowds; for that reason, the manifestations never occurred when Henry was in school or when large groups of people came to the house.

But the Lundes came to another, even more amazing, conclusion. They told Mert P. Peavy, then editor of *The Dodgeville Chronicle* that Henry had been hypnotized by someone and left in a trance!

If many accepted the notion that Henry James Brophy was possessed of strange, supernatural powers, others did not. Henry's family had consulted a number of physicians in addition to Dr. Kingsley after they noted he seemed to be running a high fever and was losing weight. His mother said he was also experiencing mood swings; at times he would not talk to anyone.

Among those who thought Henry was a fake were Dr. N. C. Evans and former sheriff G. E. Mickelson. The two men visited the Lundes one night at the peak of the excitement. They were seated with their backs to the kitchen doorway when two pieces of sausage, a bar of soap, and several chunks of coal flew into the room from the direction of the kitchen. They knew Henry was in the kitchen. Dr. Evans whirled around and asked Henry, who stood in the doorway, if he had thrown the articles. The boy did not give a direct answer. He hid in the kitchen, his grandparents said, because he was shy.

On another evening, Dr. Evans was in the sitting room and Henry was again in the kitchen. Suddenly a ball of yarn sailed into the room. The doctor was convinced that Henry had thrown it from the kitchen.

Another medical man at the time, Dr. Clarke Gapen, was asked for his opinion on the Brophy case.

"It is nonsense to waste any time on such cases unless it be to explode or expose them," Dr. Gapen was quoted as saying. "They can always be explained away and have been time and again exposed."

The Strange Case of Henry James Brophy

However, churchmen in the community were far less certain. A prayer meeting was held at the Lunde house to exorcise the demons, but, according to those present, the services only resulted in an increase in manifestations.

What are we to believe in the case of Henry James Brophy?

Parapsychologists insist that many cases cannot be explained away and that young children such as Henry are often the focus of poltergeist activity. Some research suggests a child unconsciously creates such disturbances to vent repressed hostility. That may make some sense in this case. Henry had lived with his grandparents since he was two years old. The loss of daily contact with his natural mother and her remarriage may have had a negative affect upon him that was unconsciously expressed in propelling objects through the air.

As a baby, Henry had been struck by a horse-drawn wagon. Although he finally recovered from his crippling injuries, he remained delicate and sickly throughout his childhood. Poltergeist activity has sometimes been attributed to youngsters with histories of physical weaknesses.

Henry James Brophy left Mt. Horeb sometime in 1914 or 1915. Edwin Offerdahl of rural Mt. Horeb thought Henry eventually got married and moved to California. Others said he left for Madison or Milwaukee.

In the years that followed the Brophy furor, community opinion was strongly divided about its authenticity. Josie Evans thought the poltergeist business was all a fake. Her brother, Jake Evans, thought maybe not. They both agreed that neither really knew what had gone on. Another resident at the time, a Mabel Espeseth said many of the stories were "made up." She later lived in the old Lunde house and claimed that she never gave a thought to supernatural activity. But Jan Kogen, who also later lived in the house, recalled that strange things did happen—she said a camera the family owned kept taking pictures on its own and finally had to be replaced.

The only point on which all agree is this: Henry James Brophy created a sensation nearly a century ago in that little town west of Madison. Wittingly or not, Henry built a memorial to himself that no one who knew him or of him has ever forgotten.

A DANEFUL OF GHOSTS

Ghost Hill in Dane County's Burke Township was most appropriately named. For years on end, and at the stroke of midnight, a lean figure clad in white appeared astride a pale horse racing across the top of the hill going in the direction of Blooming Grove. Neither harshness of weather nor darkness of night kept the horseman from its appointed rounds. He, or rather it, could be seen plainly, a white cape fluttering in the breeze like some sort of spectral streamer.

Early Burke Township residents could not recall the origin of the mysterious specter—called that since there was general agreement it was not of this earth. Ghost Hill itself was on the former Messerschmidt farm in the northeast corner of Section 19 on the old road from Madison to Token Creek.

Some witnesses thought the horseman was the angry spirit of an early pioneer who had been robbed and murdered near the hill. The man's ghost was condemned to wander through the night seeking revenge for his brutal death.

At least one documented effort was made to identify the ghost—or at least verify its existence. George Armbrecht of Madison told a newspaper reporter in 1936 that he and several other brave companions camped on the hill one night to see the horseman for themselves. Midnight arrived, but unfortunately on this occasion no ghost appeared.

The hill was partially excavated when a quarry was opened to supply stone for the Dane County airport. With time's inevitable changes to Ghost Hill, the legend of the horseman nearly vanished from Burke Township.

• • •

Madison Sheriff Van Wie held the kerosene lamp high as he made his last rounds on that late November day of 1873. The nine prisoners were either fast asleep or resting on their beds. All seemed well. Sheriff Van Wie returned to his own quarters in another part of the jail building and went to bed.

A wild shriek slashed through the silence. The nightshirt-clad Wie leaped out of bed, grabbed up his lantern and raced to the cellblock. Two young prisoners named Foster and Sheevy were thrashing about in their bunks, their eyes wide with fright.

Wie unlocked the cell door and demanded an explanation. The men said they'd just settled down for the night when they heard a noise in the doorway. The sound increased in intensity then seemed to move through the iron bars. As the reverberation seemed to surround them, a blinding strong light filled the cell. Then they claimed an ill-defined form screamed and brushed against their beds.

Wie thought the men had obviously concocted the tale but he conceded the young men seemed genuinely frightened. They demanded to be moved. Wie refused. He said the men could work out their own salvation.

Came the next night and the disturbances continued. But this time Wie remained snug in his bed. Foster and Sheevy did get their chance, however, to tell their tale to a reporter. They claimed that the light had again filled their cell. To escape both it and the wild wailing, they dived onto their bunks and wrapped their heads with blankets.

Wie told the same newsmen he thought Foster had a hand in the commotion. Young Foster had been accused of setting fire to several of Madison's flour mills. Sheriff Wie was convinced that Foster spent his time behind bars planning pranks to frighten the wits out of Sheevy, apparently quite a superstitious man. Yet, both men seemed genuinely frightened by the experience.

The episode—and the men—gradually faded from the news. There was no follow-up investigation so whether it was an attention-getting device on the prisoners' part or truly the vestige of a long-forgotten prisoner sentenced to roam forever the cold, gray halls of Madison's jail will never be known.

• • •

Albert J. Lamson was a farmer who lived near Lake Wingra in Madison. On one particular dark and starless spring night about 100 years ago, Lamson stepped out to his front porch and heard the unmistakable thwack of an ax—the clear, ringing, rhythmic swing of an expert woodsman at work.

As Lamson listened, he was certain the sound was coming from Bartlett Woods, later known as Noe Woods, on the southwest side of the University of Wisconsin Arboretum.

Lamson couldn't figure out why anyone would want to fell a tree in the middle of the night. Yet he knew he was not mistaken. He heard the blade bite into the trunk, stop occasionally, and then resume its steady work.

The next morning, Lamson's curiosity got the best of him. He climbed a fence near the present Curtis Prairie and the Arboretum Administration Area. Though he searched the area, he found no recent ax marks on the trees, no wood chips anywhere on the ground.

Several nights later, he heard the woodchopper again. He summoned his hired man—who also claimed to have heard the ax man at work—and together the men went into the woods. But again, they could find no evidence of recent timbering. Lamson questioned his friends and neighbors. Several said they also heard the noises and some, like Lamson, unsuccessfully searched the woods for its source.

Periodically during the summer and fall, the chopping came from Bartlett Woods. Travelers who heard the story avoided the "ghost road" that ran by the Woods. A search party with lanterns was finally organized to go into the woods at night to locate the woodchopper. But after several faint-hearted volunteers dropped out, the hunt was cancelled. Lamson was too superstitious to go back into the dense woods after dark.

The woodchopper—or whatever it was—finally abandoned his night work. His identity and the purpose of his work were never learned and remain a mystery to this day.

• • •

There is more than one "ghost road" in Madison. Seminole Highway is now a quiet residential street of spacious lawns and stately trees. The only ghost one is likely to see is a small child costumed for Halloween. But in the late 1800s, when the highway was known as Bryant Road, unearthly apparitions appeared to teamsters and pedestrians alike.

Most described the ghost as a luminous white vapor that would appear suddenly from the brush on either side of the road, follow the unsuspecting for a short distance, and then vanish as quickly as it had appeared.

A few others claimed that the vapor had the form of a Native American astride a pony that would walk behind them for a little way, then disappear. Sometimes late at night people fancied that they heard the clatter of a pony's hoof beats as the ghostly rider charged up and down Seminole Highway in pursuit of an unseen something remembered from a distant past.

A Daneful of Ghosts

The phantom never harmed anyone. Nor was its identity learned. Some said the Native American had been killed in battle and was looking for revenge. Others thought it was a man who had been buried in the cemetery near the old Bryant barn at the east end of the highway.

But no one knew the reason for its return.

By the time the horse and buggy gave way to the Model T, the troublesome ghost had disappeared, leaving stories of Madison's "ghost road" alive only in the memories of an older generation.

WAYFARING STRANGERS

Tales of early American wayside inns inevitably stir visions of romance and danger. And ghosts.

It seems inevitable that where there was so much turbulent life there would be some afterlife—guests who refuse to ring down the curtain on the final stage upon which they played.

Perhaps the very transience of those wayfaring lodgers invites speculation about their purposes. The weary traveler may have been on horseback when he emerged from the woodland trail to see the welcoming glow of oil lamps through curtained windows. Or perhaps he peered through the stagecoach window as the team of horses pulled up under the signboard rocking in the wind on the blustery night, announcing that through the heavy oaken door was offered hot food and cheap lodging. The implied offer of geniality and warmth was a welcome respite, even though the bed was made of straw and thrown upon the cold floor, and the food a nearly inedible gruel made palatable with liberal shots of cheap liquor.

Even worse for the unwary visitor who seemed to have money or possessions or both was the threat of sudden, deadly violence by those without a conscience, whose greed for quick riches meant a quick stiletto between the ribs, a razor-sharp blade across the neck, a quick bullet in the back of the skull. Those wayside inns provide the stuff of which ghost legends are made.

THE INTRUDER

Ethel Van Patten was child of eight when her parents bought the Evansville House in 1894 and converted it to a boardinghouse. The 60-year-old former hotel had innumerable rooms, halls, and musty corners, which the curious girl reveled in exploring. An old barn, once used as a livery stable, held a glimpse of pioneer life with its hand-hewn log rafters and windowsills. On the veranda, which stretched halfway around the house, little Ethel would sit for hours listening to the legends and mysteries connected with the antique structure. One particular story came startlingly to life.

Wayfaring Strangers

As Ethel was told the tale by an eccentric boarder, Patrick McGlinn, the Evansville House served as a stagecoach stop on the road between Madison and Janesville, Beloit, and other points southward. A number of servants were employed to look after the guests, cook their meals, clean their rooms, and generally attend to the numerous chores connected with the bustling hostelry.

A certain young and willing chambermaid, McGlinn told Ethel, had the misfortune to fall in love with a married salesman who made the Evansville House a frequent stop during his travels. The liaison continued for several months until the salesman, despairing of his inability to marry his love and not wanting his sweetheart to marry another, strangled the chambermaid late one night. The salesman fled the inn to jump aboard a passing freight train. Instead he fell under the passing cars and was crushed to death.

Little Ethel Van Patten was thrilled by the tale. Less enthralled were her parents who, as good, skeptical Yankees, placed little credence in McGlinn's narrative and were upset at the man's earthy language and rough ways. He was not, they thought, the best influence on their daughter. But Ethel didn't care. Mr. McGlinn told terribly exciting stories filled with history and romance and danger.

Even Patrick McGlinn may not have known the full impact of his story for on one winter's cold night the long-dead salesman may have been on the prowl once again.

Mr. and Mrs. Van Patten heard footfalls descend a staircase near their bedroom. It sounded like a man wearing heavy boots walking down the steps. Night after wintry night the scenario repeated itself—footsteps echoing through the quiet halls at about 3:00 A.M.

At first the family suspected McGlinn, figuring he was adding a bit of mischief to his morbid talltale. Further, he claimed to be a former sea captain and habitually wore heavy brogans.

Van Patten confronted McGlinn, but the merry Scotsman in his rich brogue and heavy vocabulary steadfastly denied that he was the culprit.

All that winter the Van Pattens heard the footsteps. Their pattern never altered. One night the couple settled down in bed and listened for their mysterious intruder, determined that on this occasion they could catch McGlinn in the act and put an end to this nonsense. Right on schedule they heard the footfalls ... down the staircase ... into an office on the first floor … and finally the distinctive sound of the front door slamming shut. Mr. Van Patten raced down the stairs. The outer door was bolted from the inside. He unhitched the latch and looked outside. A fresh snow cover bore no visible footprints. It was undeniable: No one had passed through the front door, despite what the Van Pattens had heard.

Undeterred, Mr. Van Patten scurried back upstairs and threw open the door to McGlinn's room. In the bed near the wall he lay, sleeping soundly in his nightshirt and snoring quite loudly.

And what's more, the mysterious intruder was never heard from again. Future owners of the place were reportedly never troubled by the phantom … or at least never admitted that they were. Perhaps it was only Patrick McGlinn adding a bit of playful sound effects to his tale. Perhaps … not.

MARK OF DEATH

Much to the chagrin of one Simon Brechler*, a badly weathered, run-down inn was the only available lodging in the village. He had spent weeks scouting for a homestead and now that he had found the site, he decided to spend the night in the nearby settlement. Simon's family awaited word from him in New York State and so he was quite alone on the Wisconsin frontier.

All that could be said of the old inn is that it provided a roof over his head, a cheap meal, and a dry room. Perhaps tomorrow he would find something better.

He was tired after weeks on horseback searching for tillable land and went directly to his room. The furnishings were sparse—a bed and washstand—but for one object that seemed terribly out of place in the rundown hostel: an immense, ancient bookcase holding scores of dusty volumes stood against a wall.

Brechler hardly noticed; he fell asleep before the sun departed the horizon. The night was not half gone when Brechler awoke with a start, sensing more than seeing movement in the corner of the dark room. He lay perfectly still, not sure if his inner alarm had not been triggered by a dream. He rolled over in bed to stare more intently around the room. The moonlight filtering in through the dusty, window without a curtain fell upon a cloaked figure huddled near the bookcase. Silently and methodically she—for Simon was quite sure it was female—lifted books from the case and placed them in piles on the floor. When the last shelf had been emptied, she reversed the process until once again the book-case was full. With that, the figure faded away.

To say Simon Brechler was astonished, puzzled, and distressed by his night caller is quite an understatement. He did not have a clue as to her iden-tity, or what she may have been searching for. Perhaps in the morning a few discreet questions asked of the locals might help him solve the mystery.

After breakfast, he found an old man willing to talk about the specter. Yes, there was such a thing in the hotel, the codger admitted.

"But don't you never speak to it!" he warned Brechler. "I say that in earnest, sir. It's plain awful what's happened to them who did."

Really not wanting to chance another night in the hotel, Brechler looked for other lodgings but could find nothing. At sundown he reluc-tantly retreated to his room. Sleep came in fits and starts. Then, as on the previous night, he heard a faint rustling near the bookcase. She was back —hunched over the bookcase, performing the same bizarre ritual as the night before.

"What in Heaven's name do you want?" Brechler cried. "Who are you and why do you so disturb my sleep?"

The figure in the dark, hooded robe stopped what she was doing and turned slowly toward the bed. She glided silently toward him. Brechler drew back in horror. He was looking not into the face of a woman but rather the hollow eyes and gaping mouth of a skull. The form bent slow-ly over the cowering homesteader and raised its bony hands. The wraith's thumbs came down upon his forehead and pushed him deep into the mattress. And unconsciousness.

How long he had been insensible he did not know. When he did regain his senses and look around it was daylight and the apparition was gone. His head burned and ached as if a flaming log had been dropped on his skull.

He struggled out of bed and looked into the mirror above the wash-stand. Two black thumbprints were burned into his forehead. Simon Brechler carried those scars until the day he died.

THE DELL HOUSE

The Wisconsin Dells is the most popular single vacation destination in Wisconsin. Tens of thousands of tourists flock each year to this spectacu-lar terrain of towering bluffs and deep ravines sculpted over the millennia by the Wisconsin River. The 21st century visitor enjoys water ski shows, boat rides, dozens of campgrounds, novelty shops by the score, man-made attractions too numerous to mention and faux Indian pageants.

Little does the modern visitor imagine that this corporeal entertainment would pale beside the supernatural entertainment once provided at the Dell House, an 1837 river inn near the Narrows in a glen close by a sandy beach and fresh water spring.

A man named Allen built the inn with an eye toward providing the rivermen with a bit of entertainment, 19th century style. The temptations were those of the flesh — bad whiskey, crooked gambling, bawdy songs, and frontier ladies more than willing to exchange what was left of their virtue for a few dollars. More often than not, violence capped the evening's "festivities." The churning, muddy waters of the Wisconsin River claimed the earthly remains of not a few luckless revelers.

The days of the raftsmen passed quickly and the Dell House lost its reason for being. By the turn of the 20th century, the hostelry was abandoned, its empty hulk mute testimony to an earlier, vanished — but not mourned — way of life. Only a few adventurous tourists and locals camped in the glen.

By daylight the old place had what one early resident of the Dells described as "an indescribable charm of romantic interest."

But nightfall brought stories of unquiet nights amid the decaying Dell House. Some campers swore that cursing and drunken laughter and crashing crockery joined the sighting of vague, fleeting figures in the moonlight. The violent and bloody history of the inn comes startlingly to supernatural life.

The legacy of the Dell House ended for good late one night in 1910 when what was left of the place burned to the ground. The towering brick chimney and a fireplace as tall as a man remained for many years, until they, too, were claimed by the forest.

FERRY HOUSE OF MERRIMAC

Peace officers were scarce on the early Wisconsin frontier. The only law was that which pioneers established among themselves. Justice was usually meted out swiftly to those transgressors unfortunate enough to be captured.

So it was that the Ferry House Inn in Merrimac came to be associated with a "galloping ghost" during the 19th century. The grim visage raced along the road near the inn astride a coal-black stallion.

Those who claimed to have seen the mounted, spectral horseman believe he was in some way connected with a bloody murder at the inn, though official records fail to show such an event. Victim. Perpetrator. We will never know.

LAYTON HOUSE INN

Strangers passing through Hale's Corners on the Janesville Plank Road a century ago often spent the night at the Layton House Inn, built in 1844 by the founder of Milwaukee's famous Layton Art Gallery.

The brick inn fell into decay many years ago and was eventually incorporated into another building that still stands. But during the days the inn sat idle, forgotten by all but a few old-timers, passers-by would often report sounds from within the empty, decrepit hotel.

Almost as if the inn had never closed. As if some guests had never left.

THE HORSE OF DEATH

How do we learn of death? A relative's letter, yes. The newspaper obituary column, of course. But other, more bizarre messages from beyond the grave have been recorded by man from the earliest centuries.

The ghastly routine of the angel of death has been the subject of many lively stories. None is more bizarre than the legend of the Devil's Hitching Post.

Years ago, a large stone near the Wisconsin Dells, now called Elephant Rock, had the eerie name of the Devil's Hitching Post. Whenever a death occurred in the area, a man riding a coal-black stallion would stop at the Hitching Post and tether the animal. The stranger would then stride across the hills to the doorstep of the deceased. The dead man and his unearthly guide would then depart.

Did anyone ever actually see the black stallion and his rider? Yes, but the witness did not live long.

The story is told of a traveler passing by the Post who noticed the horse tied nearby. He had never seen a more magnificent beast and decided to go up to the animal for a closer inspection. But as he drew near, the horse's master suddenly appeared on a nearby bluff. The horse reared and his lethal hooves struck the traveler, killing him instantly.

Whether it is a vague feeling of doom, a ghostly visitor in the dark of night … or a phantom black stallion, we can be warned in a number of strange ways that the messenger of death is near.

A PLACE OF GHOSTS

The premiere ghost hunter in southwest Wisconsin should be expected to have had at least a few supernatural experiences. Writer and folklorist Dennis Boyer does not disappoint the expectant listener. He has ghosts skulking about his own farm near Dodgeville.

"We live on a dirt road a mile and a half long," Boyer says by way of setting the scene at his home along Bethlehem Road. "The only other thing on the road is the abandoned Bethlehem Lutheran cemetery. There used to be a church there, but it burned down a long time ago. One day as I passed that cemetery [I] saw a young woman out in the middle of the cemetery who looked to be in a lace nightgown, kneeling down. Now, I can't say that what went through my mind was 'ghost,' but it seemed like an odd occurrence. What was she doing out there? It was toward dusk, but there was sufficient light to see."

Boyer, the author of several books, including *Driftless Spirits*, a collection of ghost stories from that hilly, nonglaciated region of Wisconsin, discovered that the out-of-place woman in the cemetery might in fact have been a ghost. A neighbor told him that some 60 years earlier a young woman escaped from the nearby county home and sought refuge in the now-vanished church next to the cemetery. She is thought to have been responsible for burning it down.

The other ghost frequenting Boyer's neighborhood is an irascible old man that some believe is Tommy Lee, an early pioneer who farmed a little and fished a lot.

"People see an older man," Boyer says about the sightings in his farm's wood lot. "It's taken on a life of its own. About a dozen people have seen him in the woods wearing his old blue coat."

Alas, Boyer has not yet caught a glimpse of that apparition.

For a man who has been an avid listener to people's stories for most of his life and a serious collector of ghost and other folk tales for nearly two decades, Boyer is predictably nonplussed at encountering specters so close to home.

"I'm open to a lot of different possibilities. I don't know what the explanation of these things might be. Who knows, maybe science will provide some of the answers. But ghost stories are one of the most durable forms of folklore."

Boyer grew up in a Pennsylvania Mennonite family with a tradition of storytelling dating back several hundred years. Many of the stories he heard as a child were from his coal miner grandfather who enthralled his grandson with tales of apparitions left over from the French and Indian Wars in the late 17th and early 18th centuries, and from the Revolutionary War. Boyer's family had ancestors in both those conflicts.

But a pivotal experience in his childhood, and the one that became a defining moment in his lifelong pursuit of American folk stories, came when he was just seven years old. It was 1956 and Boyer was in the first grade. He remembers that he had just learned about Abraham Lincoln and George Washington when his grandmother took him to see her own great-aunt who was then over 100 years old and living in a nursing home.

The old woman started reminiscing about her father taking her down in the direction of Philadelphia to see Lincoln's funeral train. She talked about the Black freemen and the Union soldiers crying in the rain as the bands played.

"She had a vivid memory of that time," Boyer says. "That really struck me because it was such a very long time ago. But she was there! That impressed me."

Boyer says his great-great aunt noted his astonishment.

"That's nothing, she told me. Then she talked about how her own grandfather told her about seeing the Pennsylvania Militia escort Washington away from the Continental Congress on that same road her father had taken her to see the funeral train."

Even though he was a small child, Boyer found himself profoundly moved by the woman's stories. He set off on a course that would include successful careers in law and in lobbying, as a social activist and an environmental preservationist. But all the while he maintained an abiding avocational interest in documenting the stories, legends, and folk beliefs of ordinary people and then sharing them with the wider world through his writing.

Although Boyer has a broad interest in all sorts of folklore, ghost stories are among his favorites, especially those that occur in the rural out-of-doors, away from the traditional haunted mansions of legend. Therefore,

A Place of Ghosts

perhaps not surprising, Boyer finds many of his best stories from men and women best known for enforcing hunting and fish regulations.

"Per capita, the best story sources for me have been conservation wardens," Boyer notes. "They see everything. If there's a legend of an odd creature in the swamp, they've heard it. If there's a UFO over some lake, they've heard about it. Most of them are wonderful storytellers themselves."

Unfortunately, conservation officers also end up as the subject matter of some stories. He knows of one "warden ghost" and another legendary specter of a "warden's special," or auxiliary conservation officer. Boyer says both ghosts are from northern Wisconsin, above what he and others have termed the "tension line." Sometimes that's thought to be north of U.S. Highway 8, which slices across the top quarter of the state from St. Croix Falls in the west to Iron Mountain, Michigan, in the Upper Peninsula near Lake Michigan.

"There's something that fascinates me about a sense of place and how that connects to storytelling. To me there's a story line in Wisconsin almost at the same place as the 'tension line.' Things are kind of pastoral south of there, in a rural sense. North of there stories get edgier; either they have macabre content or they incorporate themes that may not necessarily be supernatural but are the source of some discomfort and dissatisfaction."

Some northern ghost stories even contain what might be termed "political" content. The storytellers have complaints about government or big business, and those gripes are incorporated into the stories they tell.

"I talk to rural people predominantly, and they're mad at the DNR (Department of Natural Resources), they're mad at the U.S. Fish and Wildlife Service, or the paper companies or the mining companies. I think it's inevitable when someone tells stories that [those complaints] are filtered through the lens of how they view the world. And up there I find more of that sense of grievance."

Northern Wisconsin also hosts a fair number of logger ghosts, given that industry took quite a human toll a century ago. In other parts of the state, Boyer says, ghost stories are generated by what he terms "industrial themes," such as railroading, which has resulted in tales of vanishing brakemen and ghostly steam trains.

Phantom hunters seem to be a bit more prevalent in Wisconsin than, say, phantom hitchhikers, one of the most frequently recurring ghost tales in other parts of the globe.

Haunted Wisconsin

"Quite often there is a fatality involved, sometimes due to a tragic accident, sometimes something even more sinister," Boyer says of hunter ghosts. "It's usually something with some local inspiration."

Boyer believes these particular hunter stories have an underlying theme. In feudal Europe all wild game belonged to the crown, so commoners caught hunting could be prosecuted for poaching. The punishment could have been imprisonment, torture, or even death. Immigrants to Wisconsin had little tradition of hunting game and embraced it "with a vengeance," Boyer says.

"Ghostly hunter stories are told with zeal. And people can be proprietary about them. They're told within families. The family goes to the same hunting shack every November and grandfather tells the story of the ghost hunter who's still seen out in the forest."

Boyer quite naturally points to his own region, southwest Wisconsin, as being particularly rich in ghost stories.

"Among those early miners there was a wild-west environment that didn't exist elsewhere in Wisconsin, and probably one that didn't exist much of anywhere else east of the Mississippi. It was almost a Dodge City milieu. When you hear about the knifings, the shootings, the card brawls, it was pretty wild and wooly. And there were public executions that drew thousands of people. In a way, that doesn't even seem like Wisconsin."

In 1842, for instance, an estimated 4,000 people descended upon little Mineral Point to witness the hanging of William Caffee for the murder of his friend. A scaffold was erected in front of the Walker House and it was to that execution site that Caffee rode in the back of a buckboard, astride his own casket, tapping out a funeral march to the rhythm of the spoke wheels. It is his ghost that still haunts the old inn. A former manager reportedly saw Caffee's ghost—minus its head—sitting on a bench on a second floor balcony. A former Walker House kitchen worker told Boyer that "half of what goes on in the Walker House is ghost fighting and fussing."

For all of Wisconsin's ghosts, however, most of them are far gentler folk than those in other regions of the United States.

"That's what surprises me about Wisconsin, compared to the stories I heard years ago in Pennsylvania," Boyer notes. He said that the ghost stories he heard as a child had an edgier, more macabre plot line. "Here people look at [ghosts] as they would guardian angels. By and large their experi-

A Place of Ghosts

ences are fairly benign. I've found only a few in the tradition of the Legend of Sleepy Hollow, where there's some relentless pursuer. Other than that, they are watchful, sentinel types that appear to be looking after things. Even the ones that are agents of mischief don't seem that malignant."

Nearly 40 years ago, folklorists Robert Gard and L. G. Sorden claimed that Wisconsin had more ghosts per square mile than anywhere else in the United States. While a supernatural census has never been attempted—and is probably not even remotely possible—Dennis Boyer thinks Gard and Sorden were right.

"I think it is unusual," he says about the number of ghost stories he's tracked down. "You might have a few pockets elsewhere such as in New England, or maybe in the old Tidewater South, that might rival Wisconsin, but I don't think any other state has more ghosts."

Although he cautions that most of his conclusions are tentative, he believes the reason may have more to do with the state's diverse ethnic mix than with a climate particularly well suited for hosting visitors from the beyond.

"I'm not trying to have a ghostly version of Frederick Jackson Turner's view of the frontier, but I think that as people came up from Missouri, and the Yankees were coming out here from the East, at the same time you got all the settlers from Norway and Germany bringing with them lots of traditions."

But that's only part of it, Boyer thinks, especially for those ghost stories with strong rural themes.

"We have a stronger legacy from the original Native American population than many other states. In the East, their Native populations are so far removed in time that the influence on stories is very weak. Out West, I think the transition was even more violent, more unsettled, perhaps more antagonistic. Here in Wisconsin, despite the Blackhawk War and the short-lived Winnebago War, there were more protracted interactions [between Native Americans and white settlers] from as far back as the time of the French voyageurs. Because I focus on the environment, many Native American legends mesh easily because there are many natural themes, such as the names of places where spirits are alleged to inhabit."

Boyer has noted that when European Americans retell a story that began as Native American legend, the story itself moves from having a spiritual context in which the tribe might have placed it to a more lighthearted, ghostly European format. The ghost at the center of the tale shifts from being a religious icon to the source of a good scare. That's particularly true of the spirits that evolved from benevolent beings in Native American accounts to malevolent forces of evil-doing in the European settlers' retelling.

Whatever the source of the ghost story, Boyer believes most have served specific purposes in their repeated telling.

"They reinforce values, or tell people the rules. It's my suspicion that the story of a haunting has to do with dissuading people from some activity, whether it was to keep children away from a mine shaft or uncovered well, or away from a barn that was about to fall down. I think that was one function. But there are others, too. The entertainment one, obviously, but there's the uplifting function, too, where these stories have something that touches people on a deeper level. Some would call that spiritual, although some are loath to use the word in that way."

Among Dennis Boyer's favorite yarns are those he's culled from people on the lower Wisconsin River, roughly from Sauk City down to Prairie du Chien. He says there is a story milieu there that exists in only a few other places in the state. It is also along the river where he has found a recurring character that goes by various names—sometimes just the Old Man—but who might be called the Wisconsin variation of the trickster, a prank-playing spirit found in legends of various cultures for thousands of years.

"Any sort of mishap gets attributed to this fellow," Boyer has found. "He's usually described as somebody with one eye."

A common version of this tale has two buddies fishing the river. One opens the cooler aboard their fishing boat but finds it empty.

"I thought you put the beer in there," he says to his partner.

"No, I didn't," his buddy replies.

The trickster ghost has been at work.

He will also steal the biggest fish anyone catches, be responsible for accidents at the boat landing, and sometimes even capsize a boat if he's irritated enough.

Boyer says: "Any sort of mishap gets attributed to this fellow. My theory is that it must go back to some older Ho-Chunk trickster. There must have been a time when these people who lived outdoor lives, trapping and so forth, must have come in contact with Native Americans. I

A Place of Ghosts

have a feeling the [trickster] story started in the area around that time."

The trickster tradition in the American ghost story is rather common, Boyer notes. He has found different versions among Native American peoples as well as Europeanized accounts from along the Wisconsin River. But today, the story may be used more as a "cover" for a practical joke than an authentic ghost story. "Some guys delight in getting a friend to put his boat in the water and then getting him off on some sort of errand. When he comes back, he discovers that his boat is filled with water." His friends try to persuade him that a "ghost" was responsible.

Nevertheless, the trickster is still blamed for human failings. "In farming country it's what sours the cow's milk, it's why the ham is missing from the smokehouse—never mind that the hired man left yesterday for parts unknown," Boyer says.

Boyer, an attorney by profession, says that he is not particularly concerned with "truth" in his avocational pursuit of folk tales. "I would never look at a ghost story in the same way that I would look at an evidentiary matter in a worker's compensation hearing. I couldn't treat them in that fashion. I do believe that most of the people I've talked to are sincere, that something did happen to them. It's then a question of interpretation. Often what they saw were variables—an unusual light in an abandoned house, or a noise in the barn, or some recurrent physical phenomena outdoors. A glow maybe, or any manner of things."

That's not to say, however, that Boyer has not been gripped by a first-person account of the supernatural. After all, he has had his own experiences in that realm. But the one true anecdote that sticks in his mind was told to him several years ago as he was collecting stories along the Wisconsin River.

"An elderly man in Avoca, on the southern shore of the river, told me a story of what happened to him when he was a young man. This must have been World War I or maybe before. One morning he was trapping in the backwater when he walked across the ice and fell through. He claimed to have just about given up any chance of surviving when a hand reached down and pulled him out. He thought he saw an old man in front of him on the bank. He coughed and sputtered and wiped his eyes, but nobody was there."

ARTHUR

Shortly after A.J. Nielsen moved into her house at Sparta, she wished she had not. She was to recall many times over the next months the odd hesitancy by the previous and now elderly owner before agreeing to the sale of the place that had been vacant for 15 years. A.J. had been inexplicably drawn to the house; she especially admired the charming large and airy rooms on the two floors.

The troubles began almost immediately. Uneasy sensations at first. Then scratching that A.J. and her two children attributed to mice or bats in the large, walk-in attic that occupied a third floor, except that searches never revealed any evidence of rodents or flying mammals.

But that all changed one night when A.J. arrived home from work at 10:00 P.M. She found her son and daughter armed with baseball bats, their faces filled with fright. They said they had been watching television when they heard something jumping up and down from somewhere on the floors above. The chandelier in the dining room was actually swinging back and forth, they said.

With flashlights and ball bats, the trio climbed the staircase to search the bedrooms and attic above.

"The chill was terrible upstairs," A.J. remembers. "We all held our breaths as we opened the attic door."

Stacks of unpacked boxes were exactly where they had been placed earlier. Nothing had fallen. Nothing had been disturbed.

And then things got much, much worse.

Small items placed on a table one minute were gone missing the next. Locked doors swung open. Doors left ajar suddenly slammed shut.

"When I was in the bathtub there would be doors slamming and footsteps all over the house," A.J. recalls with a shudder.

Every family member was awakened during the night at one time or another by scratching noises or loud, thumping sounds. A.J.'s son often bounded downstairs to say he had felt some presence at the top of the stairs icily staring at him. His sister sensed her brother's presence on the stairs one night as she watched television. Expecting him to pop into the room and

Arthur

play a joke on her, she flung open the door that led out into the hallway and the staircase. A blast of cold air hit her in the face, and then a hissing. The girl ran upstairs and found her brother fast asleep in his bedroom.

Early one morning, A.J.'s daughter awakened to the pressure of a hand pushing against her side. "That was the last straw for her," A.J. says of her adult daughter. "She moved out and got her own apartment."

The Nielsen haunting also affected the family's social life. A.J. hesitated to invite friends over given the nightly commotion and sudden, unpredictable chills that swept the house. Two acquaintances who did drop in told A.J. they had felt uncomfortable during their visit.

An electrician hired to rewire the house started on a day when A.J. was not home. But from then on out, he refused to work there unless she was home. He told her he felt someone breathing on his neck, watching from over his shoulder as he worked.

A.J. 's former husband stopped by to visit his son. The boy had not yet returned from school and A.J. left the house to run an errand. When she got back, her ex-husband was standing outside pale and shaken. "I don't know what happened," he told her, "but something made me get out. It's just like ice in there."

So onerous was her life there that A.J. began to doubt her own sanity. On a day when the turmoil seemed unceasing, she ran to the bone-chilling attic and fell sobbing to the floor.

"Why are you doing this to me?" she cried out to her invisible tormentor. "I have never hurt you. I have no other place to go!"

A remarkable calm filled the room. She felt the pressure of a hand on her shoulder, but this was a reassuring touch that conveyed a warmth and understanding. A.J. thought that at that moment a kind of truce had been reached with whatever the source of the haunting had been.

But if A.J. thought it was over, she was mistaken. Although the unexplained noises and sudden cold spots subsided, she was to face a new ordeal.

An apparition materialized in the form of a slight man in a dark suit and white shirt. His pant legs were narrowly tailored; a large, orange cat stood by his side. The faint image was always wrapped in mist.

In the days and weeks to come, A.J. caught glimpses of her resident ghost gazing out a window or slipping quietly up the staircase. She took to calling him Arthur, for no particular reason, and even held what turned out to be one-sided conversations with him. Occasionally, she asked him to watch the house while she was gone!

A.J. didn't see Arthur one week, but the cat was still very much around.

"He'd rub against my legs when I was cooking at the stove," A.J. says. "When I'd look down I'd see this shadowy figure just disappearing" through the doorway. Sometimes she'd hear him jump to the floor from a windowsill, the curtains fluttering at the sudden movement.

A J. knew Arthur had returned when she heard the front door slam shut. She came into the hall just in time to see his murky form going upstairs carrying a leather valise with strap bindings.

Although A.J. had begun looking for another place to live, she continued to fix up the house. Arthur seemed to approve of the work. He was helpful and protective toward her.

On one occasion, she slipped off a ladder but unseen arms caught her and lifted her to safety. Another time she was running late for work and misplaced her car keys. She called upon Arthur for his help. A slight clunk and the keys suddenly appeared on the table.

A.J. found another key when cleaning the kitchen cupboards. It didn't appear to fit anything in the house, but she slipped it anyway on her key ring for safekeeping.

After her watch broke, A.J. said Arthur guided her to the attic where she found a small, gold wristwatch with a woman's strap in the middle of the floor. In all of her trips to the attic, she had never seen it. A jeweler told her that all the watch needed was a good cleaning to run like new. A.J. wondered to whom the watch had belonged. Perhaps it had been someone important in Arthur's life and now he wanted to share it with someone else.

Though she longed to ask the former owner questions about Arthur, she kept to herself. After all, she reasoned, if word got out that peculiar events were occurring in the house, who would buy it?

With the passing weeks, Arthur became even more audacious in his appearances. He often sat on the kitchen stool when A.J. was baking or washing dishes. The conversations were still one-sided—A.J. chatted away; Arthur remained silent. He seemed to like her but still resented her friends. When they visited, the chandeliers swayed and icy breezes swept through the rooms.

A.J. became quite fond of Arthur, yet she knew she had to move

Arthur

away. She yearned for a normal lifestyle, one free of unwanted ghosts. At the same time she was fearful that he might in some way try to prevent her from leaving. She need not have worried.

Finally, she found a suitable new house, bought it from the builder and moved right in. A.J. claimed that to her astonishment the key she found in her kitchen cabinets fit the lock on the front door of her new house!

During the months before the old house sold, A.J. made regular trips back to clean and keep it secure.

"I could still feel his presence," she said. "But he was much quieter than usual, almost a little sad."

Arthur made far fewer appearances during her infrequent stops at the house. Eventually the house did sell, presumably ghost and all.

On the day when the new family was moving in A.J. paid her last visit. Two little girls were playing outside.

"Look," one of them called out. "There's a man in your upstairs window!"

A.J. looked up. Arthur stood gazing down at them. His cat was perched on the sill. "Good-bye," she whispered. He raised his hand in farewell and was gone. The cat remained in the window a moment longer and then he, too, was no more.

CASSANDRA

Not all family ghosts are kept in the closet. Take the case of B.T. Jutes* of Crawford County for example. She had the live-in kind of ghost, a friendly, solicitous woman who watched over the children and helped B.T. with her genealogical research.

According to B.T., the ghost's name was Cassandra and she first appeared in a kind of psychic tableau on a bedroom wall one frosty January night. She wore a shimmering, swirling red dress and, with her bearded companion, stood before an open, horse-drawn carriage. Her jet-black hair was parted severely down the middle and pulled back tightly over her ears; dark eyes twinkled above a veil that concealed the lower half of her face. She suddenly dropped the veil and stepped into the carriage with her partner. With that the image vanished.

"I kept thinking I was dreaming, but yet I knew I was awake," B.T. said. "My husband was snoring all the while this was going on. I was awake. And I was frightened."

She got up, checked on her children, and then walked through the entire house, checking on the security of each window and door from the basement to the top floor. Still uneasy, she went back to bed but did not sleep well.

The next night the identical scene returned to the wall, but this time it was in black and white, not the colorful depiction of the night before. A new feature was added, however—the mysterious woman lowered her veil, turned to B.T. and smiled.

Sometime later, B.T. was invited to attend a séance. When she told the story of the mysterious woman and her companion, she was warned by the others present that because of the veil the woman was a negative spirit and not to be trusted. They suggested she put a mental "red circle of truth" around herself, her loved ones, and her home.

It was after midnight when she returned from the séance. "I was scared to death. I wanted to leave all the lights on," she said. The mental red circle of truth she'd been advised to create didn't seem adequate.

"I knew I wasn't keeping anybody out because they were already in!" she reasoned.

As B.T. opened her front door, the woman from the ghostly montage was standing in the hallway. "She looked exactly like she had looked on the wall, just like a real person except that I could see right through her," B.T. said.

"Why are you so afraid of me?" asked the vaporous visitor. Before B.T. could reply, the specter had another surprise in store: She was, she said, B.T. 's great-great-great-grandmother, Cassandra, and that she had lived as a child in Virginia and Maryland a century and a half before.

B.T. thought she certainly didn't seem like an evil spirit; in fact, Cassandra offered to guide and protect the family.

Later that day, B.T. told her husband and children about Cassandra. Although none of them would ever see her, they sometimes felt her presence, like that of an invisible babysitter.

Little Danny, who was four-years-old at the time, was particularly unperturbed. "I know she's here to help me," he said. One morning the boy awoke in his top bunk bed with his back bruised and cut. The ladder to his bed was on the floor and there was a fresh dent in the bedroom wall that B.T. believed was made by the force of the falling ladder. Neither B.T. nor her husband had put their son back into bed. Danny had no recollection of the incident. The boy also survived a near drowning in a local swimming pool with Cassandra's help, B.T. maintained.

B.T. was a veteran genealogist when Cassandra first came on the scene. However, she had been unable to locate several branches of her family. In those years before the explosion of interest in genealogy and Internet resources, B.T. said some birth certificates could not be found and important marriage certificates were seldom available. The family had not kept a family Bible in which ancestors might have noted family names and significant dates. B.T. said Cassandra supplied the missing links, giving her facts about family members that she was later able to verify through official documents.

B.T. believed that might have been the reason for Cassandra's appearance. Ghosts have been reported to leave familiar surroundings to travel great distances, bringing missing information or intervening in a crisis.

For instance, Cassandra disclosed her own maiden name and the date and place of her marriage.

"I wrote to that county in Ohio and I (now) have her wedding license. When I gave a photocopy of the certificate to my grandmother, she was flabbergasted because she didn't know this woman's maiden name," B.T. said.

Cassandra supplied the names and birth dates of all her children, as well. B.T. went directly to census records. "I wanted to see if that was my imagination that was telling me that or she was. And, by golly, those names showed up …" she said. Cassandra had had two daughters and several sons.

Sometimes names and complete addresses of living relatives came to B.T. "out of a clear blue sky—people that I had no inkling of any connection with us. I didn't even look up the addresses. I just wrote."

Incredible still is the notion, according to B.T., that she has twice visited Cassandra's home. Each visit represented an instantaneous transition. "I disappear and I am there," she said. The two women have talked in Cassandra's sitting room. B.T. has even seen Cassandra's daughter, Mary Jane, who was later killed in a horse riding accident.

When she is in Cassandra's home, B.T. said the experience is entirely real, but that when she is with the ghost in her own home "everything is in a haze."

Some parapsychologists say human beings can leave their bodies and describe people and places that the person has never actually seen.

B.T. thought Cassandra was in the Jutes' home long before she appeared on the bedroom wall. She seemed to spend a lot of time by the front door, watching the children come and go. Cassandra also followed B.T. upstairs to tell her the phone is ringing downstairs or that someone is at the door.

Cassandra was a real and loving presence for B.T. Far from being the evil spirit others warned against, Cassandra was always a positive force, bolstering B.T. 's spirits in times of need and pushing her to do more than she ever thought possible.

THE RIDGEWAY GHOST

The year is 1842. Wisconsin is still six years away from statehood. Towering pines blanket the virgin forests, lumbering is an infant industry, and settlers are only now reaching into the remote corners of the wilderness that stretch endlessly across the horizon. The precious element lead has been discovered in the rolling limestone hills of southwestern Wisconsin. For a new nation, still struggling for survival, the soft, bluish-gray substance represents a valuable commodity in the world market; perhaps more importantly, the veins of lead could help produce the bullets and other products with which Americans would tame the rugged land.

The opening of the mines attracted rowdy, tough, dangerous men whose job it was to wrestle the lead from the earth's grasp. From Wales to Ireland, Germany and Cornwall, and the American South miners spread into the lead district surrounding the pioneer outposts of Mineral Point, Dodgeville, Blue Mounds, and countless other small villages. At the height of the mining era, nearly 40,000 pounds of lead would be hauled each year to markets in Milwaukee, Dubuque, Chicago, and Galena.

Roads were cut through dense forests over which the lead wagons would roll. Alongside the rutted paths another industry grew—saloons and roadhouses catering to the raucous appetites of the miners. These establishments had names like McKillips (near Ridgeway), the Messerschmidt Hotel (five miles west of Dodgeville), and Markey's. There were over 22 saloons on the main route, called the Military Ridge Road, between Blue Mounds and Dodgeville, a distance of only 25 miles.

Drunken fist fights, robberies, clubbings, and murder were not uncommon along the Ridge Road. The immigrant miners were joined by various criminal elements, gamblers, and prostitutes to foment a way of life usually short and often fatal. Burial services for the unluckiest victims were informal. The corpse would be dropped unceremoniously into a convenient pit with a few hasty words mumbled over the departed one's body.

For over two decades wagons carrying lead for the processing mills rolled down the Ridge Road. The saloons, bawdy houses, and inns thrived. But all that ended in 1857 when the Chicago and Northwestern

Haunted Wisconsin

Railroad completed a branch line into Mineral Point. Lead could be shipped out more easily by rail, and traffic along the Ridge Road declined. The notorious hangouts eventually closed down.

At the height of the mining era, however, wagon masters and way-farers had more to fear than a chance meeting with a highwayman. Beginning about 1840, a series of bizarre, often puckish, and generally unexplainable encounters with ghosts and phantoms beset those who lived or worked along Ridge Road. The small community of Ridgeway, halfway between what was then called Pokerville (now Blue Mounds) and Mineral Point, became the center of activities for what has come to be known as the Ridgeway ghost.

The Ridgeway ghost, it must be said, was not one spirit but rather a mischievous phantom that could change its appearance at will. The ghost would appear as dogs, horses, pigs, sheep, and several different human forms, including a headless horseman. The ghost roamed the countryside frightening farmers, miners, and travelers alike. It would accompany buggy riders or lead haulers as they ventured out along the Ridge Road after dark, terrify farmers returning from fields, and generally frighten the wits out of anyone unlucky enough to cross its path.

But is there any basis in fact for an appearance by a ghost haunting the country around Ridgeway? We may never know for a certainty, although there are scores of stories about the ghost and several different versions of how the apparitions began. We must go back more than a century and a quarter, to the early 1840s, to begin the tales of the Ridgeway ghost.

One of the seedier establishments along the Ridge Road was Sampson's Saloon and Hotel. Many a traveler risked his earthly future in this pit of human scum. The Ridgeway ghost may be the earthbound spirit of one naïve wayfarer who stopped at Sampson's.

A peddler checked into Sampson's after a long day's ride, unaware of its unsavory reputation. He was seen entering his room but then vanished. Early the next morning, his fully saddled horse tried to enter the saloon-hotel. The animal failed in its attempts and was soon chased off, never to be seen again.

Soon after the peddler's apparent demise, people began reporting a bizarre apparition on the road near Sampson's. A giant black horse would gallop along the roadway, and on the horse's back was the torso

The Ridgeway Ghost

of a headless man mounted backward in the saddle. The headless horseman would keep pace with and often pass the frightened travelers. If anyone tried to converse with the macabre apparition, unearthly groans would issue from the incomplete body.

One buggy driver encountered the headless horseman in a most unusual way. As the driver rode along, he heard the sound of an approaching horse. Turning in the wooden buggy seat, the man beheld a stallion upon which rode a figure in black—minus its head. Instead of passing the buckboard, the horse reared and planted its front quarters firmly in the wagon box. Frightened nearly senseless, the wagon driver whipped his team of horses forward but the horse and rider kept pace. The beast's front legs were still in the wagon only inches behind the driver. When (or if) the wagoneer reached safety is not recorded.

McKillip's was the name of another, even more notorious, tavern about five miles west of Ridgeway on what is now Highway 18-151. Some accounts of the origin of the Ridgeway ghost stem from a horrifying incident at this saloon in the early 1840s.

Two teenage brothers, ages 14 and 15, ambled into the establishment one winter day and promptly became the subject of jest by the drunken customers. The ridicule soon turned to murder when one boy was grabbed and thrown into a blazing fireplace. He was burned alive. The other youngster managed to escape out the door but was never seen again. The next spring his frozen corpse was found in a field.

After the boys' murder, a small, gray-haired woman would be seen wandering aimlessly along the road near McKillip's. She would vanish as soon as a stranger approached. Those who saw her speculated that she might be the mother or grandmother of the murdered boys looking for their bodies. Variations of a female specter abound in the Ridgeway vicinity.

A retired railroad man, Lyle Kramer, told a story passed down by his father. The older Kramer said he often saw two old women on an isolated section of the railroad tracks flagging down a passenger train as it moved along the Ridge Road. When the train stopped to pick up the women, they would float away into the forest.

On another occasion an unidentified man was driving his team of horses along near Ridgeway when he sighted a woman walking in the road directly ahead. She was going in his direction, in the center of the road. He yelled at her to move but she didn't respond or turn. She continued to walk. The horseman drove to the side of the highway to pass, but as he did so the mysterious woman moved to block his approach. He whipped his team into a faster gallop. The woman somehow managed to stay ahead. He reined his team to a halt. And she stopped. After several miles of this frustrating exchange the woman vanished.

Others said an old woman would appear shuffling along the road. She would then disappear into a ball of fire.

McKillip's Saloon also figures into another Ridgeway ghost tale. A local man was riding home after a visit to the village. As he approached McKillip's he passed a large white oak tree. A sudden gust of cold wind enveloped him. His horse reared, nearly tossing the rider onto the ground. The man managed to hang on as the animal raced wildly all the way home.

The death of the pastor at Ridgeway's Catholic church has prompted another version of the origin of the ghost.

The priest was walking down the steps of the church when he fell and struck his head on the stone steps. He died soon after. For many years, on the anniversary of his death, people claimed blood would appear on the steps of the church and hideous sounds reverberated from within the building.

The church mysteriously burned to the ground several years later.

Whichever version one chooses to believe there is little doubt that the ghost became the subject of more tales than nearly any other specter in this country. It played no favorites and assumed various disguises to frighten unwary victims. The following stories recount some of the Ridgeway ghost's more infamous appearances.

The long-vanished Messerschmidt Hotel in Ridgeway was the scene of several hauntings by the ghost.

The hotel's founder, George Messerschmidt, was member of the county board in 1855. The railroad was to be built from Warren, Illinois, to Mineral Point, and board members had decided to raise the necessary capital by issuing county bonds.

Soon after Messerschmidt decided to sign the bonds, strange creakings and groanings began to be heard in the hotel. Messerschmidt couldn't sleep. Night after night the sound grew in intensity. A voice was even heard echoing through the night, "Don't sign the bonds. Don't sign the bonds."

Perhaps a disgruntled taxpayer had discovered a political use for the Ridgeway ghost! Or perhaps the spirit realized the railroad would take

The Ridgeway Ghost

away the traffic along its favorite haunt, the Ridge Road.

Throughout the hotel's history, customers would hear moans coming from the walls and the sound of dragging chains.

• • •

An early Irish settler named Kennedy accumulated quite a sum of money and used part of it to build a large home on some land he owned near the old Porter Grove cheese factory.

One evening he visited the nearly completed house. Kennedy unlocked the front door and strolled through the many rooms. Upon entering the dining room, however, he saw the misty form of a human being seated at the table. The old man fled, never to return. He built a smaller house nearby and lived there the rest of his days, convinced the Ridgeway ghost had taken up residence in his mansion.

Other stories are told about Kennedy. Like many eccentric people, he had a penchant for burying his wealth in the ground. Kennedy deposited his in the earth near the railroad tracks and would check on its safety each day. One night after visiting his cache, he was walking home when he saw a light mysteriously dancing up and down, sometimes dim, at other times quite bright. A train? Or flagman? Perhaps. But Kennedy didn't wait to find out. He fled across the fields.

In the end, Kennedy's death was attributed to the nightly visitations at his earthen bank. As the years passed, his hearing deteriorated. One night a train struck and killed Kennedy as he sat on the tracks. What became of the money? No one knows for sure.

Years later a local character named Rocky Jim Ryan moved into the old Kennedy house. Rocky Jim claimed that at night he could hear the old man's boots tromping through the rooms. Rocky Jim finally moved out the morning after "something" pulled the covers off his bed.

• • •

The Reilly house now stands near a Catholic church in Ridgeway. But, when it was built nearly a century ago, the house was located several miles west of Ridgeway near the railroad tracks. A ghostly history is connected with the house.

An old gentleman named Peavey once lived in the house when it was on its original foundation. After Peavey moved away, the place burned down. Another house was built on the foundation, but the new owners left within a few days. A large black dog would appear, tired and panting, under their dining room table every night after dark. The animal would disappear as suddenly as it had come.

The house was eventually moved to its current location in Ridgeway. The dog never reappeared. Some people think it was the original foundation, or the area in which the house was first located, that caused the canine apparition.

But recent tenants of the Reilly place reported some unusual sounds. When their daughter was young, she would become frightened at a noise like that of children playing with marbles. It came from the attic. The "marbles" would roll across the floor for several minutes on end. Nothing was ever found that would explain the incident.

• • •

There are two versions of Evan "Strangler" Lewis' mysterious death.

Lewis was a well-known wrestler of immense size with a fearlessness that matched his physical strength. When he wasn't winning bets in the wrestling rings, he supported his family by farming and helping neighbors butcher stock. It was after a day of butchering on a neighboring farm that Lewis took a fateful walk.

Lewis had been warned not to travel home after dark because of several recent episodes involving the Ridgeway ghost. Lewis sneered at the reports, citing his strength, agility, and the butcher knives he carried as protection enough against any would-be phantom.

One version of what happened next says Lewis was walking across a field when a white horse with a driverless carriage charged at him. Lewis jumped out of the way and as he did so the horse and carriage rose and disappeared into the sky. He ran all the way home.

The second tale also has Lewis crossing a large pasture. He suddenly felt something warm breathing on his hand. Lewis turned and stared directly into the red eyes of an immense black dog. He tried to chase it away but the beast kept following at a distance. A few yards farther along Lewis again felt the panting beast at his heels. This time he aimed a kick directly at the dog, but his foot flew through the empty space where the dog had been only seconds before.

Running now, Lewis thought safety was within his grasp. Darkness was now complete as he crashed through the brush. His cabin only a hundred yards away, Lewis again felt the pressure of the black beast at his back. This time Lewis extracted one of the butcher knives and slashing at the dog, hitting nothing but air. He continued to fight off the dog until he was within sight of his house when the canine disappeared.

When Lewis reached home he was dripping with sweat, shaking and exhausted. His family sent for the doctor. Upon examining the still-traumatized Lewis, the physician stated that the man's heart has moved nearly two inches from its original location.

Lewis died on May 8, 1874, two days after his run-in with the phantom dog.

• • •

All sorts of strange animals have been sighted as part of the Ridgeway ghost stories. Pigs, sheep, horses, dogs, and "critters" are part of the ghost lore in this corner of Wisconsin.

One night many decades ago, Mr. and Mrs. Buckingham were returning home from a day of shopping. As their buckboard approached Markey's Saloon, two miles west of Ridgeway, Mrs. Buckingham noticed what she thought was an animal on the road. Her husband squinted into the gloom and said it looked like a new breed of dog. Whatever it was, the couple claimed the entire area around the animal was illuminated with sparks flying from its back. The horses nearly bolted at the sight. The apparition slowly vanished. The Buckinghams never discovered the creature again.

• • •

Boo Tesch and his dog were returning home about 12:30 A.M. following an evening at a friend's house. As they passed a low bank of earth Tesch heard a sound. Looking at the top of the ridge, Tesch saw a huge, snarling dog crouching as if ready to spring at any moment.

Tesch's dog took one look at the creature and scampered down the road, tail between its legs, whimpering all the way. Tesch was left alone. He looked for something to use as a weapon and found a stone, which he hurled at the grotesque animal. The rock missed its target and the dog was now circling the hapless Tesch. And then, just as suddenly as it had appeared, the dog vanished.

For 50 years after the incident, until his death, Tesch could not rationally explain what he saw or forget that night.

• • •

Sailor Dave Jones often courted his future wife at her home in what is now part of Governor Dodge State Park, north of Dodgeville.

Jones was returning home one evening when he heard sheep bleating on the trail behind him. He stopped his horse and a herd of sheep passed on either side of the startled rider. Behind the sheep rode two silent men. They did not look at Jones or say a word. The sheep and their stoic herders faded into the distance.

Soon after the incident, a group of men examined the trail but could find no sign of sheep of the riders.

• • •

George Russell, a farmer near Ridgeway, had arranged with another man to purchase a pig. Russell agreed to meet the man in Ridgeway where he would pay cash for the pig. The two met, the pig was transferred into Russell's crate on the back of his wagon, and the seller left. Russell performed a few errands in the village and finally hitched up his team for the drive home.

At his farm, Russell backed the wagon up to the chute and opened the crate, but, instead of the pig, a large dog emerged. To this day no one knows how the exchange took place, whether it was the work of the Ridgeway ghost, or whether a practical joker had some fun at Russell's expense.

• • •

Interestingly, one of the phantoms often sighted near Ridgeway was a pig or a drove of pigs.

One particular teamster reported that he encountered several pigs on the Military Ridge Road. As he approached, they dissolved into a cloud of dust.

• • •

Wagon drivers would often stop at one (or several) of the saloons for "courage," knowing they were within the stamping grounds of the Ridgeway ghost.

John Riley was one of those who stopped regularly at a saloon near Ridgeway. His team of oxen would stand outside with a load of pig lead destined for Galena.

One night after finishing his brew he stepped outside the door and beheld a strange spectacle. His oxen had been rehitched to the rear of the wagon. And walking down the road was the Ridgeway ghost with a whip in one hand and a lantern in the other.

John Riley spent the night in the tavern.

• • •

There is a "haunted grove" west of Ridgeway on Highway 18. During the era when it was known as the Ridge Road a phantom would often appear to startled passers-by.

The Ridgeway Ghost

One story recounts the tale of a man on foot who encountered a team of huge black stallions pulling a black carriage. The apparition charged directly at the immobilized walker and, incredibly, passed directly over the man, leaving him lying prone in the dirt, dazed and frightened.

Other travelers going through the "haunted grove" would report that a strange white apparition flew out at them from the forest before disappearing into the brush. Some heard an eerie, wailing scream from the bowels of the grove. No one ever ventured in to investigate.

• • •

One old gentleman didn't believe in the Ridgeway ghost. The fellow took a short cut through the Ridgeway cemetery one evening. A bright light suddenly shone upward from a tombstone and ghastly screams pierced the night air.

From that day forward the elderly gent was reportedly afflicted with a nervous disorder.

• • •

A young girl was returning home from a visit to a neighboring farm when she saw a light coming from within a barn her family used as a horse stable. Thinking it was her father checking on the animals, she approached the barn but the light suddenly vanished.

Inside, she could find no one. And yet she claimed to have felt a presence. Perhaps the Ridgeway ghost looking for a new horse?

• • •

The Ridgeway ghost apparently took various human forms.

A young man named Jim Moore was visiting his sweetheart near Blue Mounds. The young lady lived in a large two-story frame house with an outside stairway leading to the girl's apartment on the top floor. It was dusk when the suitor climbed the steps to the apartment. He paused at the top landing to catch his breath before knocking on the door. From there he looked down and saw an old man perched atop a rusted stove lying in the yard. Moore had never seen the elderly man before and thought there was something strange about him. Moore went inside and told his story about the visitor in the yard. The girl was concerned and, as the night progressed, tried to persuade her beau to spend the night. Moore didn't think it was proper and declined.

Moore left and started home on foot. Suddenly the old gentleman was at his side matching Moore's stride step for step. The vaporous figure did not speak a word and stared straight ahead. As Moore neared his house he heard a small explosion and the old man vanished.

Moore broke into a run and made it safely into his house. As he leaned panting against the kitchen door, he realized the Ridgeway ghost just escorted him home.

Jim Moore never visited that girl again.

• • •

In the era before automobiles, young couples would often walk short distances to visit friends. So it was that a young man and his new bride accepted an invitation to a party at a home a few miles away near Wakefield.

The night became dark and still. The only light blazed from their swinging lanterns, pointing the way through the heavy woods. The air had not yet cooled from an unusually hot day in early autumn. No breeze stirred the air. Freshly fallen leaves formed a dark carpet upon which their footsteps made a faint rustling sound.

Without warning, something stirred in the path a few yards ahead. Thinking it was a neighbor also walking to the party, the young man called out a greeting, but there was no answer. Abruptly the night air turned cold. Their lantern's glow reflected upon leaves fluttering in the air for no apparent reason. The sound of footsteps reached their ears, and looking down they could see the imprints of a man's shoes.

Although they saw nothing, the couple claimed to have felt a presence in the forest. The Ridgeway ghost out for an evening stroll?

• • •

Willy Powell passed a pleasant evening with his girlfriend in Ridgeway and was returning home in his buckboard hitched to a fine pair of coal-black horses. The winter night was particularly cold with masses of swirling snow drifting across long stretches of the road.

Hurrying the animals along, Powell turned in to the drive, which led to the warmth and safety of his cabin. Without warning, his horses reared suddenly and the cutter overturned, tossing Powell into a snowbank. As Powell looked up he saw the object of his horses' fright: a towering black figure stood in the doorway of his barn. Powell scrambled to his feet and raced for the cabin to rouse his sleeping brother.

The pair returned to the barn to find the door closed and no signs of an intruder. The horses were not found for several days.

• • •

An old man who lived by himself reported that the Ridgeway ghost

The Ridgeway Ghost

visited him one night during chores.

The fellow had walked out to the pump to fill several buckets with water. On his way back into the house he turned and saw that the pump handle was still vigorously moving up and down. At once he realized the ghost was getting a drink. The terrified farmer ran into his kitchen and bolted the door.

• • •

Country doctors were regularly called out at night to isolated farms to deliver babies or look after the sick. Doc Cutler, who tended the people of Ridgeway for years, took the ghost stories quite seriously.

Cutler would avoid the main Ridge Road if at all possible since the ghost was known to frequent the area. On those occasions when he had to travel the highway, the Ridgeway ghost would always keep him company. The phantom would spring from the brush and perch on one of the doctor's horses or stand on the tongue of his buggy. Cutler tried whipping his horses into a faster gait but the ghost would not be deterred. And, all the while, the ghost would stare up at the frightened physician with its hollow, vacant eyes.

After one late night call Cutler claimed that he overtook a man walking beside the road. He asked the stranger if he wanted to ride and the man climbed into the doctor's buggy near the edge of town and vanished into the night.

Doc Cutler was convinced that he gave a lift to the Ridgeway ghost.

The ghost, it is said, was particularly attracted to anyone who worked with blood.

• • •

A man was riding home one afternoon in the hills near Ridgeway when he thought he saw movement in a deserted cabin. He dismounted and walked into the ruins. Sitting in a chair was a vague, white, human-like form the visitor immediately recognized as the Ridgeway ghost. He struck at the phantom with his whip and the ghost vanished.

The next day, the man noticed there were clear impressions of his fingers in the handle of the whip. Fright had placed them there, he realized.

• • •

Johnny Owens, a Welsh miner, was out for an evening stroll on the Ridge Road. Rounding a bend he saw several dark objects swinging from a limb of a tall oak tree. As he approached more closely, the moonlight clearly revealed three human bodies hanging by their necks. Owens ran all the way home.

The next day Owens returned to the spot with three stout friends. There were no bodies hanging in the tree.

• • •

One day in the late 1840s, a lead miner encountered the Ridgeway ghost as he trudged along the road west of Ridgeway.

As the miner walked, the man realized he was being followed. He turned and saw a hazy form some distance behind. The miner said it was the specter of the Ridgeway ghost. He quickened his stride. So did the phantom. Always keeping the same distance behind the frightened miner, the ghost matched the strides step for step. Frightened badly, the miner began to run, and so did the ghost.

Finally, after several hundred yards, the miner slumped exhausted on a log at the side of the road. The ghost sauntered up and sat down at the other end. For one of the few times in history the ghost spoke.

"That was some fine running you were doing back there," the spirit said.

"Yes," acknowledged the miner. "And I'm going to be doing some more in a minute." And off he sped with the phantom in pursuit.

• • •

Three men were sitting in a Blue Mounds saloon, nearing the end of a stud poker game. The stakes were high and a considerable sum of money was riding on this final deal. A miner with a full house won the pot. As he reached across the table to gather up the winnings, a man appeared in a vacant seat, grabbed up the cards, and began to deal. The uninvited stranger wore black clothing with a wide-brimmed hat pulled down low over his eyes, obscuring his face.

The cards began flying from the stranger's fingers and seemed to dance across the room before floating down to the table.

The tavern keeper dove behind his polished bar and hid for the duration of the stranger's visit. The poker players were thoroughly frightened at the card antics and stumbled over each other in their headlong rush for the door.

The money on the table vanished, along with the phantom in black.

• • •

When traffic declined on the Ridge Road following the completion of the railroad in 1857, the Ridgeway ghost also became less active. In fact, it

The Ridgeway Ghost

is said that the phantom was seen leaving town on the cowcatcher of a freight train passing through Ridgeway. Others claim the ghost died in a fire that consumed nearly all of the Ridgeway business district in 1910.

But there are other more skeptical believers, who say the ghost has never left.

Jeanie Lewis lives near Wakefield and has collected stories about the ghost for some time. She is not convinced the ghost has truly departed, citing several bizarre experiences that seem to defy explanation.

Shortly after the birth of her first child in 1959, Mrs. Lewis arose at 2:00 A.M. to give the baby an early feeding. As she sat rocking the child in the darkened living room, Mrs. Lewis heard the kitchen door open. Turning to look, she saw newspapers that had been placed on the freshly waxed floor float through the air. The sound of footsteps echoed in the air, but no one was visible.

Mrs. Lewis ran to the bedroom to rouse her husband. Together they heard the footsteps and the kitchen door slam shut. And then silence. The couple walked cautiously into the kitchen but found nothing disturbed. The newspapers were still arranged neatly on the floor and the damp ground outside the door bore no impressions of footprints.

This incident could be called "The Case Of the Wandering Jacket." Mrs. Lewis says her husband once owned a jacket given to him by a former girlfriend. About three years after Mrs. Lewis and her husband married the coat disappeared from a clothes hook in the stairwell where it was always kept. Mr. Lewis insisted that his wife had destroyed it; she just as strenuously denied any involvement. Mrs. Lewis searched the house thoroughly but could not find the coat.

Several years passed. Then one afternoon as Mrs. Lewis walked down the stairs she saw the coat hung, as always, on the peg. But the garment was nearly in shreds. It was as if someone had worn it nearly every day since its disappearance.

• • •

An old schoolhouse in Wakefield has been converted into a recreation center. This new center, along with the Folklore Village Farm, provides neighborhood youngsters with a great gathering spot. But some peculiar incidents have taken place there.

At about the time the school was undergoing its face-lifting, Jeanie Lewis, who lives within sight of the place, happened to glance toward the sky one evening. On the eastern horizon she noticed a bright, colorful object directly over the Wakefield cheese factory. It hovered over the factory and began to descend. Then it took off to the north and stopped over the old schoolhouse. While Mrs. Lewis watched, the lights appeared to descend into the chimney of the old building.

Several times since that night, children and others visiting the schoolhouse have reported strange sounds from within the chimney. It is said the Ridgeway ghost visits there every so often.

Meanwhile, a bleak, abandoned farmhouse on the old Petra property is said to be the permanent residence of the Ridgeway ghost. It sits surrounded by weeds past the pioneer Ridgeway cemetery south of town and looks just like the sort of place a ghost would inhabit. Doors hang from their hinges, windows are broken—altogether an ideal haunted house.

Was there really a Ridgeway ghost? Or did the Old World settlers bring their superstitious ways to the new land, recreating in slightly altered form the vampire, banshee, and werewolf? The Ridgeway tales and any truth upon which they might have been built are now lost in the mists of time. We will never know for sure, but the legends will live as long as there are listeners willing to believe.

Bibliography/
Index

SELECTED BIBLIOGRAPHY

BOOKS

Boyer, Dennis. *Driftless Spirits: Ghosts of Southwest Wisconsin*. Madison: Prairie Oak Press, 1996.

Chapin, Earl. *Tales of Wisconsin*. Compiled and edited by M. Wayne Wolfe. River Falls: University of Wisconsin–River Falls Press, 1973.

Cole, Harry E. *Stagecoach and Tavern Tales of the Old Northwest*. Cleveland: Arthur H. Clarke, 1930.

Conard, Howard Louis, ed. *History of Milwaukee: From Its First Settlement to the Year 1895*, Vol. 1. Chicago and New York: American Biographical Publishing Co., n.d.

Gard, Robert, and Sorden, L.G. *Wisconsin Lore*. New York: Duell, Sloan, and Pearce, 1962.

Gilman, Rhoda R. *Historic Chequamegon*. 1971.

Holzhueter, John O. *Madeline Island and the Chequamegon Region*. Madison: State Historical Society of Wisconsin, 1974.

Lewis, Jeanie. *Ridgeway: Host to the Ghost*. Dodgeville (Wis): Dodgeville Chronicle, 1975.

Napoli, James. *The Coasts of Wisconsin*. Madison: University of Wisconsin Sea Grant College Program, March 1975.

Owen, A. R. G. *Can We Explain the Poltergeist?* Chicago: Regnery, 1954.

Strait, William E. *Camp Fires at La Pointe: An Historical Journey Through the Centuries in La Pointe*, n.p., n.d.

Stresau, Marion. *Tomorrows Unlimited*. Boston: Branden Press, 1973.

Thurston, Herbert, S. J. *Ghosts and Poltergeists*. Chicago: Regnery, 1954.

Williams, Mentor L., ed. *Schoolcraft's Indian Legends*. Westport, Conn.: Greenwood Press, 1956.

PERIODICALS

Bednarek, Jim. *"The Legend of Mary Buth."* Germantown Press, September 1, 1977.

Burnett County Sentinel (Grantsburg), October 4, 1889.

Cummings, Gerald. *"The Mysterious Hitchhiker."* FATE Magazine, August 1992.

Daily Milwaukee News, August 9, 1874.

Doehlert, Betsy. *"Do Ghosts Walk Arboretum Glades?"* Capital Times (Madison), October 31, 1977.

Dunn County News (Menomonie), September 13, 1873; October 25, 1873; November 8, 1873; November 2, 1994.

Durand Weekly News, September 12, 1873; September 26, 1873; October 3, 1873.

Franklin, Dixie. *"New Light Shed on Odd Light."* Milwaukee Journal, August 6, 1978.

"The Ghost Hunter's Handiguide." Wisconsin Week-End, October 1978.

Heinen, Thomas. *"Tragedy Stalks a Farmhouse."* Milwaukee Journal, October 25, 1977.

Henningfield, Julie. *"The Double Meaning in Spirits."* Excursions. October 22, 2000.

Hudson Star and Times, December 8, 1869.

Selected Bibliography

Lenz, Elmer, *"Have You Seen the Light?"* Milwaukee Badge, July 1977.

Madison Daily Democrat, December 5, 1873.

Miller, Willis. Editor's Column. *Hudson Star-Observer*, September 14, 1944.

Milwaukee News, October 16, 1873.

Milwaukee Sentinel, August 11, 1875; September 26, 1878; February 14, 1897.

Mt. Horeb Times, March 18, 1909; March 25, 1909; April 1, 1909; April 8, 1909; April 11, 1909; April 15, 1909.

Olson, Kathy. *"'Something' is out there in Flowage."* St. Paul (Minnesota) Pioneer Press, July 5, 1992.

Orton, Charles W. *"The Haunting."* Wisconsin Trails, Autumn 1976.

Orum, Alma. *"Octagon House Has Spirit, But No Ghost."* Milwaukee Sentinel, January 3, 1960.

Oshkosh Weekly Times, November 25, 1873; December 3, 1873.

Pease, Harry S. *"A Different Northern Light."* Milwaukee Journal Insight Magazine, November 30, 1980.

Peterson, Gary. *"Time Plays Tricks With Memory of 1909 Mt. Horeb Poltergeist."* Capital Times (Madison), October 26, 1978.

Pett, Mrs. W. F. *"A Forgotten Village."* Wisconsin Magazine of History, September 1928.

Reuschleim, Harrison. *"Mischief on High Hill Where Jenny Lies Buried."* Wisconsin Week-End, December 7, 1977.

River Falls Journal, September 23, 1873; October 31, 1873; December 12, 1873.

Rogo, D. Scott. *"More About the Poltergeist: The Power Behind Teenage Tantrums."* Human Behavior, May 1978.

Smith, Susan Lampert. *"Where Ghosts Gather: Book Describes Spooky History of Iowa County."* Wisconsin State Journal (Madison), June 14, 1993.

Tschudy, Kim. *"Explanation of Light in Barn Near Postville."* Monticello Messenger, November 20, 1991.

Waukesha Freeman, July 18, 1918; July 25, 1918.

Wisconsin State Journal (Madison), August 11, 1874; March 30, 1909; April 2, 1909.

UNPUBLISHED WORK

Dettloff, John. *"Indian Trail Resort: A History"* n.d.

Madison, Wisconsin. The State Historical Society of Wisconsin. *Charles E. Brown Papers.* Wisconsin Mss. HB, Boxes 7 and 9.

Nielsen, A. J. *"He Came With the House."* May 9, 1977.

Orton, Charles W. *"Ridgeway Ghost Tales."* n.d.

Owens, Dick. *"A Graveyard Tale"* n.d.

Owens, Dick. *"The Happenings."* May 8, 1991.

Van Dyke, Madge Patterson. *"The Story of Kilbourn and Its Vicinity"* Bachelor's Degree thesis, University of Wisconsin, 1916.

INDEX

Index of Selected Place Names

(All locations are in Wisconsin unless otherwise indicated.)

Place Name   **Page Number**

Index

223

Index